Chieftains of the Highland Clans

. .

A History of Israel
in the Twelfth and Eleventh Centuries B.C.

ROBERT D. MILLER II, S.F.O.

WILLIAM B. EERDMANS PUBLISHING COMPANY
GRAND RAPIDS, MICHIGAN / CAMBRIDGE, U.K.

Nihil Obstat:
Rev. Michael L. Barré, S.S.
Censor Librorum

Imprimatur:
+Most Rev. W. Francis Malooly, D.D., V.G.
Archdiocese of Baltimore
May 16, 2003

© 2005 Wm. B. Eerdmans Publishing Co.

Wm. B. Eerdmans Publishing Co.
255 Jefferson Ave. S.E., Grand Rapids, Michigan 49503 /
P.O. Box 163, Cambridge CB3 9PU U.K.

Printed in the United States of America

10 09 08 07 06 05   7 6 5 4 3 2 1

Library of Congress Cataloging-in-Publication Data

Miller, Robert D., II.
Chieftains of the highland clans: a history of Israel in the 12th and 11th centuries B.C. /
Robert D. Miller II.
p.   cm.   — (The Bible in its world)
Includes bibliographical references and index.
ISBN 0-8028-0988-X (pbk.: alk. paper)
1. Jews — History — 1200-953 B.C. 2. Excavations (Archaeology) — Palestine.
3. Palestine — Antiquities. 4. Iron age — Palestine. I. Title. II. Series.

DS121.55.M55   2005
933′.02 — dc22

2005040486

www.eerdmans.com

Chieftains of the Highland Clans

THE BIBLE IN ITS WORLD

David Noel Freedman, *General Editor*
Astrid B. Beck, *Associate Editor*

THE BIBLE IN ITS WORLD series offers an in-depth view of significant aspects of the biblical world. Reflecting current advances in scholarship, these volumes provide insights into the context of the Bible. Individual studies apply up-to-date historical, literary, cultural, and theological methods and techniques to enhance understanding of the biblical texts and their setting. Among the topics addressed are archaeology, geography, anthropology, history, linguistics, music, and religion as they apply to the Hebrew Bible/Old Testament, Apocrypha/Deuterocanonicals, and New Testament.

Contributors to THE BIBLE IN ITS WORLD are among the foremost authorities in their respective fields worldwide and represent a broad range of religious and institutional affiliations. THE BIBLE IN ITS WORLD series will interest anyone who seeks a deeper understanding of the Bible and its world.

For Robert S. Kinsey, ז״ל

Contents

Acknowledgments

This monograph is the outgrowth of a dissertation presented to the Department of Near Eastern Studies of the University of Michigan. I wish to thank the many individuals and organizations who aided in the pursuit of this study in the areas of funding, access to unpublished field data, and comments. The earliest form of this study was a seminar paper prepared in 1991 for Ron Tappy at the University of Michigan, whose early comments were highly valuable. Portions of Chapter 9 appeared in a seminar paper prepared in 1991 for Joseph Jensen at the Catholic University of America, whose insights were also helpful. Another person who provided comments and advice at that early stage was David Hopkins of Wesley Theological Seminary.

Some of the greatest help for this study outside my dissertation committee itself came from Gus Van Beek, Curator of Old World Archaeology at the Smithsonian Institute Museum of Natural History. Through my Academic Internship in 1995, and in his subsequent comments on the study, especially Chapter 5, his help was indispensable.

This monograph would not have been possible without the opportunity to reside in Jerusalem for two-and-a-half years. The first portion of this stay was funded by a Junior Scholarship-in-Residence from the Tantur Ecumenical Institute for Advanced Theological Study, the latter portion by a fellowship from the Samuel H. Kress Foundation administered through the W. F. Albright Institute of Archaeological Research and the W. F. Albright Institute's James A. Montgomery Fellowship. Dr. Hamdan Taha, Director of the Palestinian Department of Antiquities, graciously provided a permit to survey in the West Bank. This survey was funded by the Catholic Biblical Association's Archaeological Research Stipend. Preparation of the text was supported by a Rackham Dissertation Fellowship from the University of Michigan.

Many people were helpful in gaining access to unpublished archaeological data. I want to acknowledge here Israel Finkelstein, Chair of the Nadler Institute of Archaeology of Tel Aviv University, for access to the unpublished version of his "Highlands of Many Cultures" survey (Finkelstein, Lederman, and Bunimovitz 1997); David Livingston of Associates for Biblical Research, Inc., and Baruch Brandl for unpublished information on Khirbet Nisya; Bryant Wood and Gary Byers of Associates for Biblical Research, Inc., for unpublished information on the ongoing excavations at Khirbet Mukhatir; Moshe Kochavi of Tel Aviv University for permission to see the Israel Antiquities Authority files on Izbet Sartah; Zvi Gal of the Israel Antiquities Authority for permission to see the Israel Antiquities Authority files on Keren Zeitim (Tirat Zvi); Nancy Lapp for permission to use and assistance in examining materials from Paul Lapp's work at Tell el-Ful and James L. Kelso's work at Beitin housed at the Pittsburgh Theological Seminary Kelso Bible Lands Museum, where she is the curator, as well as at the Rockefeller Museum and Birzeit University's Palestinian Institute of Archaeology; Edward F. Campbell of McCormick Theological Seminary for permission to see materials from Tell Balatah housed at the Rockefeller Museum and Albright Institute; Roger Boraas for information on the Tell Balatah pottery he is currently publishing; the late James B. Pritchard for permission to examine materials from el-Jib housed at the Albright Institute, Birzeit University, Rockefeller Museum, and the Jordanian Department of Antiquities; Alain Chambon for permission to examine materials from Tell el-Farah North housed at the École Biblique et Archéologique Française and an enjoyable afternoon of assistance with those materials; Gary Pratico of Gordon-Conwell Theological Seminary for permission to examine materials from Joseph Free's excavations of Tell Dothan housed at the Rockefeller Museum, St. George's College Benshoof Cistern Museum, and the Jordanian Department of Antiquities; Museum Director Alon Goldberg for access to materials from Tel Amal at the Museum of Regional and Mediterranean Archaeology, Gan HaShlosha; Aren Maier of Hebrew University for access to materials from his survey of the Beth-Shan Valley; Sam Wolff for access to materials from his excavations of Ein Haggit; and Joel Drinkard of the Southern Baptist

Theological Seminary for permission to use and access to materials from the J. A. Callaway excavations of et-Tell and Khirbet Raddanah housed at the Southern Baptist Theological Seminary Nicol Museum of Biblical Archaeology. I examined the records of the Rockefeller Museum and Israel Antiquities Authority with the assistance of Arieh Rochman-Halperin, Head of the Archives Branch of the Antiquities Authority; objects housed at the Rockefeller/Israel Antiquities Authority with the permission of Acting Chief Curator Hava Katz and the assistance of Joe Zias; records housed with the Jordanian Department of Antiquities with the permission of Ghazi Bisheh, Director of Antiquities, Fawzi Zayadine, Assistant Director, and Muhammad Najjar of the Department, and with the assistance of M. Zayyat, Curator of the Jordan Archaeological Museum; materials from Tell Dothan housed at St. George's College, Jerusalem, with the assistance of then-curator of the Benshoof Museum, Dorothy Porter; and records and objects housed at Birzeit University with the permission of Khaled Nashef, Director of the Palestinian Institute of Archaeology. I also used the records and objects kept at the Albright Institute with the permission of the Dorot Director Seymour Gitin.

A two-and-a-half-year association with the W. F. Albright Institute provided an unparalleled opportunity for scholarly interaction. Many fellows, appointees, and associates of the Albright Institute provided insights and advice throughout this period. Everyone with whom I came into contact deserves credit, but I would like to single out for special thanks, in no particular order: Jeffrey Zorn, Jeffrey Blakely, Glenda Friend, Hayim Lapin, Garth Gilmour, Justin Lev-Tov, William Schniedewind, Bruce Routledge, Susan Sheridan, Robert Haak, Robert Mullins, and Alycia Fisher. Muhammad Al-Zawahra of Birzeit University also answered many questions on zooarchaeology.

The members of my dissertation committee deserve the utmost thanks. I was privileged to have studied with Peter Machinist and honored to write his final Michigan dissertation long after he had left for Harvard. It was he who taught me how to question. Brian Schmidt taught me to pose those questions universally, and I was delighted to be his first completed Ph.D. student. Professor Charles Krahmalkov taught me what the rare answers look like, and throughout my time at Michigan Henry Wright showed interdisciplinary cooperation at its best as he shared his brilliance as an anthropological theoretician and as a teacher with an *Alttestamentlicher* like myself.

ACKNOWLEDGMENTS

My wife Anne-Marie and sons William, Patrick, Joseph, and James, who endured this study and its revision more than I, deserve my total gratitude and thanks for their patience and encouragement. I have dedicated this monograph to the late Dr. Robert Kinsey, himself a student of W. F. Albright. A friend of my family since before he officiated at the wedding of my parents, he first introduced me to archaeology and the ancient Near East as a young child and took an active interest in my dissertation up to his death in 1996. I hope this study is a worthy tribute to him.

Preface

One might call the 12th and 11th centuries B.C. (Iron Age I) the new "Dark Ages" for those examining the Palestinian highlands and the community commonly known as Israel. The beginning and end of this period have had no end of ink spilled on them. During the past three decades or more biblical scholars and archaeologists have rigorously considered questions regarding the emergence of Israel at the end of the Late Bronze Age.[1] More recently, but foreshadowed by some earlier work, scholars have done much work based on archaeology and on archaeology in conjunction with the biblical text on the formation of the state and the dawn of the Monarchy in the ancient Israelite community (e.g., Flanagan 1988; Ahlström 1993; Finkelstein 1994).

This lacuna is not because this "gap" offers little of value. Rather, scholars have been so eager to get "From Nomadism to Monarchy" (the title of Finkelstein and Na'aman 1994) that few have taken a long look at the intervening period except as it illuminates the earlier or later ones.

Nevertheless, an understanding of the functioning of the immediate pre-state Israelite community is in itself a valuable goal; it is a historical subject that can be explored profitably by the historian of the ancient Near East. The reader in a hurry to get to a history of this community should go directly to Chapter 7, "A Social History of Highland Palestine, 1200–1000 B.C."

There is really no term readily available for this period, and one must

---

1. For an excellent but seldom cited summary, see Lemaire 1990 (esp. 258-82).

be coined, such as Epimonarchic or Antemonarchic Israel — "Pre-monarchic," without further qualification, implies too broad a chronological range. The Israelite community may have been in Palestine before 1200 — the Merneptah Stele is evidence that it clearly was. Perhaps it was present quite some time before 1200, in fact. And perhaps the sociopolitical nature of the highlands does not change until the end of the 10th century. But the 12th and 11th centuries are a self-contained archaeological unit in the highlands of Palestine, and since this is the final pre-state society, certain anthropological models are suggested for understanding this society.

Ethnographic evidence from diverse cultures shows a high probability that complex chiefdoms immediately preceded state formation. This suggests the systemic anthropological model of social structure known as the "complex chiefdom" for the 12th-11th centuries in highland Palestine. I will define this model in detail in Chapter 3. Comparative anthropological evidence commends the application of the model to the communities that preceded state formation in the highlands of Palestine ca. 1000 B.C. To ascertain the sociopolitical nature of Israelite society for this period, I will apply this anthropological model to the material culture of 11th- and 12th-century highland Palestine.[2]

Despite the seeming applicability of the model, in the past chiefdom models have only rarely been applied to or assumed for this community, and often in a vague and ill-defined manner. This study will interact with the current presentation of the model as it is given by the anthropologists themselves, examining its various incarnations. Chapter 3 will both summarize important early research and integrate more recent findings by scholars who have drawn on their predecessors.

The complex chiefdom model describes pre-state societies with ascriptive rank and more than one level of political control above the base community, with a schematization of the tributary economies and political hierarchies. Archaeological correlates to this, detailed in Chapter 4, include settlement patterns, land usage, mortuary practices, architectural styles, and distribution of wealth. These correlates will help to focus the study of the archaeological record of the highland settlement in the 12th

2. This should be distinguished from attempts to apply anthropological models directly to the biblical text, such as those of Crüsemann (1978:201-8), Thiel (1985:101-18, 150-64), Hauer (1987:18), Flanagan (1988:301), Lemche (1988:93-100), and Bendor (1996) — or to the biblical text "paired" with archaeology, such as those of Stager (1985a), Yamauchi (1994:1, 5), and V. Fritz (1996:96).

and 11th centuries B.C. on specific relevant subjects, which I will catalogue exhaustively in Chapter 5.

In Chapter 8 I will use the archaeologically based reconstruction of highland Israel to identify morphologically analogous cultures of the ancient Near East and elsewhere. There I will examine how these cultures recorded their own histories in "textual artifact" — where they preserved a textual memory of the past and the "depositional" process of that textualization. I will make an attempt to expand the modified complex chiefdom model further to include processes of "textual deposition" — how sociopolitical reality becomes textualized, if at all, in this type of society. I will try to use these analogies to understand how Israel's own supposed historiography — the Hebrew Bible — reflects on the period in question. I will show, however, that such a taphonomic approach proves incapable of describing the depositional process of the text from Iron I to final form. In Chapter 9, in a second approach to the biblical material, I will proceed from comparing and contrasting the anthropological/archaeological reconstruction of Iron I with some reconstruction(s) of Iron I presented by the Hebrew Bible. Finally, in Chapter 10, I will propose some ways to enrich the social history of the hierarchies and economy of the 11th and 12th centuries and suggest a more intellectual and cultural history, an ideological content of the societal structures and symbols not otherwise accessible.

List of Figures

List of Figures

Abbreviations

AASOR	Annual of the American Schools of Oriental Research
ABD	*Anchor Bible Dictionary*
ADAJ	*Annual of the Department of Antiquities of Jordan*
ANET	*Ancient Near Eastern Texts Relating to the Old Testament*
ASA	Archivo storico dell'arte
ASOR	American Schools of Oriental Research
AST	*Analecta Sacra Terraconensia*
ATD	Das Alte Testament Deutsch
BA	*Biblical Archaeologist*
BAR	*Biblical Archaeology Review*
BARInt	Biblical Archaeology Review International
BASOR	*Bulletin of the American Schools of Oriental Research*
BASORSup	Bulletin of the American Schools of Oriental Research Supplement Series
BBB	Bonner Biblische Beiträge
BTAVO	Beihefte zum Tübinger Atlas des Vordern Orients
BZAW	Beihefte zur Zeitschrift für die alttestamentliche Wissenschaft
CANE	*Civilizations of the Ancient Near East*
CBQ	*Catholic Biblical Quarterly*
DMOA	Documenta et Monumenta Orientis Antiqua
EA	*El Amarna Tablets*

Abbreviations

EI	Encyclopedia of Islam
ESI	Excavations and Surveys in Israel
HA	Hadashot Arkheologiyot
HTR	Harvard Theological Review
IEJ	Israel Exploration Journal
JAOS	Journal of the American Oriental Society
JARCE	Journal of the American Research Center in Egypt
JBL	Journal of Biblical Literature
JEA	Journal of Egyptian Archaeology
JESHO	Journal of the Economic and Social History of the Orient
JNES	Journal of the Near Eastern Society
JPOS	Journal of the Palestine Oriental Society
JSOT	Journal for the Study of the Old Testament
JSOTSup	Journal for the Study of the Old Testament Supplement Series
KAI	Kanaanäische und aramäische Inschriften
MANE	Monographs on the Ancient Near East
OBO	Orbis Biblicus et Orientalis
OrAn	Oriens Antiquus
PEFQSt	Palestine Exploration Fund Quarterly Statement
PEQ	Palestine Exploration Quarterly
RA	Revue d'Assyriologie et d'Archéologie Orientale
RB	Revue Biblique
SBLSP	Society of Biblical Literature Seminar Papers
SBT	Studies in Biblical Theology
SJOT	Scandinavian Journal of the Old Testament
TA	Tel Aviv
UF	Ugarit-Forschungen
UT	Ugaritic Textbook
VT	Vetus Testament
VTSup	Vetus Testamentum Supplements
ZAW	Zeitschrift für die alttestamentliche Wissenschaft
ZDPV	Zeitschrift des deutschen Palästina-Vereins

CHAPTER 1

Identifying Early Israel

A study of the political and social nature of "Israel" at the close of the 2d millennium B.C. involves many distinct issues, demanding what some may call faddish methodological preoccupation. It is not my intention here to engage in "a preoccupation with selecting and defending methods to the exclusion of the actual substance of the story being told" (Janesick 1994:215), but the issues of theory are not simple, and "unreflective archaeological practice [read also "history writing" or "biblical scholarship"] is now simply unjustifiable, unprofessional, and, indeed, a dangerous threat to the past" (M. Shanks 1997:398).

To begin with, the term "Israel" implies much baggage that merits more extensive treatment. The use of "Israel" in no way implies a hegemony of the biblical reading of the history for the region. Without oversimplifying what is an intensely complex issue, at the outset I should state that the loose use of the term "Israel" in this study refers to a sociocultural polity and not to a geographic region. The geographic region will remain "Palestinian Highlands" — again, not for any political reasons but only because it is easier than calling it something like "Upper Retenu," "Tzahi," or "Canaana."

The use of "Israel" as the designation of Iron I highland society is problematic. If the term is to be used as the ethnic designation for the community, it must be done so critically. I have discussed extensively the issues involved in identifying ethnicity in the archaeological record elsewhere (R. Miller, 2003), but can make brief comments here.

The overall homogeneity of the highlands suggests that the high-

1

lands do constitute a self-contained ethnicity on stylistic grounds. The nature of the Iron I settlement patterns defined later in this study will further support this thesis. The Merneptah Stele is direct positive evidence that the term "Israel" was used for some entity in the highlands of Palestine in the parlance of Late Bronze IIb sources (this stele will be treated more fully in Chapter 6). In another sense, it makes no difference what the Iron I highlanders called themselves: they were the direct antecedents of Iron II Israel and, thus, "Proto-Israel." There is direct continuity from the Iron I highlands to Iron II Israel and Judah in pottery, settlements, architecture, burial customs, and metals (see, among other things, the extensive literature by W. Dever and I. Finkelstein on this issue). So whatever the Iron I highlanders called themselves, by their continuity with Iron II they were nevertheless "those elements that were not yet Israel, but which went into or led up to the creation of Israel" (Thompson 1987:33). Yet since the Merneptah Stele records that the name of this community, or at least part of it, was Israel, once archaeology has established the continuity to Iron II, there is no reason to retain the prefix "Proto-."

CHAPTER 2

Writing Israel's History

This study will incorporate, or rather use as its entry point, an anthropological model. Someone may object at this point that to begin with a model is in a sense to shoot arrows into a wall and then draw bull's-eyes around them. There is an entire literature on the applicability of models in the fields of both anthropology and history.[1] Let me affirm at the start that models do "not conclude a study, but summarize current thought or help raise new questions" (Herion 1986:7-8). Thus it is appropriate that the model introduce this topic and bring analytical focus (Carr 1991:226; Thuesen 1996:53), although it will not conclude it. There are inherent limits to all models and comparative analogies: they can obscure any uniqueness of the society in question (Wilson 1984:53).

One can argue, however, that a historian always has a model in mind (see, e.g., Albright 1966:11; Yoffee 1981:25; and Provan 1995:595), if by a model one means mental paradigms, guiding assumptions, definitions, values, or principles (Gadamer 1987:126). When it is defined this way, stating a model is at least explicit, but to deny having one is self-deceiving (J. Fritz and Plog 1970; LaCapra 1978; 1982; Yoffee 1981:25; M. Shanks and Tilley 1987a; White 1990; Carr 1991:223; Kincheloe and McLaren 1994:154).

This discussion has serious implications for truth seeking and the question of what *kind* of history of Israel we seek here. Many have argued

---

1. Lamentably, the biblical and ancient Near Eastern contributions to the discussion of models are decidedly few: Albright 1966:5; Yoffee 1981:25; Jamieson-Drake 1989; 1991; Lemche 1996b:277-78; and Dever 1997d:300.

that biblical scholars should abandon the goal of being historians (Redford 1992:263; also potentially Lemche 1991a). This may be due to their narrow definition of historiography as historicism (as in Neusner 1981) — of all history writing as a quest for Leopold von Ranke's *"wie es eigentlich gewesen war"* ("just as they really happened"). If historicism is taken to mean literal objectivism, one can honestly say that "real" historians (if one may so dub them) outside biblical studies have not sought historicism since von Ranke (F. Stern 1973). There is an extensive literature on what history as a discipline means today, and it is not a historicist enterprise (LaCapra 1978; 1982).

Although the issue of just what biblical or Israelite history is has been raised implicitly, and occasionally explicitly, since the advent of critical scholarship, debates over Israelite historiography seldom recognize literature on the critical theory of history itself. I have discussed elsewhere current notions of the nature of history writing in comparison with those of biblical scholars (R. Miller 2005). The key to writing a critical postmodern history of Israel, avoiding Rankean empiricism and naive biblicism while including a moderate postmodernist skepticism about the approachability to any external reality, is the construction of well-argued plausibilities, of possible pasts that are available to further testing and examination and that challenge other possible pasts, yielding better-informed reconstructions. We must always clearly distinguish what it is possible to know and what it is possible to propose. This investigation will be explicit with its models, open to revision, and seek not *wie es eigentlich gewesen war,* but *was wir eigentlich sagen konnen,* "what we can really say."

Perhaps someone will object that the model proposed in this study is borrowed from unrelated periods and regions far afield (S. Talmon 1978 finds such nonproximate analogies particularly disturbing). In support of this use of ethnographic comparison, the skeptic should refer to discussions by I. J. Gelb (1980) and A. Malamat (1973), who thoroughly explain the acceptability and utility of ethnographic analogy, as well as more recent discussions by Lemche (1985:75; 1988:219; 1992:533; 1996a:539) and Jamieson-Drake (1989; 1991), although the treatment by Albright (1966:6ff.) reads as fresh as anything coming out of current anthropology.

If scholars are to reject typological analogy (true analogous types, as opposed to mere resemblance) as a method, and they still may do so, it must be for reasons other than lack of proximity. Following Foucault, many poststructuralist historians have rejected the comparative method and its quest for universal laws. This is because societies are simply not pushed out of a mold that renders only three or four distinct "types" of society (White 1990; Ginzburg 1989). Still, even those anthropologists who in this vein reject analogy as a wholesale explanatory tool for summarizing and concluding analyses accept analogy for formulating beginning models and introducing sets of questions at the onset of a study, to be tested against the data (Kramer 1979; Gould 1980; Hodder 1982). As Jacques Derrida has put it, such taxonomies "are neither inscribed in the heavens, nor in the brain, which does *not* mean that they are produced by the activity of some speaking subject" (1981:9; italics added). He means that although taxonomies are not an inherent part of what they describe, neither are they simply the mental constructions of a particular interpreter. And, further, Derrida holds that "the necessity of certain contexts will render strategically indispensable the recourse to a model known elsewhere" (1981:18). Endless variation of forms is not exclusive of large-scale comparability (Reisch 1995:54-55, 57).

It is such an approach that I will take in this study: the model of complex chiefdoms will introduce the examination and generate the questions to be asked. The model will elucidate and focus the data without forcing a square peg into a round hole. "The question to be asked of the model . . . is not 'is it true,' but 'is it useful?'" (Renfrew 1974:72) — does it explain a significant body of the data? "Considering how few pixels of the real image of the past are available, we find ourselves in a situation where our chances for reconstructing or exploring the past within a narrow chronological frame of [e.g.,] five hundred years, are fragile" (Thuesen 1996:54).

CHAPTER 3

The Complex Chiefdom Model

There is a long history of attempts to understand the premonarchic "structure" of the "Twelve Tribes" of Israel. Mendenhall (1973 and earlier) and de
Geus (1976) had already drawn on ethnographic models for understanding. The problem was that the English term "tribe," used by nearly every
modern translator for Heb. *šēbeṭ*, was misleading. When biblical scholars
(e.g., Lemche 1985:212-24, 236; Sigrist and Neu 1989) turned to the anthropological literature on "tribes," they did not realize that anthropologists
had in mind a primitive mode of organization without any permanent hierarchy (e.g., Braun and Plog 1982). This led biblical scholars to mistaken
conclusions. For example, because he was looking at the literature on
tribes and saw that they are far from being states, de Geus concluded that
tribes could not become states and that there must therefore have been
huge Israelite cities in Iron I that archaeology had missed (1976:209).
Flanagan (1981b:11-12), on the other hand, tried to develop tribes into
states. Other scholars became so confused that they decided "tribe" was a
meaningless term (Frick 1979:238; Gottwald 1993:179; Lemche 1996a:110).

Only in more recent years have efforts been made to study early
Israelite society under the rubric of the "chiefdom" (e.g., Jamieson-Drake
1991:144). Usually, what anthropologists mean by a chiefdom is a society
with ascribed rather than achieved rank. This means that rank is assigned
based on birth or family and not because of personal accomplish-
ments alone. This distinguishes chiefdoms from tribes (non-ranked or se-
rially ranked "Big Man" societies), a distinction extensively documented
ethnographically (Carneiro 1981; H. Wright 1984; Creamer and Haas

1985:742-43). But additionally, a chiefdom is a society where there is no specialized administrative control apparatus and legal system. A chiefdom's decision-making hierarchy lacks internal differentiation (H. Wright 1977:381; Earle 1990:76). This distinguishes chiefdoms from states (H. Wright 1984; 1985). Chiefdoms also differ from states in that states, like tribes, base status in part on achievement. That is, a chiefdom is "kinship politics taken as far as it can go" (Maisels 1990:9), while in states position is often a matter of political appointment and advancement and less of kinship or of ritual sanction (Taylor 1975:45; Yoffee 1992:65, 69). There is not a total dichotomy between societies with achieved and societies with ascribed rank, but rather a continuum between these two; exclusively achieved rank and exclusively ascribed rank are equally rare (Feinman and Neitzel 1984:61).

The office of chief exists apart from the individual holding that office. Not only are chiefdoms led by figures with ascribed rank, but the entire descent group of the chiefs is ranked above the commoners and is therefore endogamous (Barth 1961:74; Spencer 1987:376; Spriggs 1988:69; Mudar 1993:11). The chiefs are the landowners, and "have special relations with the gods which are denied commoners, which legitimize their right to demand community support and tribute" (Flannery 1972:403).

Unfortunately, the few biblical scholars and Syro-Palestinian archaeologists who have read any anthropological literature on chiefdoms (e.g., Mendenhall 1973; Flanagan 1981a; Lemche 1985:210-16) have relied on the outdated anthropological theories of Raymond Firth (1950), Elman Service (1962, esp. p. 144; 1975), and Marshal Sahlins (1963) for their understanding of chiefdoms. Sahlins generalized the analyses of Firth and others of various Pacific societies and created the chiefdom model with ranked patrilineages interrelated through redistribution (Sahlins 1963:296). Service reworked this general model. Yet holes began to appear in this construct when Lewis Binford (1965) showed that 17th-century mid-Atlantic chiefdoms could also be built inside a range of kin structures, not only patrilineal ones (e.g., matrilineal descent reckoning in Binford's Mid-Atlantic societies). Subsequent work by Earle (1977), Peebles and Kus (1977), and Steponaitis (1981) eliminated any remaining applicability of the redistributive model. Among historians of ancient Israel, only a few have noted this newer work (e.g., Frick 1985:74-84, 90-92; Jamieson-Drake 1991).

Much current theory describes chiefdoms as either "simple," those having only one level of control above the kin level, or "complex," those having an intermediate level or levels of "subchiefs" between the paramount and the people, although literature on this distinction has yet to be noticed by Syro-Palestinian archaeologists.[1] It is complex chiefdoms that develop into states and that one would expect to find in Israel on the threshold of Monarchy. Although evolutionary schemes will be avoided in this study (unlike Frick 1987:249), if a society did become a state (as, e.g., Israel), odds are that it would not immediately prior have been a simple chiefdom (Spencer 1987:378).

In addition, the Israelite complex chiefdom(s) would be neither primary nor pristine. That is, its development was not independent of contact with other cultures, nor was it the first complex chiefdom to emerge in the locale. Given the pre–Iron I history of Palestine, the Israelite chiefdom(s) would be greatly influenced by sociopolitical predecessors in the locale (Higgenbotham 1996). It is this "secondary complex chiefdom" that we will examine here, and that is important. But chiefdoms are *usually* secondary developments, and so the model may automatically handle this (Kristiansen 1991:25; Pauketat 1991:22). Characteristic attributes of secondary chiefdoms include an emergence more rapid than that of pristine, primary chiefdoms, less emphasis on entrenched ideological mechanisms to maintain elite power (D. Anderson 1990:29), greater reliance on overt use of force, at least initially, shorter durations of the centralized stages, and less likelihood of leadership positions having hereditary origins (D. Anderson 1990:32). Perhaps the closest analogy for Israelite society will be northern Mesopotamia from the upper and middle Khaibur drainages to the Assyrian plains east of the Tigris during the Ninevite V period (3100–2500 B.C.; G. Schwartz 1994). This region, like Iron I Palestine, had witnessed a devolution and regionalization when expansion by outside great powers (in the Mesopotamian case, Late Uruk) ended, and settled back into a chiefdom society (G. Schwartz 1994:154, 163).[2]

Earle (1977) and Peebles and Kus (1977) have shown that there are three main characteristics of complex chiefdoms: tribute mobilization, cy-

---

1. Without noticing the anthropological literature on this distinction, Stager did conjecture "'little chiefs' whose domains replicate on a smaller scale that of the . . . 'big chief'" (1985a:25).

2. The specifics of Schwartz's scenario, however, are questionable: a center at Tell Leilan is too far away to administer tributary sites at Nineveh, Tepe Gawra, and Tell Billa (as per G. Schwartz 1987:94). Perhaps Nineveh and other sites like Yurgan Tepe are the centers for Tepe Gawra and Tell Billa.

cling, and sacralization. Each of these can be summarized separately. That a paramount's role is mobilization and not redistribution means that, rather than dispensing the communal goods as needed, local units are in fact self-sufficient (Earle 1977:219; 1978:10; Spencer 1987:375). The chief mobilizes the distribution of native finished goods as signs of favor (Steponaitis 1978:420). Earle, along with Peebles and Kus, based much of this understanding on observations in Hawaii, where the paramount makes a tribute extraction for political and ritual reasons, not economic (Earle 1977:225). The model has been applied successfully elsewhere, as I will describe below.

The second characteristic described by Peebles and Kus, the cycling feature, involves a cycling between two and three levels of control (Kristiansen 1982:245; D. Anderson 1990:13, 35). When there are three levels — the centralized stage — the paramount (e.g., Basseri *khan*, Panamanian *quevi*, Tahitian *matahiapo arii*) rules supreme and has subchiefs (e.g., Basseri *kalantar*, Panamanian *saco*, Tahitian *raatira ariie*) below him (Feinman and Neitzel 1984:41), with the producing masses further below. The paramount chief is regarded as the residual owner of all land by patrimonial domain (Drucker 1951:248; E. Wolf 1966:50; Ruddell 1973:260, 264; Earle 1978:15; 1991b:74; A. Johnson and Earle 1987:233), although he does not control the means of production, which remain vested in kin groups (Maisels 1990:266). It is to the paramount's advantage to remove or at least bypass his subchiefs, and so there will often be three levels of control in ideology — chief, subchiefs, people — and so in text and mortuary evidence, but only two in practice — chief and people — and so in residential hierarchy (Spencer 1987:374-75; H. Wright 1984:50; Bard 1992:3).

A complex exchange takes place in this centralized stage (see the diagram in Welch 1991:17; see also Earle 1977:215-16; H. Wright 1984; Welch 1986:12-13). Subsistence tribute is usually cash crops such as olives, although occasionally tribute takes the form of single-season conscripted labor (Schwerin 1973:11; Mudar 1993:18), and moves from the people to subchiefs and from the subchiefs to the paramount chief, a portion being reserved at each stage (Ruddell 1973:260; Earle 1978:181; 1987a:66). Often the paramount only symbolically receives all this produce, and actually takes only what he needs to live (Drucker 1951:251), although conspicuous consumption to excess by the chief can be a demonstration of his social distinctiveness and economic authority (Earle 1978:181). In either case, it is not necessary to draw a distinction between tribute as "commodities," when consumption is involved, and tribute as "currency," when it is not, as do Wapnish and Hesse (1988:34). Either the tribute may be sent to the chief, or the chief may travel to the tributary sites to receive it (Earle 1987a:69).

This tribute is not seen as repaid by the chiefs through material redistribution, but rather repaid through sacred powers and activities such as intercession (Drucker 1951:257-58; E. Wolf 1966:52; Peebles and Kus 1977:426-27; Steponaitis 1978:420; Kristiansen 1982:245; Earle 1987b: 298; 1990:81; Pauketat 1991:24). Simultaneously, locally made exotic craft ("sumptuary") goods are made by the people, given up to the subchiefs and paramount, and then traded with foreign groups for their finished fancy goods (Welch 1991:180). The local craft or "sumptuary" goods vary in nature from society to society but are typically items of wide distribution not used in daily sustenance (cf. Bard 1994:72 for examples from early Egypt). The imports, occasionally along with some locally made sumptuary goods (Earle 1978:182), are then distributed in a reverse direction from paramount to subchiefs and thence to the people to build or maintain political support and to deny the existence of real power differences (Drucker 1951:247; Earle 1977:226; 1978:181; Peebles and Kus 1977:425; Kristiansen 1982:259; Brumfiel and Earle 1987:7; Paytner and McGuire 1991:8; Welch 1991:191). Necessities are not redistributed, as Service and Sahlins maintained (Wason 1994:52). Because trade occurs at the top, the paramount will have first access to foreign products, which may be visible in their relative abundance in his residence and grave goods (Brumfiel and Earle 1987:8; Dewar and Wright 1993:449; Bard 1994:107-8). This is, in effect, what Rowton has described (1977) for dimorphic chiefdoms: the elites interact with neighboring societies. There is a vicarious association of the elites with those traders who travel to get the foreign sumptuary goods. In this way, the chiefs can evidence their power both by possession of these goods as marks of exceptionality and, through the act of accumulation, as the fountainhead of the society's prosperity (Helms 1988:166-67; 1993:136; see G. Schwartz 1994:162 for evidence of this in northern Mesopotamia).

The two processes, the mobilization of subsistence goods and the tributary/distributary movement of prestige goods, are really independent. The one does not convert into the other, and prestige goods cannot be used to buy sustenance in a market sense (Earle 1987a:69). Nevertheless, wealth (prestige goods) symbolizes rank, which equals the rights to sustenance (Earle 1987a:69). Some items may be difficult to designate as specifically "subsistence" or "sumptuary," and may fall somewhere between — items such as salt, terebinth resin, and honey, known, for example, from texts at Ugarit and archaeologically from the Ulu Burun shipwreck. It is unclear how the movement of items such as these fits into the above model.

Any society has limits to its productivity. While the limits of production are approaching but devastating ecological changes such as deforestation undertaken in an attempt to increase the amount of "usable land" have not yet occurred, the production of the sumptuary goods — which are products of only part-time craft workers — will cease first, so that more time may be devoted to the production of sustenance goods (H. Wright 1984:45). When the production of sumptuary goods diminishes, the paramount has less opportunity to distribute sumptuary goods to his subchiefs (H. Wright 1984:45). Unless the paramount can gain more land and tribute by a victory in war or the like, a rebellion will likely follow, and the system will break down (Ruddell 1973:264-65; Earle 1978:184; Steponaitis 1978:430; Kristiansen 1982:260; H. Wright 1984:45-46; A. Johnson and Earle 1987:234).

A two-level decentralized system of subchiefs and subjects, but without a paramount chief and with little external exchange, is the result (Kristiansen 1982:261). The main center is now moot, and each subchief rules his portion, often warring with the other subchiefs (Barth 1961:83; D. Anderson 1990:81). Although each subchief receives craft goods and useful tribute from his subjects and gives them finished fancy goods, it is in much smaller amounts than in the centralized stage. One of the subchiefs probably will assume the status of paramount after the conflict is resolved (if not, the chiefdom will fragment into smaller units permanently; Schwerin 1973:7; D. Anderson 1990:82). Just which subchief takes over might be decided based on which one can begin giving his fellow subchiefs redistributed fancy goods (Kristiansen 1982:262; Pauketat 1991:14; Welch 1991:191-92). And this may be related to his ability to make outside trade connections and to muster his own economic resources most effectively (Kristiansen 1982:265; Helms 1988:153; Welch 1991:192). On the other hand, as the trickling down of foreign fancy goods to the people has become less because of the disruption of foreign trade and in the wake of social disintegration, it cannot serve as the sole motive for their production of local goods and food to send back up through the system. The locals have to be producing *before* the subchief-cum-paramount has anything to trade on the foreign markets. So perhaps foreign trade is not really the great stimulus for who becomes the paramount and is more a result of other processes of local motivation to internal efficiency and of military victory over competing subchiefs (Matthews 1978:155; Spriggs 1988:70; Earle 1991a:8).

With a new paramount, the process repeats. This cycling is evident not only in Hawaii, where it was initially observed by Earle (1977) and Peebles and Kus (1977), but also for the Natchez Native Americans (Steponaitis 1978) and, archaeologically, for Moundville II in Alabama (ca. A.D. 1250; Steponaitis 1983:156, 167-68) and southwestern Iran of the 5th millennium B.C. (H. Wright 1984).[3] Other ethnographic examples of complex chiefdoms, many secondary, include Tonga, Samoa, Tahiti, the Choctaw, Powhatan, Nootka, Arawak, and Cuna groups of Native Americans (Debo 1934:20-21; Swanton 1964:54; Helms 1976:29; Feinman and Neitzel 1984:63), pre-Colombian Panama (Helms 1976:27), 14th-16th century A.D. Madagascar (Dewar and Wright 1993:450), and the Basseri of Iran (Barth 1961:72; A. Johnson and Earle 1987:238). The Cherokee roughly belong in this group, but show so many idiosyncrasies owing to the fact that they were battered by European contact as to be of little use for analogy (Feinman and Neitzel 1984:63). Other archaeological examples include the Mexican valley of Oaxaca in the Rosario Phase (700-500 b.c.[4]), the valley of Mexico in the First Intermediate Phase 3 (200 B.C.-A.D. 1; Drennan 1991:271), Amratian/Nagada II Egypt (3600-3000 B.C.; Bard 1994:101), and such secondary post-state chiefdoms as late- and post-Mycenaean ("Dorian") Greece and the non-sovereign Western Semitic "tribal" elements described in the Mari texts (Rowton 1976:243-44; Anbar 1991). In the latter, the $sugāgum$ and $šibūtum^{meš}$ (and possibly the $maliku$ as well, given their Amarnan glossing as $rābiṣu$) might be subchiefs under paramount $abbūtu^{meš}$ or $šarrānu^{meš}$.

From ethnographic case studies, it appears that these cycles last about fifteen years. Every hundred or 150 years there is a larger cycling in which a new dynasty might be established, bringing with it a new center and new symbolism (Kristiansen 1982:247, 263; H. Wright 1984:51; D. Anderson 1990:19). Commonly, the most efficient territory size for a single paramount's domain would be one with a radius of about a half day of travel from the regional center (Spencer 1982:6-7).

3. Here Susiana Phase c and Susa Phase A are the centralized periods, and the intervening Susiana Phase d and Susa Terminal Phase A are times of decentralization.

4. The abbreviation "b.c." (lower case) refers to unadjusted radiocarbon dates.

The third of Peebles and Kus's characteristics, the sacralization process, is directly linked to the cycling, in the following way. Genealogical manipulation is a key to legitimizing rule. It is important that each new paramount be seen as the legitimate senior descendant of the eldest line, and so rewriting of genealogies takes place (Barth 1961:55, 63; Ruddell 1973:258; Steponaitis 1978:419; Maisels 1990:248-49). Younger descendants of the chiefs' line become almost a middle class, creating the characteristic "conical clan" (e.g., the Nootka; Drucker 1951:245). The genealogies become more complex as the chiefdom continues to cycle. The dynastic founder becomes merely an eponymous ancestor. Eventually, the paramount's descent as eldest in the eldest line from a distant patriarch may be mythicized into descent from a demigod (Friedman 1975:172-78; D. Gibson and Geselowitz 1988:24). The chief's relation to this god gives him a sacred legitimacy, which makes his support obligatory for the people (Helms 1979:71; Earle 1987a:71; Spencer 1987:376; Maisels 1990:244).

Complex chiefdom cycling may continue for some time without state formation. "Pre-state societies with two or three levels of control hierarchy persist for centuries, with intense competition and much replacement of centers and no doubt of paramounts, but with little or no increase in social complexity" (H. Wright 1985:357).

However, these types of complex chiefdoms usually eventually become states (Schwerin 1973:7; Brumfiel and Earle 1987:8). The exceptions (e.g., Samoa and Tonga) are nearly all islands (northeastern South America contains continental exceptions) where intrusive, achieved-rank "hero" individuals (e.g., the Panamanian *cabra*) do the actual ruling, whereas the paramount chief reigns only as a figurehead (Helms 1979:12-13; 1993).

No attempt will be made here to elaborate on the process of transformation from chiefdom to state (for fuller treatment see Earle 1987b:280). The complex chiefdom model stands on its own logic, and is not justified by any reference to the later development of states (Spencer 1987:379; Feinman 1991:230-31). Here the criticisms of chiefdom theory by Yoffee (1992) are therefore not valid, as his critique is of the evolution-to-state framework (Yoffee 1992 passim, esp. 61-62, 64).

One must give serious consideration, however, to other arguments against the chiefdom model. Yoffee also objects to the classification of societies into ethnological "types" (1992:71), taking a more historical-particularistic view. It is not the goal here, however, to come up with a phyletic-type "chiefdom" that can be compared to homologous "chiefdoms" throughout history and space (Hodder 1984). Yoffee is correct that "Societies do not form phyletic stages. . . . cross-cultural comparison can best proceed through analogy rather than homology" (1979:7). But there is still validity in typologies. Steward's dictum holds true that "there must be a typology of cultures, patterns, and institutions . . . for formulating cultural regularities" (1949:3) — or irregularities, one might add (Gould 1980). The kind of "types" needed allows the researcher "not to identify fossilized natural classes, but rather to deal with a series of sociocultural variables, which are seen as analytical categories, which can be combined and recombined into numerous societal constellations" (Yoffee 1979:28). Yoffee himself has not been averse to using such "types," calling them "sociocultural forms" (Yoffee 1979:27) of "comparable socioeconomic complexity" (Yoffee 1981:2). The complex chiefdom model, contrariwise, has actually focused attention *away* from a societal type of chiefdom and onto political process (Earle 1989:87; Pauketat 1991:11).

CHAPTER 4

Archaeological Analysis
of the Iron I Highlands

A society that operates as described by the complex chiefdom model will leave characteristic archaeological remains. The archaeological correlates are not telltale traits that demarcate the developmental level of chiefdom (Yoffee 1979:44) but merely the inevitable archaeological results of the sociocultural functioning described in the model (Yoffee 1979:28; Carr 1991:224). Much of what is visible archaeologically is also the result of intentional actions on the part of the chiefdoms' leaders (and probably the subaltern groups as well; Brumfiel 1992:556). These individuals are real cultural agents, not passive elements (Renfrew 1986:154).

In this chapter, the aforementioned list of potential archaeological correlates to the model focuses the study of the archaeological record of the Israelite community in the 12th and 11th centuries B.C.

Geographic Scope

It is first necessary to delimit in a preliminary way the geographic scope of this archaeological discussion. It is the archaeology and its interpretation that will, in the end, define the "boundaries" of the Israelite settlement in Iron I, and so no effort will be made to decide which sites are Israelite before assembling the data. Because the entire question of what is "Israel" remains an open one, this archaeological section will include geographic areas that must certainly be *outside* proto-Israel. The drawing of ethnopolitical boundaries around Israel will need to be a separate issue entirely (to be addressed in Chapter 5). Yet we must focus on a limited geographic area, and there is a weight of evidence to suggest it. Archaeologically, a distinct settlement occupied the highland area between Jerusalem and the Jezreel Valley (Redford 1992:295; A. Mazar 1994c:39-57). The "Judean" area south of Jerusalem was sparsely inhabited, largely by seasonal sites, compared with the densely populated north-central hill country (Finkelstein 1993a:124). This north-central region was bounded on the north by a line of Egyptian, Amorite,[1] and Philistine city-states running from Dor to Beth-Shan (Dor, Ein Haggit, Yoqneam, Megiddo, Taanach, Ibleam, Afula, and Beth-Shan), and on the south by a similar line from Gezer to Jerusalem, which exhibit material cultures distinct from the highland unit until the late 11th century (Herrmann 1985:49; Gal 1994:45; Donner 1995:139-40). A similar line can be drawn on the western edge, from Socho to Aphek to Jaffa (Herrmann 1985:49; Astour 1995:1416). On the eastern edge, although it is assumed that the Jordan River was a sufficient boundary on topographic bases (for the effect of a water boundary on lines of trade, see Hodder and Orton 1976:59-60, 78-80), there is a similar line partway down the river from Beth-Shan to Rehov to Hamath to Tell es-Saidiyeh to Deir Allah.[2] All of

---

1. I have chosen the term "Amorite" because "Canaanite" is quite problematic. As early as Yeivin (1971:90n.18), scholars were suggesting that it had no specific ethnic, linguistic, or political connotations. Recent discussions have emphasized this (e.g., Ahlström 1986; Lemche 1991c; 1993). The evidence of Nibbi (1989) is even more damaging to any attempt to reconstruct a consistent meaning of the term (although all "Canaan" references are certainly not to the Nile Delta). Its ancient use certainly had various referents, but at some point it *was* a term for the Late Bronze Age inhabitants of Palestine (Yeivin 1971:90n.18; Na'aman 1994), and "Canaan" was a nonethnic geographic term behind that appellation (Ahlström 1995:587) as well as an Egyptian province (*piati ša Kina'i; EA* 36:15). Nevertheless, because of the heated debate over the loaded use of "Canaanite" (Lemche 1991a:107), in this study I will replace the term with the appellation "Amorite," an even more meaningless term (although its blanket usage is supported by Josh. 10:6).

2. Each of these municipal principalities will be dealt with in Chapter 5. The only ones not treated there are the following: Yoqneam — Tel Jokneam/Egyptian 'Ain(i)qan'am-(m)u<'Ain(i)-yiqn'ammu (Ahituv 1984), Levels 14-13 are 12th century (Raban 1982:11); Ibleam — Khirbet Belameh, the Egyptian *Yabla'amu* (Ahituv 1984), a nine-hectare city in Iron I (Peterson 1977:221; Zertal 1992:116); Ein Haggit guarding the Nahal Tut pass between Dor and Yoqneam (S. Wolff 1994:3; 1995:54); Socho — Khirbet Shuweikhat er-Ras, mentioned as *Socho* in the Karnak List of Thutmose III, lines 67a, b, and c, the Spoleto List of Seti I, line A19, the Memphis Annals of Amenhotep II, 1306:2, the Soleb List of Amenhotep III, line 7B3, the Amarna West List of Rameses II, lines 70 and 91, and #38 of the Shishak List, which I surveyed August 31, 1996; Jaffa — Joppa V-IV, the Egyptian port of

these lines are of sites whose material culture is totally unlike that of the highlands: lowland sites, most much larger than those of the highlands, have locally made Egyptian pottery forms, large amounts of Cypriote-made Mycenaean IIIc pottery, large numbers of incense stands, cuneiform tablets, hieroglyphic door lintels, and unique pottery forms such as "beer jugs" — the differences from the highlands are quite clear. For an excellent treatment of these issues see Dever (1998:47-48) and Killebrew (1998).

It is a separate question whether a 12th- and 11th-century Israelite community was confined to the highlands. Nevertheless, the greatest number of Iron Age I sites is found within this north-central hill country of Palestine (A. Mazar 1990:335). Therefore, I will not examine areas such as Galilee or any supposed Israelite coastal settlement around Tel Hefer and Tel Zeror in this study. Yet to define the boundaries of highland Israel exactly, the archaeological analysis extends in all four directions, beyond sites that "appear" Israelite to sites that do not, so that many may be eliminated at a later point by criteria other than a "pots equal peoples" dichotomy of material culture.

Methodology

Information from archaeological excavations and surveys on settlement patterns, mortuary practices, architectural styles, and distribution of wealth provides a basis for comparing the specific cases of highland Palestine with the complex chiefdom model. Archaeologists have defined six phenomena that result from complex chiefdoms (Peebles and Kus 1977:431-33). This list is useful for initiating the study of the highland set-

---

Yapu abandoned in the 11th century with a small Philistine settlement in the late 11th century as Level IIIB (Singer 1994:307-8); Rehov — Tel Rehov/Tell ez-Zarem (Zori 1962:176-78; 1975:14; Singer 1994:310; A. Mazar 1998), the *Rehob* of Thutmose III Karnak List 22.8, Seti I's Beth-Shan Stele 12.10, Seti II Year 1 Papyrus Anastasi 4 17.3, the 20th-Dynasty Papyrus Turin 102, and Shishak's #17, with pottery identical to Beth-Shan in all Iron I phases; Hamath — Tell el-Hamme, *Khamath* of the Seti I Stele found at Beth-Shan, Seti I Karnak XII.50, Seti I Karnak XIV.52(55), Seti I el-Qurne North and South Sphinxes #14, and Rameses II Karnak #27, with three Iron I strata (Cahill et al. 1989:38), also with pottery identical to Beth-Shan; and Tell es-Saidiyeh — Egyptian Level XII displaying the largest wall in the southern Levant since the Middle Bronze Age (Tubb 1988:440), followed by Level XIA in the 12th century (Tubb 1988:38; Weinstein 1992:145).

tlement, although the paper of Peebles and Kus is somewhat dated and tends toward a *Kulturgeschichte,* grocery-list approach to the model (match the list and you've got a chiefdom; Yoffee 1979:24).[3]

First, according to Peebles and Kus, ascriptive rank, as opposed to achieved, must be documented. It has been suggested that "no single category of archaeological data will prove as useful for social inference as burial remains" (Tainter 1976:91; cf. Bard 1994:104). Mortuary evidence for ascriptive rank would be cases where grave goods suggesting social rank occur independently of age or sex (Tainter and Cordy 1977:97; Peebles 1978:371). Stimulated by the American Anthropological Association's Social Dimensions of Mortuary Practices Symposium organized by James Brown in 1966 and its subsequent publication (Brown 1971), seminal essays by Saxe (1970), Binford (1972), and Goldstein (1980) outlined how mortuary practices relate to economic and political stratification (Larsen 1995:247). Their assumption was that the living choose to use funerary symbols, and that these must be congruent with the roles the dead had when they lived. Presumably, but falsely, the role of most power that people had while alive will be most emphasized in their death (Saxe 1970). Studies such as Tainter's (1973; 1976; 1980) understood the Saxe-Binford-Goldstein program narrowly as an act of reading each burial as a terminal social statement that one could quantify, without synchronic or diachronic dimensions (O'Shea 1984). The generalization that a wealthy child burial equals ascribed rank, regarded as a truism since Peebles and Kus (1977), is a popular corollary to this work, although its popularity rests on internal logic and not on a great deal of concrete evidence either cross-culturally or historically (Larsen 1995:250). In the end, mortuary evidence can be used only for advancing part of the larger argument, contributing to the larger chain of data of different kinds (Trinkaus 1995:55).

Earle argues that although mortuary evidence may illustrate the theoretical structure of society, residential evidence is more apt to show the actual operational hierarchies (Earle 1987b:291). Residential evidence is the second of Peebles and Kus's correlates — indications of differences in scale and wealth between households. In complex chiefdoms, "there will be segregation by neighborhoods or in special communities of elite," but no palaces (H. Wright 1984:44; Creamer and Haas 1985:742). Taken together,

---

3. The grocery-list tendency is evident in Frick (1979:243; 1985:87), who has, however, been one of the few biblical scholars to read modern chiefdom literature.

mortuary and residential evidence has been found to correlate only slightly (v = .40) with the actual functions of a chief (Feinman and Neitzel 1984:60, 77), although the correlation is strong (v = .95) with the number of administrative levels in the society (Feinman and Neitzel 1984:68). Furthermore, although a chief may often have much power and few archaeological markers, rarely will an individual have the trappings of power without the power (Feinman and Neitzel 1984:60).

Thirdly, settlement hierarchy must be established. This involves identifying the centers of administrative control, the number of such centers, and the hierarchy of these centers. It is assumed that one can measure the degree of political centralization by determining the ratio of the amount of tribute controlled by the central authority and the amount of tribute controlled by the next lowest administrative level. It is further assumed that this ratio can be seen on the ground by differences in site size, since larger tribute received, particularly comestibles, will result in larger populations and therefore larger site size (G. Johnson 1986:23). One might therefore conclude that a complex chiefdom would require three levels of settlement hierarchy, two above the producer (H. Wright and G. Johnson 1975). There is a danger here, however, in that occasionally the paramount's center may not be the largest site, and the subchiefs' capitals may not even be the largest sites in their zones. Other evidence, such as foreign goods and residential evidence, must support the identification of centers (Dewar and Wright 1993:448).

Fourth, Peebles and Kus maintain that settlements should be found where there is an abundance of resources for sustenance, although they are vague at defining such abundance.[4] Fifth, there should be monumental architecture or similar constructions that would have required conscripted labor, designed to discipline a population (Paynter and McGuire 1991:9). One must be careful here of mistaking a state society, which can also have conscripted labor, for a chiefdom (Haas 1982:215-26). Only regional-scale contributed labor of no more than one season's duration is characteristic of chiefdoms (Creamer and Haas 1985:742-43).

Sixth, and finally, there should be evidence of warfare or defense (Drennan 1991:279), although the distinctiveness of chiefdoms in this regard is debatable (Steponaitis 1983:172; Creamer and Haas 1985:743).

---

4. It seems difficult to imagine any type of society where "inhabitants prefer the isolation and protection of ecological niches that have marginal agricultural potential and require labor-intensive cultivation" (Flanagan 1988:154). Certainly not a chiefdom.

Beyond the list of Peebles and Kus, the search for the archaeological correlates of complex chiefdoms begins with regional analysis. Regional settlement patterns can reveal social organization (C. Smith 1976:4; Parsons 1990:13). In this study I will draw the settlement map for this geographical unit for the 12th and 11th centuries, complete with locations and periods of occupation. Full-coverage surveys alone can provide the identification of centers and objective data that may show unexpected settlement patterns (Parsons 1990:13). This use of settlement patterns must go beyond simply looking for the history of the settlement process in dating when the Israelites moved into different environmental zones (as done by Finkelstein 1996c:390). It must interact with discussions of settlement patterns in the literature of locational geography (Gregg, Kintigh, and Whallon 1991:152).

As the complex-chiefdom model suggests a mobilization of subsistence goods to support the elite, the lines of transfer of tribute and sumptuary goods will be determined. The interaction between sites is mapped using the Gravity Model, as Plog has found this formula particularly applicable to chiefdoms (1976:255). The Gravity Model holds that the interaction between two sites is directly proportional to the product of the population of the two sites and inversely proportional to a function of the (time) distance between the sites (the linear distance adjusted to topography; Cliff, Martin, and Ord 1974:186, 281; Curry, Griffith, and Sheppard 1975:289, 295).[5]

This Gravity Model–driven interaction map will then be compared with various possible locational-geographical scenarios. Steponaitis (1978) has taken the features of the complex chiefdom model and from them determined how the settlement pattern of complex chiefdoms should look. The result is mid-level sites found between smaller sites and the main center instead of uniformly around the center, with the smaller sites, in turn, grouped uniformly around those mid-level sites — as one would find in classical Central Place Theory (the so-called k = 3 or even k = 4; Christaller 1966:72).

This interaction map can be expanded by looking at the assemblages, particularly ceramic, from each site to illustrate patterns of exchange, eco-

---

5. Admittedly, if sites are of different types, their interaction may have more to do with the interplay of site functions than merely with their distances apart (Crumley 1979:147-52).

nomic relations — direction of tribute, storage on a regional level,[6] and political structure — how nonlocal goods enter the community, and how they are distributed (Creamer and Haas 1985:742-43; Welch 1991:21). It will be determined whether different components of the community use or have direct access to grossly different sets or mixtures of resources and if there is strong evidence of net movement of subsistence into and out of the subsidiary centers to provision the elites (Welch 1991:79-80, 103). Sumptuary goods made outside the community ought to be the prerogative of the paramount (Creamer and Haas 1985:743; Bard 1994:107-1). Occasionally, other objects will act as symbols of hierarchy (Wobst 1977). An ethnographic example is the occurrence of mace heads in Nagada II Egyptian graves (Bard 1994:100). However, these symbols may not always be identifiable, either if they are perishable (e.g., costumes) or if they are not clearly luxuries but are instead important for their ritual connections of great power (Brown 1981:37).

Such information can be examined diachronically to show temporal change. This could show the cycling of the complex chiefdoms, particularly in "patterns of expansion-regression, settlement densities and systems of land use, degree of and means of economic exploitation, and to some extent, systems of rank and ritual" (Kristiansen 1982:247). It may be possible to analyze the breakdown phase, when established hierarchic structures and tributary systems collapsed in the prelude to state formation.[7]

---

6. Such regional storage has been argued for subsidiary sites of possible Ninevite V chiefdoms at Telul eth-Thalathat Tell V and, in a separate polity, to a lesser extent at Karrana 3 (G. Schwartz 1987:96).

7. Brumfiel's work (1976), as developed by Steponaitis (1981), suggests that when plotting all the sites within a given chiefdom on a population vs. productivity graph one will discover one line of sites below the line expressing the maximum population supportable for a given productivity level and another above the line (Bernbeck 1994:59). The lower line, where there is more productivity than is needed to support the immediate population, represents the tributary sites (Creamer and Haas 1985:742-43). The higher line, where productivity is not enough to sustain the populations, illustrates the centers supported by the tributary sites (cf. Creamer and Haas 1985:742). There may be a third level for the paramount's center (Steponaitis 1981:330; 1983:156, 168). This method thus eliminates large noncenters that might be mistaken for centers; they will now not show up as centers unless they are not only large but larger than their catchment can support on its own.

Another method that has proven empirically impressive for identifying sociopolitical and economic structure is rank-size analysis (Dacey 1966:31-33). Rank-size analysis involves graphing the size of the sites of each rank to show how large the main centers are in compar-

Inherent Difficulties

We must carry out each of these procedures in examining the archaeological realia of the Iron I highlands of Palestine, in addition to other methods presented in the following section. Several issues, however, really render all conclusions drawn from such analyses tendentious, and the tasks themselves all but impossible.

Survey Coverage

Meager amounts of survey data involving broad and unquantifiable aspects — and it can be argued that this is what one has from the survey data of Syro-Palestine — yield only trivial results when forced through statistical computations (Kennedy 1978:99-100). To begin with, even full coverage surveys "are ill-suited to discover small settlements, particularly unobtrusive farms and camp sites, that might lie buried in wadi bottoms" (Banning 1996:38; Aston 1985:98 with examples). Many small settlements are simply missed by the survey methods used (S. Gibson 1995), although Banning's own work involving two-millimeter-deep test pits across the landscape found that many sites buried at the wadi bottoms could *never* be located by *any* surface survey method, and Israel Finkelstein has recently noted this (Finkelstein, Lederman, and Bunimovitz 1997:8). The impact of missed sites on the kind of regional analysis undertaken and proposed

---

ison to lower-ranked settlements. It lacks, however, a good theoretical basis and ignores the fact that different sites may have different needs and contacts (Crumley 1979:147). Rank-size graphs could be constructed for the highland settlement, and there are some good experiments in this (Jamieson-Drake 1991:63-64, 212; and Ofer 1993:fig. 94 — both for the highland region south of Jerusalem). The rank-size curve for complex chiefdoms is primo-convex. That is, it begins primate for higher-ranking sites (a quick dropoff in size from the first-ranked site) since the capital monopolizes external trade and has little economic or political competition, and then bends convex for lower-ranked sites (lowest-ranked sites are not as small as the early slope of the line suggests) characteristic of multiple subsystems largely outside the economic control of the first-ranked sites (e.g., Early Uruk; Sumner 1990:108). Cf. the log-normal curve for Late Uruk, Early Bronze III Palestine, and Monte Alban II in Mesoamerica and the primate/concave state curve for Iron II Palestine (Bradford and Kent 1977:60-61, 64-65).

But for reasons that will be outlined below, neither of these methods can be used for the Iron I highland settlement.

here would be severe. Gravity Models will be wrong, Theissen polygons wrong, rank-size curves misleading, and so on (Kennedy 1978:99-100). So it must be stated at the onset that although, *as it is currently meant,* all Iron I sites within the geographic scope have been identified, this is most definitely not so in reality.

Site Size

Almost as important for these manipulations as not missing any sites is having sizes for each site. The Gravity Model, rank-size curves, population vs. productivity graphs and the like all rely on size measurements for the sites. So, in most studies of this sort, sizes are given for the sites included in the study for the period in question (e.g., many studies from Stager 1985a to Finkelstein 1996f). Yet one can argue that it is not possible to give sizes for sites from survey data for a given period except single-period sites.[8]

Usually, archaeologists simply present the size for a site in a given period, with no indication about how they arrive at this figure (e.g., Stager 1985a; Otto 1997:11). One may presume that usually the "size" figure for the site is simply lifted from the survey. In this case, this is the *modern* size of the site. Issues of erosion and so forth aside, the modern size of the site will only be equal to the size in the period of interest if that were the time of the site's largest occupation. Thus a five-hectare site, according to its modern measurement, may have been five hectares in Iron I, or it may have been one. A five-hectare Byzantine town may overlay it. This is known as the "Palimpsest Effect" (Zvelevil, Green, and Macklin 1992:196-97).

In response to this problem, some archaeologists have attempted to weigh the modern sizes by the pottery they find in surveys (e.g., Ofer 1993). To find the size in a desired period, the modern size will be adjusted according to the percentage of pottery (or of rims) from that period. In this case, a site that is ten hectares in the present may be surveyed with a pickup of 10 percent Early Bronze pottery, 10 percent Iron I, 50 percent Iron II, and 30 percent Byzantine. The researcher would then declare the site to have been one hectare (10% of 10 ha.) in Iron I. Or perhaps they would admit

---

8. Outside of Syro-Palestinian archaeology, this idea has been suggested before (e.g., Rihll and Wilson 1991:69).

that the site may not have been exactly one hectare, but use the figure of "one" as a comparative index to compare with other sites (as per Jamieson-Drake 1991:56, passim).[9]

Yet this method is also meaningless. The percentage of pottery from a given period is proportionate to many more conditions than simply the amount of occupation from that period. A site occupied in the Early Bronze and Late Bronze periods and then terminally as a one-hectare village in Iron I will have a much higher percentage of Iron I pottery on the surface than a one-hectare Iron I village reoccupied in the Iron II, Hellenistic, and Crusader periods. But lest one think that by somehow incorporating into the calculations of modern size and percent from the desired period a factor of the number of subsequent occupations (or years), as suggested by Portugali (1982:171), studies have shown that the decrease of early sherds on the top of a site is less proportionate to the number of later occupations than to the height of the site-top itself, and that earlier levels will not leave sherds at all if buried more than five meters deep (A. Rosen 1986:246; Finkelstein, Lederman, and Bunimovitz 1997:14).

Portugali (1982) has attempted to deal with the issues of both "proximity to the top" and varying expanses of earlier settlements. Simply put, his proposal involves using topographic maps to make "shelf maps" of a given site, and then surveying each shelf proportionally. Mapping out what period dominates each shelf, one can determine what period each shelf "sticking out" comes from and determine that periods for which pottery is found but never dominating any single shelf must be totally sealed inside the site and therefore smaller than the smallest exposed shelf (Portugali 1982:183-84). This idea is particularly attractive since it would deal with the varying forms of layering sites can take — sites with successive settlements of equal size, and all variations of larger-on-smaller and smaller-on-larger and so forth (cf. A. Rosen 1986:47).

However, apart from the fact that Portugali's method cannot help with sites already surveyed by traditional methods and that surveying in the field by his method is too time-consuming, its presumptions are mistaken. Although, unlike most other archaeologists, Portugali does account for varying site form, he does not take into consideration leveling, erosion, or deposition (A. Rosen 1986:9-10; Finkelstein, Lederman, and Bunimovitz 1997:16). As a concrete example, shelf surveying at Khirbet Seilun by

9. And, in fact, the latter method was tried in earlier versions of this study.

Finkelstein using Portugali's method revealed 0 percent Middle Bronze sherds directly above the richest Middle Bronze deposit of the site (Finkelstein, Lederman, and Bunimovitz 1997:14). In the first place, using modern topographic contour lines at all is pointless in the severely eroded areas of southwest Asia (Rapp 1996). As Arlene Rosen has shown (1986; also Sharon 1995:57-59), the formation of debris on top of an Iron I settlement, for example, is a complex process of accumulation of rubble, refuse, and sediment, plus soil development, competing against a downward deformation from the complex process of slope erosion. Contrary to Portugali, slope erosion is not a simple process. It is possible to model the process, as Portugali has not done, and such a model would suggest a combination of Slope Decline — erosion as it is usually imagined, especially on the eastern faces of sites — and Parallel Retreat, where sediment is removed and there is therefore no change in slope, especially on the northwestern, rain-facing faces (A. Rosen 1986:27). One could use this combination model to adapt Portugali's method, except that it works only on sites undisturbed after the last occupation — with each new occupation the process is interrupted (A. Rosen 1986:29-30). Moreover, there would still be no accounting for varying depositional processes, nor for the fact that mud brick, sandstone, basalt, limestone, and other building materials erode at different rates, nor for the varying ways erosion occurs in different climates (A. Rosen 1986, chaps. 2-3). Allowing for most of these conditions is possible, using what is known as the Universal Soil Loss Equation (USLE). This equation incorporates the building matter and soil type, the slope of the site, the slope length, the type of covering vegetation, and the rainfall conditions, and computes the interplay of deposition, soil formation, and erosion (A. Rosen 1986:34). Without all this information, one cannot reconstruct the tell's evolution as Portugali does or as Ofer does implicitly. Nevertheless, even using the USLE, no allowance is made for occupational interruptions in the process, for quarrying, for variations in rainfall intensity or direction over history, or for changes in the nature of vegetation over history, and one cannot assume that these were constant for the last three thousand years. Except for single-period sites, one cannot give precise size data from surveys.

Excavated sites, even those with "full exposure," may still not give accurate size information. For example, it now has been shown that Tell el-Ful in the Iron I period was not confined to the tell but extended down the lower eastern slope, likely all the way down into the Wadi Zimri (S. Gibson

1996; see Chapter 5 below), and this means that the real size is much larger than previously believed.

But instead of abandoning all hope of Gravity Modeling, rank-size graphing, and the like, one can partially alleviate the problem of size (but not that of missing sites). By looking at survey data from single-period Iron I sites, of which there are several (Abu Rish, Wadi Hamdan, etc.), and critically looking at excavated sites, classes of sites can be set up (Finkelstein 1996b; 1996f; Finkelstein, Lederman, and Bunimovitz 1997:15). This is based on the postulate that rather than running the gamut of sizes uniformly, sites tend to group in discrete, size-based classes. These classes could be used for Gravity Modeling, population vs. productivity graphing, and other manipulations, although for something like rank-size curves the presumptions made are extremely dangerous. For Iron I, the classes used herein are as follows (Finkelstein 1996f; Moore 1997:301-3): Class A villages, from five houses up to 0.2 ha.; Class B to 0.7 ha.; Class C1 to 1.35 ha.; Class C2 to 2 ha., and Class D to 4 ha. In figures included in this study, Class A is indicated by a dot, B by a triangle, C1 by a hollow circle, C2 by a square, and D by a hexagon. To which class a site belongs has been determined on the basis of nonmathematical examination of modern size, percentage of pottery, position in the depositional sequence, erosional nature, duration of occupation, time since abandonment, and the like (Finkelstein, Lederman, and Bunimovitz 1997:15-16), and then for calculations the modal values are used instead of site-specific ones.

Dating Concerns

Israel Finkelstein has raised a serious challenge to the dating of Iron I over the past several years (beginning with 1995b; 1996a). Without detailing Finkelstein's argument, one may say that one element of it sets as 10th century Beersheba VI, Arad XII, Megiddo VIA, and the like, all of which are small, underdeveloped sites. By moving the dating of these strata previously called 11th century later by a hundred years, one also brings their pottery repertoires, previously "Iron I," down into Iron II, complete with the collared-rimmed pithoi and the Iron I cooking-pot rims. Collared-rimmed pithoi, for example, survive until 900 B.C. This means that since the end of Late Bronze II does not change, sites previously surveyed as "Iron I" may be 10th century. It also means that some excavated sites dated to Iron I may now really date from around 950, while others may still be in the 12th century. For the purposes of this study, contemporaneity of sites may be lost, rendering everything from settlement patterns on meaningless and the quest for the 12th and 11th centuries insurmountable. Finkelstein has suggested that as a result the conclusions of his own highland Iron I work (1986; 1988a) may in this way be meaningless.

Many responses to Finkelstein, replies to these responses, and rejoinders to the replies are in print. The reader should consult A. Mazar (1997c) and subsequent studies. The burden of proof still seems to be on Finkelstein, and his revisions will not be accepted here.

Another chronological issue for settlement patterns is that even in a two-hundred-year Iron I period, all "Iron I" sites may not be contemporaneous (Berry 1968:29; Parsons 1972). This is not as much of a problem as it would be for periods of long duration, but even in two hundred years sites can be founded and abandoned. One need not assume that all Iron I sites on the map were occupied simultaneously (Dewar and McBride 1992:230-37). Nevertheless, this study will assume that they were, first because Iron I is a comparatively short period, and second because long-term environmental benefits and cultural/ideological notions tend to give sites "inertia" and prevent quick abandonment and movement in a single society (Portugali 1984b:47; Naʿaman 1986a:32; Wandsnider 1992:279; Sharon 1995:97-98; Grosby 1997:1).

Residuality

The final subject of concern for the archaeological data is one that seems innocuous on the surface but may actually be the most damaging of all, and in many ways may confirm the vanity of "New Archaeology" in the Levant. A recent essay by Jeff Blakely (1996; also Camili and Ebert 1992:115-31) discussed two cases of "residuality" in ceramic remains, cases where pottery appears in strata long after the pottery is believed to "date." Both examples are of pottery types with firm production dates of short duration. The first case is the presence of Attic Fine Ware at Tell el-Hesi (Blakely 1996:333; also 1990:240). Attic Fine Ware "dates" to ca. 400 B.C., yet 80 to 90 percent of the Attic Fine Ware found at Tell el-Hesi, even sherds found flat-lying on occupational surfaces, was in much later strata. The other example is Caesarea, concerning Pompeiian Red Ware (Blakely 1996:334-35). Again, 90 percent of the Pompeiian Red Ware found at Caesarea was residual in later levels. In fact, half the Pompeiian Red Ware came from strata two hundred years after the production of Pompeiian Red Ware had ceased.

The corollary to this is that a large portion of the pottery from a given stratum is not from that stratum. It may be from an occupation some two hundred years earlier. This does serve almost to eliminate *terminus ad quem* dating by ceramics: anything found that could be from an earlier occupation likely is. Finding a sherd that "occurs only before X" is meaningless because *no* sherd "occurs only before" any time. One cannot say that biconical jugs disappear in late Iron I (as does Amiran 1970:251), or that Cypriote Base–ring ends in 1125 (as does Van Beek 1951:28), or that because Mycenaean Cypriote Late Helladic IIIB is found as late as the end of the 19th Dynasty at Deir Al-lah, Late Helladic IIIC1a must start at 1190 (as does Iakovides 1979:461-62).

But this is more than just another wrench in the dating. If *this much* pottery is residual, one must contend with the possibility that from a given stratum seeds, bones, metal objects, gems, and all sorts of other things may be residual, and likely are (Blakely 1990:244; 1997; Hesse and A. Rosen 1988:118). If floral and faunal remains cannot be securely assigned to a given occupation, they are useless for reconstruction of economies.[10] If metal, glass, and mineral objects similarly cannot be assigned, they are useless for reconstruction of trade systems and useless for interpretation as markers of rank. And although Blakely (1990:247-48) holds out the hope that statistical modeling can reconstruct the taphonomic processes to the extent that residuality can be removed, the work of Arlene Rosen (1986) discussed above puts this hope beyond reach.

Because of all these concerns, in this study I will use Gravity Model on site class data, rather than sizes, for all regions involved, but will not at-tempt rank/size, population/productivity, and so forth; to apply these would imply a significance to the statistics that is not present. The follow-ing, then, is what can be said about the archaeology of the Iron I highlands.

---

10. A potentially more useful method might be to examine pottery that can be dated securely to the period of the stratum for "lipid biomarkers" (Evershed 1996), using Gas Chromatography–Mass Spectroscopy to identify the ancient foods contained in vessels by residual lipids. This procedure is just in its infancy, and numerous dangers exist: the con-struction of a database of molecular weight "fingerprints" needed to identify the lipids and their food sources is impossible for animals or plants that are now extinct; one is merely testing today's equivalent foods for matches. The very act of extracting these biomarkers from an artifact may alter or decompose some of the molecules (already eaten by millennia of bacteria to unrecognizable compositions).

CHAPTER 5

The Archaeological Portrait
of the Iron I Settlement

Sources

The key data for this study comprise an exhaustive catalogue of all the Iron I sites in the area under examination. The collection of these data, including all the site information referred to herein, has been published as Robert D. Miller II, *A Gazetteer of Iron I Sites in the North-central Highlands of Palestine,* Annual of the American Schools of Oriental Research 56 (Cambridge, MA: American Schools of Oriental Research, 2002). This should be considered a companion volume to the present study and consulted for more detailed archaeological information.

Settlement Map

The map of the Iron I highland settlement reveals six distinct zones of occupation, the distinction of which is more clear with the application of the Gravity Model. There are two partly intertwined zones north of modern Nablus, one centered around Tell Dothan (Site #219) and the other around Tell el-Farah North (Site #222; *Tirzah* of Shishak's List #59). A large zone is centered on Tell Balatah (Site #12) in the center of the study region. Another surrounds Khirbet Seilun (Site #1) farther to the south. To the west of Khirbet Seilun, a zone centers around Khirbet Tibne (Site #38). Finally, there is a complex matrix of sites at the southern edge of the study area in the region of el-Jib (Site #403), Tell en-Nasbeh (Site #404), Khirbet

Raddanah (Site #402), Tell el-Ful (Site #400), et-Tell (Site #401), and Beitin (Site #419; e.g., *rd* of 19th-Dynasty texts). The complexity of this last system, combined with the consecutive nature of the A-level (not to be confused with the size "Class" A) centers within it (see below), requires leaving this southernmost "Benjamin" region out of the mapping that follows. We will deal with many sites more marginal to these zones in turn.

Using the site-size classes set out in Chapter 4 as substitutes for the elusive site-size data, the Gravity Model is the basis for drawing lines of interaction between sites. As described above, this model describes the interaction between two sites as directly proportional to the product of the population of the two sites and inversely proportional to a function of the distance between the sites. Mathematically, the interaction can be quantified as the product of the two populations (or class sizes or credits) multiplied by a constant, then divided by the distance of travel time between the sites raised to a power of an attenuation constant (Hodder and Orton 1976:59-60, 78-80). One can determine the "travel time distance" by adding linear distance plus 0.4 times the number of 50-millimeter contour lines crossed, plus 0.5 times the distance (if any) over water.[1] The constant C does not matter for comparison purposes, but here the value of 1.9 is used, a figure found ethnographically to work well for preindustrial societies (Alden 1979:176). When one applies this formula to the distribution of sites, using classes, the following settlement patterns are produced (Figs. 1-5).

From these figures, the centers of administrative control can easily be seen, bearing in mind the warning that the Gravity Model tends to make the largest sites the centers. Therefore, it is necessary to note other evidence in the identification of these centers. For example, in the bailiwick of Khirbet Seilun, Tell Marjame (Site #6) is by size a center (3 ha.), but the absence of architecture (presumably its buildings were of wood) eliminates the possibility that it is an A-level (not Class A) administrative center. For each center, I will discuss evidence other than size that supports the identification as a center below in the treatment of residential hierarchy and monumental architecture.

1. Possibly erosion since antiquity is great enough to render modern contour lines meaningless in determining travel time (Rapp 1996). Rihll and Wilson (1991) argue that the location of sites itself takes topography into account and eliminates the need for contour counting. Nevertheless, we will employ contour counting here, although erosional issues again render the results even more tentative.

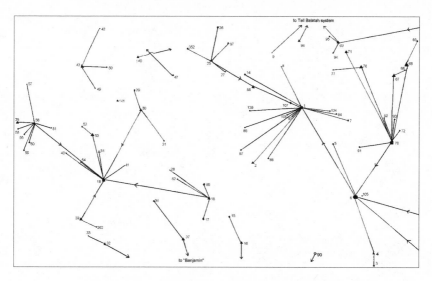

Fig. 1 System of Khirbet Seilun and Sites to the West

Fig. 2 Khirbet Seilun System

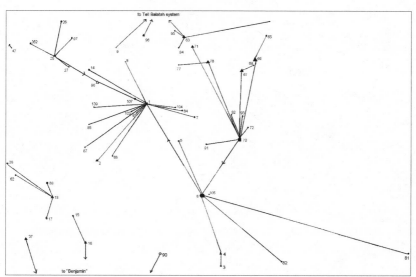

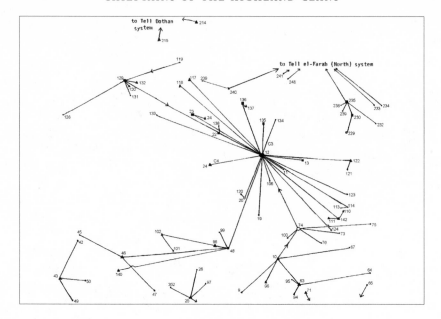

Fig. 3 Tell Balatah System

Fig. 4 Tell el-Farah (North) System

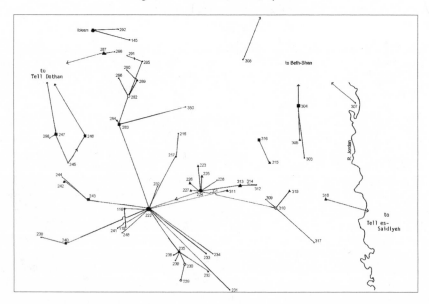

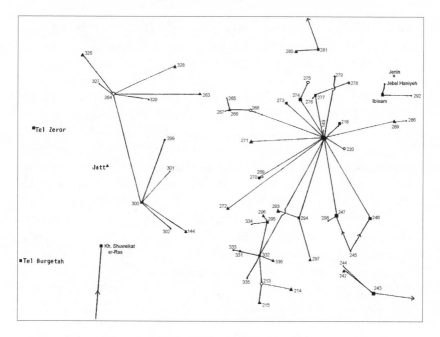

Fig. 5 Tell Dothan System

Figures 1-5, then, illustrate the systems of the hill country heartland. The system (Fig. 2) supporting Khirbet Seilun (Site #1) contains only two main "extensions" administering territory, besides numerous sites directly supporting Khirbet Seilun. To the northwest of Khirbet Seilun, the B-level sites of Khirbet es-Sur (B) (Site #86) and Khirbet Bir el-Kharayib (Site #25) control a small enclave. The site of Tell Marjame, already mentioned, is the administrative center for the whole eastern edge of the Khirbet Seilun bailiwick, although its control of the area to its north is through Khirbet Jibit (Site #70). For the entire Khirbet Seilun System, B-level centers are Khirbet es-Sur (B), Khirbet Bir el-Kharayib, and Tell Marjame. C-level centers, found only in the Tell Marjame Subsystem, are Khirbet en-Najama (East) (Site #4) and Khirbet Jibit. D-level centers, also found only in the Tell Marjame region, are Ukasha (Site #78), Sheikh Mazar (Site #69), and es-Siyar (Site #66).

Figure 1 shows how the Khirbet Seilun system fits into the broader geographic setting. To the west of the Khirbet Seilun System is a smaller-scale system centered on Khirbet Tibne (Site #38). "Smaller-scale" here means not that there are fewer levels of control, but that each ranked site is much smaller than similarly ranked sites of the Khirbet Seilun System. Thus Khirbet Tibne is supported by B-level centers Deir el-Mir (Site #56), an unnamed site at M.R. 158.154 (Site #39), Farkha (Site #30), and Khirbet Tarafein (Site #18). There are also small systems of very few sites such as the one about Khirbet et-Tell (Site #43). None of these systems, nor the Khirbet Seilun one, correlates at all with the supposed ancient roads from the highlands to the coast (to Aphek and the like), one of which apparently ran from modern Jifna to Rantis roughly along modern Highway 465 (Dar 1986:116-17), and another that ran from Khirbet Seilun along the Nahal Shillo all the way to Aphek (Harel 1984:77-78; Dar 1986:217).

The largest system of the highlands (Fig. 3) is that of Tell Balatah (Site #12). A broad east-west area south of the latitude of Mt. Gerizim is administered by an extensive network of B-, C-, and D-level centers. Although a similar situation does not obtain north of Mt. Ebal due to the proximity of the Tell el-Farah (North) System, the area to the east and west of Tell Balatah is full of tributary sites. Passing the large site of Tell Sofar (Site #22), which guards the western end of the Nablus Pass, subsystems of sites are also administered far to the northwest along the Wadi el-Burj/Nahal Alexander road to the coastal plain (Dar 1986:216). Only the region southwest of Mt. Ebal is empty of Iron I sites. This is not a gap in the survey coverage: there are in fact no Iron I sites there. This leaves no sites along the supposed direct route from Tell Balatah to the coast, following modern Highway 55 (Monson 1983:111; Dar 1986:116-17). The Tell Balatah System's B-level centers are Tell Sofar, Kuma (Site #23), and Qarqaf (Site #129), administering the northwest, Khirbet Ras Zeid (Site #48), administering the southwest, Khirbet Urma (Site #74), administering the southeast, Khirbet en-Nebi (Site #20), Khirbet Yanun (Site #142), Khirbet Shuweiha (Site #122), and Khirbet Asira esh-Shamaliyya (A) (Site #136). C-level centers are the unnamed site at MR 164.170 (for the southwest corner) and Khirbet Dawara (Site #10) in the southeast. Khirbet Dawara also has a subordinate, D-level center at Jurish (Site #63). The southwestern extension controls the road from the Watershed Route (Tell Balatah to Khirbet Seilun and beyond in both directions, following modern Highway 60; Monson 1983:111; Astour 1995:1415) along the modern "Trans-Samarian Road" (Highway 505) to the coastal plain (Monson 1983:111; Dar 1986:216), and probably also a branch of the route that swings north along the Wadi Qanah (Monson 1983:111; Dar 1986:217).

There is a chronological glitch in this system, however, in that the center of Tell Balatah was uninhabited for a portion of Iron I. The problem is with the stratigraphy of Tell Balatah. In early publications of the excavations, and some recent ones, Stratum XII was dated 1200–1150 (Toombs 1972:106; Campbell 1991:14; G. R. H. Wright 1993-94:323). This stratum was a continuation of the Late Bronze level and was represented by occupation in Fields I, III, V, VI, VIII, IX, and XIII (Toombs and G. E. Wright 1961:34; Horn 1962:11; Ross and Toombs 1962:12; Campbell and G. E. Wright 1965:416-17; Campbell 1966:6; Bull and Campbell 1968:4; Toombs 1972:106; Peterson 1977:237; G. R. H. Wright 1985:202; 1985:219; 1994:326; Boraas 1986:250; J. F. Ross, "Field III," in "Records File 24 Balata," Rockefeller Museum). More recently, however, the consensus is shifting to the view that Stratum XII is 13th century (E. F. Campbell and R. Bull "1966 Press Release"; Jaroš 1976:43; Peterson 1977; Campbell 1993:601; Seger 1997:22). The result of this is to move the later levels earlier. Thus the "intermediate phase" between Strata XII and XI, previously dated 1150–1100, moves to 1250–1200, or in some fields 1250 into Stratum XI with no discontinuity (Toombs and G. E. Wright 1961:34-36). Stratum XI, rather than 1100–1000, moves to 1200–1125. The 11th century is then entirely without occupation at Tell Balatah.

It is true that there are no secure 11th-century forms at Tell Balatah such as Pilgrim Spoon Flasks or Cypro-Phoenician Black-on-Red juglets, but, as we will see, these do not occur in many highland sites. Stratum XII and the "intermediate" stratum do contain many elements that would be glaring anomalies in the Iron I highlands: phallic images (#283 and 360 from Stratum XII, Field I[127A], Area 7, locus 3), a cuneiform tablet (from "Intermediate" Stratum, Field XIII; Seger 1997:22), a gold pin (from "Intermediate" Stratum, Field XIII; Toombs et al. 1971:16). On the other hand, the pottery illustrator for much of the Stratum XII pottery for Larry Toombs observed many cooking-pot forms that can be securely dated to Iron I (J. Blakely, personal communication). Conclusions as to the stratigraphy of Tell Balatah must await the publication of the site (this was expected in 2003). Meanwhile, the consensus of scholars associated with the Drew-McCormick excavations is that Stratum XI is 12th century, and there is no 11th. This being the case, if one looks at the rest of the sites in the Tell Balatah System, there are no B-level centers that, from exploration done so far, show any signs of serious enlargement in the 11th century indicative of their having replaced Tell Balatah as the regional center. We will assume that there is a gap at Tell Balatah, and we must conclude that the regional cohesion broke down in the 11th century, and several smaller systems with A-level centers at Tell Sofar, Kuma, Qarqaf, Khirbet Ras Zeid, Khirbet Urma, Khirbet en-Nebi, Khirbet Yanun, Khirbet Shuweiha, and Khirbet Asira esh-Shamaliyya (A) were the result. This may be seen as evidence of the "cycling" described for the complex chiefdom model.

The next system north (Fig. 4) is that of Tell el-Farah (North) (Site #222), which extends in all directions. This system, unlike that of Tell Balatah, contains one very large B-level center, Khirbet Einun (Site #224). All of the sites around Einun are large by comparison with the rest of the Tell el-Farah (North) System. Also worth noting is the extension of Tell el-Farah (North) control far to the north via the chain of centers beholden to el-Kebarra (Site #283). The list of B-level centers is: el-Kebarra, Yasid (Site #243), Khirbet Nib (Site #240), Khirbet el-Unuq (Site #235), Khirbet Einun, and seemingly Khirbet Fuqaha (Site #217), itself a fortified site (Zertal 1983a:44); and of C-levels is: Zebabida (Site #282) for el-Kebarra, Khirbet Ein Farr (Site #230) for Khirbet Unuq, and Yerzah (Site #313) and Yusuf (Site #310) for Khirbet Einun. Mhallal (Site #316) and its daughter, el-Bird (Site #315), are independent of this system.

To the northwest of the Tell el-Farah (North) bailiwick is that of Tell Dothan (Site #219; Fig. 5). This is another multilevel system, but fairly circumscribed without far extensions. B-level centers are Khirbet Rujjam (Site #268), Batn Umm-Nari (Site #270), Kom el-Ghaby (Site #332), Kheir-Allah (Site #294), Sanur (Site #247), Khirbet Kheibar (Site #246), Khirbet Umm el-Butm (Site #287), Khallet Seif (Site #277), and Tell el-Muhaffar (Site #274). C-level centers are el-Khrab (Site #266) for Khirbet Rujjam and er-Rame (Site #295) and es-Sirtassa (Site #213) for Kom el-Ghaby. The Tell Dothan System controls the northern entry of the Watershed Route into the highlands (Monson 1983:111; Astour 1995:1415).

To the west of the Tell Dothan System lies another highland system. The A-level center is at Attil (Site #300), although it is not a large site (size class B). It has one subsystem from Tel Ze'evim (Site #264), itself a fortified site (Ne'eman 1990:34*, 41-42). This small system plots by the Gravity Model to be independent of both the Tell Dothan System to its east and the lowland systems of the west (Jatt, Khirbet Shuweikat er-Ras, Tel Zeror, etc.).

To illustrate the boundaries between the disparate systems, Theissen Polygons have been drawn. Theissen Polygons on principle define economic territories by associating villages with centers by proximity, with boundaries being buffer areas of sparse villages (Jarman, Vita-Finzi, and Higgs 1972:62; Earle 1987b:289).[2] Theissen Polygons have on occasion been used in Syro-Palestinian archaeology in the past (Bunimovitz 1993:447; Finkelstein 1996f:227). They can be viewed as a corollary of the Gravity Model. Given the Gravity Model equation, the distance to the economic boundary between two sites is equal to the distance between the sites divided by the sum of the square root of the population of the first site over the population of the second and the Gravity Model–determined interaction figure (Hodder and Orton 1976:188; Hagget et al. 1977:436-37). A simpler method that results in the same boundaries is to draw perpendiculars to the "Gravity lines" at the midpoints between sites (Hodder and Orton 1976:59-60, 78-80, 187; Hagget et al. 1977:436-37).

This procedure produces Figures 6-9. These figures also show the prominent topographic formations of the region. Often the position of these features confirms the gravity-derived Theissen polygon boundaries: the boundaries determined mathematically happen to coincide with topographic boundaries. Thus the Khirbet Tibne System borders the Tell Balatah System at the mountain ridge of Jebel el-Kharayiq. The Tell Balatah System borders the Tell el-Farah (North) System along the Jebel el-Kabir ridge, and its eastern border is the Jebel el-Urma. The empty southwestern quarter of the Tell Balatah System may be due to the topographic "shadow" of Mt. Gerizim and Jebel Salmah. The Tell el-Farah (North) System is separated from the small Mhallal System by a chain of mountains. Part of its northern boundary with the Beth-Shan System is the "Har Bezek." The Tell el-Farah (North) System's boundary with sites beholden to Deir Allah is the Ras Hamsa massif. Part of the Tell el-Farah (North)–Tell Dothan boundary is determined by the Marj Sanur swamp. The southern boundary of the Tell Dothan System is the Jebel Hureish ridge, delimiting it from the Tell Balatah System. The western boundary of Tell Dothan's System, along the Attil System, runs along the dropoff of the highlands to lowlands — where the elevation goes below 200 meters. All of this serves to confirm that the Theissen boundaries are in the correct place, which in turn confirms the Gravity Model interaction scheme.

---

2. In many cases, these "boundaries" will not be between highland systems but between Israel and the "outside world." Here the issues of ethnicity again emerge. We will treat such "outside" boundaries separately below.

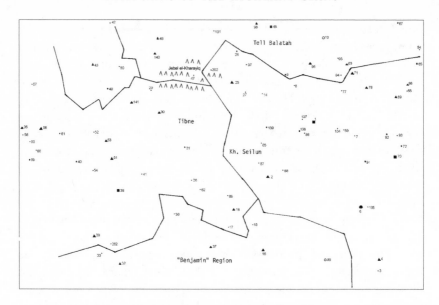

Fig. 6 Khirbet Seilun and Khirbet Tibne Polygons

Fig. 7 Tell Balatah Polygon

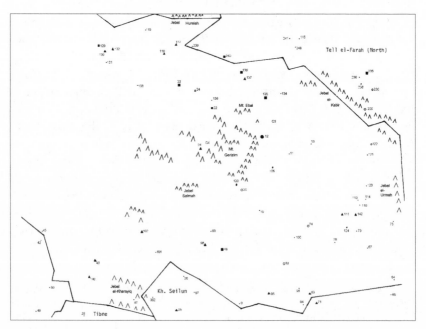

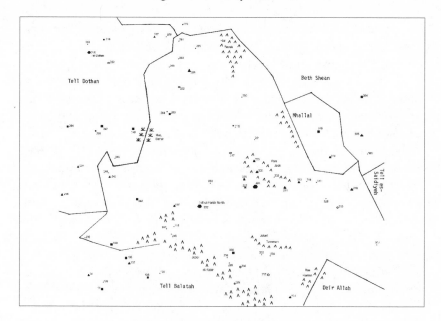

Fig. 8 Tell el-Farah (North) Polygon

Fig. 9 Tell Dothan Polygon

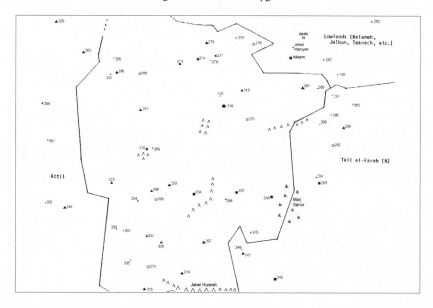

A few comments should be made about the resulting settlement maps. First, the respective settlement networks are "stacked" latitudinally, with each spanning a broad east-west area and a limited north-south one. Networks sit beside each other on the map only north of the Tell Balatah bailiwick and in the Khirbet Tibne–Khirbet Seilun area. The result is that when one matches this arrangement with the environmental map of Palestine (see below), the bailiwicks do not follow any environmental borders. Rather, they each include several diverse environmental zones (these zones will be defined in detail and mapped below). This means that a single, extended administrative entity must be involved in managing the disparate resources of several distinct production and consumption regions. Without the Gravity Model, one would see only the close clusters of sites and other isolated ones, and so reconstruct each system as covering only single ecological zones alongside a few autarkic sites (as by Kochavi 1985:56).

Comparing these settlement patterns with various theoretical patterns is now possible. As for levels of settlement hierarchy, all these systems have more than the two levels above the producer described for complex chiefdoms by H. Wright and G. Johnson (1975), except the small systems of Khirbet Tibne and Attil. Tell el-Farah (North) and Tell Dothan each have three levels above the producer, and Tell Balatah and Khirbet Seilun have four. This means that most of these systems would be multifarious enough to be a complex chiefdom, and that other evidence needs to be weighed if they are not even to be called states.

The next procedure in comparing these drawn settlement maps with various theoretical schemes is to count the number of centers of each hierarchical level down to the fourth level (if present). If this is a central-place organized state, the progression between each level and the next would be such that there are a number of r-ranked centers equal to the number of $r-1$ ranked centers multiplied by a factor of k but minus the number of $r-1$, $r-2$, and similar centers (to the 1st-ranked site) already included. Since k remains constant only in a central-place arrangement, k ought to be constant within a given system if these are states.

When the calculations are done, *none* of these systems showa a constant k. Values for k are spread widely between fractions slightly less than 1.0 and 10.0. Only in the Khirbet Seilun bailiwick can one see any semblance of consistency, with $k = 4.5$, 2.0, 4.0. Now since "$k = 4$" is a valid Central Place model (Christaller 1966:72), it is worth keeping an eye on the Khirbet Seilun System for further evidence of statehood.

When looking at the arrangement of these sites in dialogue with Steponaitis (1978) and the Central Place arrangement, the locations in both the systems of Tell el-Farah (North) and Tell Balatah, where not totally determined by topography, display Steponaitis's proposed pattern of a "tree" arrangement of sites. This is the first positive evidence for a complex chiefdom structure. The exact opposite pattern, the Central Place arrangement, is found in the system of Khirbet Tibne, which cannot be a state (it is merely one small village with a couple of daughter settlements), and at Tell Dothan (see below). The Khirbet Seilun bailiwick displays a mixture of arrangements. To its west, the Central Place arrangement is the case, while for the Tell Marjame Subsystem, the Steponaitis pattern is visible.

Another way to identify a ranked society of the complex chiefdom variety is to plot the number of dwellings against the number of sites, y sites to x dwellings (Jamieson-Drake 1991:63, 211 illustrates this for the southern highlands). A ranked society will show a bimodal distribution (Taylor 1975:103). Since the number of dwellings is dependent on the elusive size figure, size class is here substituted (Figs. 10-15). None of the regions displays anything *more* than a bimodal distribution, militating against suggestions of statehood for Khirbet Seilun and Tell Dothan. Tell Dothan's System, rather, presents the most clearly bimodal distribution of all. Tell Balatah's System also displays a bimodal curve, although not as strongly. This combines with the "Steponaitis pattern" to suggest that Tell Balatah was a complex chiefdom. Weakly bimodal curves are presented by Tell el-Farah (North), Khirbet Seilun, and Khirbet Tibne. The Attil System is not bimodal.

Distribution of Material Culture

Lines of movement of craft goods and mobilization of subsistence goods are another valuable piece of information. Petrographic analysis can illustrate some movement from the place of production. At Khirbet Seilun, most of the pottery came from only two production sites, neither near to the site (Glass, Goren, Bunimovitz, and Finkelstein 1993:283). Eighty-seven percent of the pottery in the pillared buildings of Area C (see below) came from a fast-wheeled potter using the Lower Cretaceous clays of the Wadi Farah (Glass, Goren, Bunimovitz, and Finkelstein 1993:282-83). This was

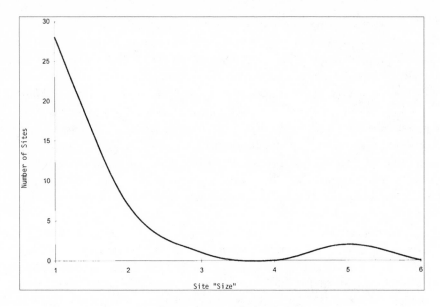

Fig. 10 Dwellings vs. Sites: Khirbet Seilun System

Fig. 11 Dwellings vs. Sites: Khirbet Tibne System

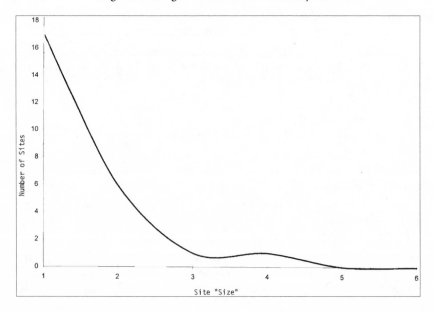

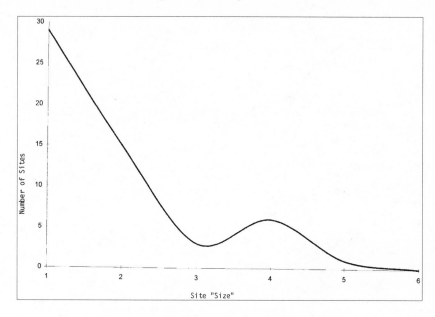

Fig. 12 Dwellings vs. Sites: Tell Balatah System

Fig. 13 Dwellings vs. Sites: Tell el-Farah (North) System

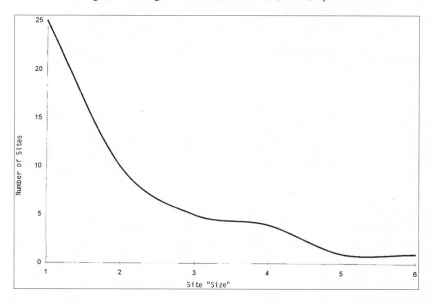

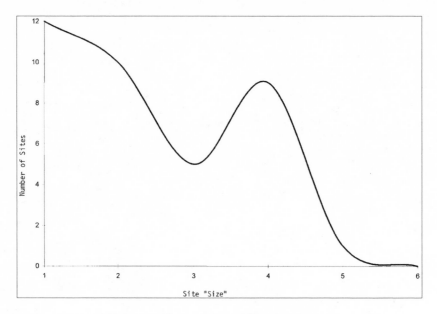

Fig. 14 Dwellings vs. Sites: Tell Dothan System

Fig. 15 Dwellings vs. Sites: Attil System

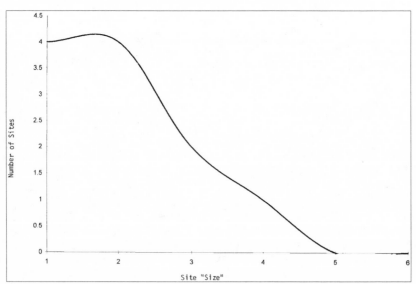

the preferred source for the earlier portion of the Iron I occupation (Glass, Goren, Bunimovitz, and Finkelstein 1993:281). Only 10 percent of the pottery of this clay is found in the later debris dumped over these buildings (Glass, Goren, Bunimovitz, and Finkelstein 1993:279-81). Eighty-two percent of this later debris pottery was from a handmade or slow-wheeled potter in the Nablus Syncline (the clay is Calcareous Sand containing Eocene limestone and Taqia marls; Glass, Goren, Bunimovitz, and Finkelstein 1993:279, 281-82). This poorer, less distant pottery accounted for only 23 percent of the pottery in the earlier subphase (Glass, Goren, Bunimovitz, and Finkelstein 1993:279-81). Thus *all* of the collared-rimmed pithoi, along with most of the bowls, lamps, pyxides, and jars, were imported from two different locations in the life of the site: first from the Tell el-Farah (North) System and later from the Tell Balatah System. All of the cooking pots, on the other hand, and one lamp were made locally of terra rosa/calcite clays (Glass, Goren, Bunimovitz, and Finkelstein 1993:277). One can note in comparison that at Khirbet Raddanah most of the pottery was locally made (Glass, Goren, Bunimovitz, and Finkelstein 1993:272).

Additionally, we have set as a goal to identify the occurrence of foreign goods in the systems, how nonlocal goods enter the community, and how they are distributed — whether they are the prerogatives of the centers (Jamieson-Drake 1991:122-28 provides an illustration for the southern highlands). The list here contains only items whose material or manufacture clearly shows that they are imports, not, for the most part, those whose stylistic elements only hint at foreign influence. Also, items from mortuary contexts will not be treated here but in a section on mortuary remains.

There is evidence that foreign goods were not solely the prerogatives of the centers. In the Tell el-Farah (North) System, the C-level center of Tell el-Miski (Site #237) shows pottery that is generally considered Transjordanian and is rare in the Cisjordan (Kappus 1968:81-82). In the Tell Balatah System, however, the presence in village site Khirbet esh-Sheikh Nasrallah (Site #13) of an Egyptian steatite scarab from the 9th [sic] Dynasty (Reg. #1670; from Area D2) is less indicative evidence since the scarab was about a thousand years old in Iron I (Jaroš 1976:57). More suspicious is a scarab found in a pit at el-Burnat Sitti Salaamiyeh (Site #135) in the Tell Balatah System, which is a Rameses II issue of a Thutmose III commemorative, dated to the late 13th century (Zertal 1986:52), and an iron nail from the same site (Zertal 1986-87:150; on iron see below). This site also shows evidence for exchange with the occurrence of a Cardium shell (*Glycymerys violacescens*), which is a Mediterranean shell (Horwitz 1986-87:173).

Another problem is Site #290 in the Tell el-Farah (North) System, Dhahrat et-Tawileh, the "Bull Site." This is a tiny village-level site in the chain of centers far to the north of Tell el-Farah (North) beholden to el-Kebarra (Site #283). The principal find here was a bronze "Zebu" (the humped-back *Bos indicus*) bull figurine 17.5 centimeters long and 12.4 meters high (A. Mazar 1982a:27; 1983:37). Although it has been argued that this figurine is unique (A. Mazar 1982a:29), an identical statuette has been found in the Ashmolean Museum from northern Syria/Lebanon from the 8th century B.C., and similar ones from Urartu, 10th-century Tell Halaf, and Late Bronze Age Ugarit (Moorey 1971:90-91). Much has been made of this figure and the site's supposed cultic nature (e.g., Ahlström 1990:78-79, but cf. Coogan 1987:1; Gilmour 1995:91-92; both the pottery and the flint assemblage are domestic; A. Mazar 1982a:41). For this study it is noteworthy that the style is clearly of foreign origin. Yet given that the bull itself was not found in a stratified context (A. Mazar 1982a; Ahlström 1993:363) and that its parallels are widely dispersed chronologically, one should be hesitant about assigning it to the Iron I occupation. Although the excavator continually calls the site single-period Iron I (A. Mazar 1982a; 1982c; A. Mazar and S. Rosen 1982), an independent survey of the site found only 5 percent of the sherds collected to be Iron I (Zertal 1992:169).

At Tell Dothan, a small copper chain was found in Area A, Level 6c/7a (early 12th century; Fig. 16). As copper objects are rarely made by remelting existing objects, the copper must have its source in the Negeb or Wadi Arabah (Muhly 1995:1510). In Area L, also 12th century, a gold earring was found (#2594; "1962 Notebook"). The closest source for gold would have been Egypt or possibly Arabia (Goffer 1996:124). In the 11th-century Level 5, Area A produced an iron ring (#2593; "1962 Notebook"). Iron, like copper, is not usually recycled, and so the possible sources must be the Golan, Syria, Galilee, the Negeb, and northern Transjordan (Muhly 1995:1510; Waldbaum 1978:59).

At Tell el-Farah (North), in Level VIIa ("Stratum 4"), the earlier Iron I phase, building #490 (rooms 487-90 in square J6, called a "temple" by Chambon; 1984:20) contained a silver-plated bronze female figurine, #1.491 (Chambon called it a Hathor statuette; 1984:20). Again, no matter where it was made, the nearest silver source is southeast of the Dead Sea

Fig. 16 Tell Dothan Area A

(Waldbaum 1978:63). In the same building was a Phoenician vase (#F3480, #PAM61-62 in the Rockefeller Museum), a cylindrical vessel with a small ring base, carinated shoulder, small opening in the neck, and two vertical handles at the carination (Chambon 1984:140; "Tell el Farʿah 1955: Notes de Chantier" notebook p. 51; "Tell el Farʿah 1955" notebook p. 350). Tell el-Farah (North) Level VIIa also produced an iron point and an iron triangle ("1946 Catalogue of Objects," pp. 23, 25; see below). A basalt mortar ("1946 Catalogue of Objects") was found in House #205 (including rooms 201, 206, 214, 215, 204, and 237) in Level VIIa. The nearest sources of basalt are Galilee and Transjordan (G. R. H. Wright 1997:363).

At Tell Balatah, Level XI (see above), Field VII in the northeast-central part of the tell produced two scarabs. In Area 5, a gray steatite scarab (#B64-478; 16 × 11 mm.) bears the Egyptian inscription $\underline{dd}$ = "stability" (Horn 1966:52). In Area 2, another gray steatite scarab (#B64-575; 19 × 13 mm.) shows a bull and uraeus (Horn 1966:54). Both suggest contact with Egypt, although they could be residual from the Late Bronze strata. In the German trench on the east side of the tell between Fields VII and I, several alabaster juglets were found (Sellin 1960?:3). Either these are again residual, or they or the alabaster raw material were imported from Syria or

Arabia (Avi-Yonah 1939:84). Residuality may be even more a possibility for the occurrence of Cypriote Base–ring II ware. Eleven sherds of jugs and juglets, mostly unpainted, were found in Field VII (G. R. H. Wright 1967:49, 52-53), and another five unpainted bowls and jugs and two painted jugs in Field IX (G. R. H. Wright 1967:55). As the occurrence of Base–ring II is a Late Bronze II phenomenon, the presence here ought to be residual. Otherwise, trade with Cyprus existed.

In the Khirbet Seilun area, the site of Khirbet Seilun produced a 4-centimeter conical black basalt seal along the city wall (Israel Antiquities Authority #K12801). The seal is of two ibexes forming a central cross, two recumbent horned quadrupeds, and the head and neck of another ibex (Brandl 1993:216; Finkelstein et al. 1985:145). Either the seal or the uncarved basalt was imported. At Area C, in a set of buildings described in detail below, an 11.3 × 25 × 18.4 millimeter hematite weight in the shape of a snake head was found (Reg. 3144, #315). The weight is 135.3 grams, which is exactly the "Egyptian gold standard" of the time (Eran 1994:152). This is again evidence of trade. Near this same house, from locus 1322, was an impression of a scarab seal depicting a sphinx (Israel Antiquities Authority #K11274; Brandl 1993:215). Also found at Khirbet Seilun were two Philistine sherds (Bunimovitz and Finkelstein 1993:160).

Outside the area here being mapped (for Izbet Sartah; see below), in the "Benjamin" region, an orange glass, ring-shaped bead (#856, p. 1132 of the "No. 2 Notebook") was found at el-Jib (*Qb'n* of Shishak's Karnak list #23; called *gb'n* on Iron II jar handles found on the site). Now glass in itself is evidence of trade. Any small site can have the facilities to form glass from the recycling of old glass objects; it requires only a furnace similar to a pottery kiln (Newton and Davison 1989:62). Still, this presupposes having the old glass objects somehow, and that depends on trade. To melt glass objects from cullets (ingots or beads or canes) requires a furnace of 800° C (Newton and Davison 1989:62), while glassmaking from sand requires 1050° C, a furnace of the size and complexity found only in Syria-Palestine in *any* period at Beth Shearim, Arsuf, and Hadera (Newton and Davison 1989:61). The glass sand must come from the Negeb, at the closest. To obtain the color orange in glass, the most readily obtainable pigment is copper or copper oxide. This must have come from the Negeb or Wadi Arabah (Muhly 1995:1510). Thus, although it is impossible to say that the el-Jib glass bead was itself imported, or that specific components were, it is evidence that somewhere along the line importation was involved — unless the bead or a glass object recycled into it had been found on the site of el-Jib left over from an earlier period.

Another item of possible import in the southern zone is a twenty-handled kernos krater from Phase 3 of Khirbet Raddanah Site R. Found in Area R.III in a room with a unique mud brick–paved floor, this krater has a channel on the upper wall leading to zoomorphic bullhead spouts on the inner wall pouring into the basin (Callaway and Cooley 1971:1; Callaway 1974:92; Cooley 1975:12). This unusual vessel is unique in Syria-Palestine, and has analogies only in Anatolia: at Inankik and Eskyaper (Allen 1980:64). There is a slightly similar vessel from Gezer with channel rim and zoomorphic spout (Allen 1980:49), but that is a jar and not a krater, and it is most interesting that the Gezer vessel is itself identical to one at Alaca Huyuk in Anatolia ("Denyer 1976" report in the Nicol Museum). Without petrographic analysis or neutron activation, it is possible to propose that the krater was made at Khirbet Raddanah, perhaps by a foreign resident. Nevertheless, it is either evidence for an import, in the end at least from Anatolia, or for the "import" of the potter. Rather than tie the form to Gezer, it is better to tie both either to some trade route from Anatolia or to the presence in central Palestine of Anatolian individuals. In any case, it is at a center, Khirbet Raddanah, that such an item is found.

A directly related issue is the presence of 47 Philistine bichrome sherds at Tell en-Nasbeh (T. Dothan 1982:44, 48, 54; Graham 1981:33). Neutron activation has found that two painted kraters and other body sherds were actually manufactured at Ashdod (Gunneweg et al. 1994:235). This is clear evidence for trade. But another six painted kraters of similar typology, along with more body sherds, were made locally (Gunneweg et al. 1994:231, 238). Someone was making Philistine pottery in the middle of the highland settlement! Yet Tell en-Nasbeh Stratum 4 was totally unfortified and cannot possibly have been a Philistine "garrison" in hostile Israelite territory (as per Dever 1992b:103). Nevertheless, here was locally made Philistine bichrome, along with imported Philistine ware, to which can be added a Philistine piece with an Aegean-inspired swan decoration (Badè 1927:6) and several Phoenician globular jugs (Briese 1985:14).[3]

A miniature copper-making installation was also found in Khirbet Raddanah Phase 3. Slag-encrusted crucibles were discovered, but without

---

3. It is not clear what Finkelstein means when he says that the ceramic assemblage of Tell en-Nasbeh is no different from that of Khirbet Seilun and Tell el-Ful (1997a:222).

smoke on the crucibles (Callaway 1974:12). This means that the ingots were smelted elsewhere and traded in, and then put in the crucibles (Cooley 1975:11). As mentioned above, the copper had to come from the Negeb or Wadi Arabah at the closest (Muhly 1995:1510). There are many bronze objects from Khirbet Raddanah and other centers, but this is not evidence of import since most bronze was made by resmelting old items — ingots are almost nonexistent (Muhly 1995). Straight copper, however, is seldom done this way, nor is iron (Muhly 1995:1510). And from Khirbet Raddanah Phase 3, there is an iron digging iron (a horizontal pickaxe similar to the American "spud bar"; Kurinsky 1991:118), along with an iron knife and iron rod (Waldbaum 1978:25). The ultimate source of the iron would be the Negeb, Galilee, or Transjordan, or farther away (Waldbaum 1978:59). Thus an iron point was found at Khirbet ed-Dawwara (Finkelstein 1990a:196), while in the north, Tell el-Farah (North) Level VIIa produced an iron point and an iron triangle ("1946 Catalogue of Objects," pp. 23, 25).

An iron arrowhead (#1079) was found at Beitin in House 310/312 (see below) from Phase 1 ("1954 Daybook 1," "1954 Daybook 2," "1954 Object Cards," "1954 Record Book"). Additionally, from various Iron I phases, iron arrowheads and javelin heads (itemized below under evidence of warfare), an iron hammer, and an iron point of unclear function were found (#338, Pittsburgh Theological Seminary #2-0187). There are many scarabs at Beitin, which illustrates at least Egyptian influence. At House 310/312 in Phase 1, there is frit/paste scarab #1012 ("1954 Daybook 1," "1954 Daybook 2," "1954 Object Cards," "1954 Record Book"). From elsewhere in Phase 1, frit/paste scarab #442 (Rockefeller Museum) shows a cobra, bent lines, and a hawk (Albright and Kelso 1968:84). Also from this phase, in Room 308 (Room 18 in an earlier numbering system), is a red stone scarab (#1073; "1954 Daybook 1," "1954 Daybook 2," "1954 Object Cards," "1954 Record Book"). From Phase 2, frit/paste scaraboid #445 shows a boat full of lotuses (Albright and Kelso 1968:84). Phase 4a contains frit/paste scarab #1012 (Albright and Kelso 1968:88), although this phase goes into the 10th century. Copper products are also abundant. As mentioned above, the copper had to come from the Negeb or Wadi Arabah at the closest. Thus there is a copper ring (#1091) at House 310/312 from Phase 1 ("1954 Daybook 2," "1954 Object Cards," "1954 Record Book"), a copper sheet from Phase 2 or 3 of Area 32 (Albright and Kelso 1968:118), and another such sheet from "Sub41" in Phase 1 (#452), copper arrowheads, a copper wire, copper bracelet #1045, and copper ring #1050 (for the latter two see "1954 Daybook 1," "1954 Daybook 2," "1954 Object Cards," "1954 Record Book"). House 35 from Phase 1 contained a Cypriote painted jar handle (#329, Pittsburgh Theological Seminary #2-206), unless this is residual from the Late Bronze occupation. Also from Phase 1, from "Sub41," was a marble bead (#451), the closest source of marble being the southern Negeb or Egypt. A small amount of Philistine pottery was found in Phase 3 (Kelso 1934:417) and in other phases (e.g., sherd #116; "1957 Room Cards," "1957 Daybooks," "1957 Artifact Book 1," "1957 Artifact Book 2"). From Phase 4a comes a basalt seal of a lion attacking an antelope (Albright 1934:13; see above on the origin of basalt), although this phase goes into the 10th century. In Room 313 (designated Room 24 in an earlier scheme), a piece of pumice was found (#1089; "1954 Daybook 2," "1954 Object Cards," "1954 Record Book"). Its function is unknown, but the closest source of pumice would likely be Galilee or the Golan.

At et-Tell, in the "Cobblestone Street" Stratum (= Level Ia = Intermediate Stratum IX = Phase II), possible evidence of importing comes from the presence of red slip-and-burnish bowls, many of them wheelmade, some with painted lines (Callaway 1980:figs. 147-50). This is a form more common in coastal "Amorite" sites (Amiran 1970:192). An iron point was also found at et-Tell (#430; "1964 Registered Objects") from the "Silo Granary Stratum" (= Level Ib). Also from this level, from Sites D and G, came a pair of iron tweezers, an iron lance head, an iron dagger, two iron knives, an iron nail, and another unidentifiable piece of iron (Waldbaum 1978:25), and from Site D, Room 10, a lugged-blade axe (Meron 1985:69). Not only is this further evidence of iron, the ore of which at least must be imported, but this form of axe — symmetrically sharpened even on the rear portion of the blade and the narrow part opposite the crest — is basically an Anatolian form that arrived in Palestine with the Sea Peoples (Meron 1985:iv, 84, 163). Phoenician globular jugs like those from Tell en-Nasbeh were also found (Briese 1985:12, 14, 16, 20).

Tell el-Ful Level II had an iron plow in Room A (A. Mazar 1994b:78; Kurinsky 1991:119; Sinclair 1960:47). Several sherds of Cypriote White Painted I, including one barrel juglet, were found (A. Mazar 1994b:78; 1994c:51). Other potential imports are the red slip-and-burnish bowls with bar handles (e.g., Albright Institute Collection #18.1), a form more at home in coastal, "Amorite" sites (Amiran 1970:192).

Highland Economy

Reconstructing ancient economies is based on accurately describing the ancient environments. In many ways the latter has been problematic for ancient Palestine. A full treatment of the issues involved can be found in my "Modeling the Farm in Early Iron Age Israel," in *Life and Culture in the Ancient Near East,* ed. R. E. Averbeck, M. W. Chavalas, and D. B. Weisberg (Bethesda, MD: CDL Press, 2002). The conclusions can be summarized here.

Researchers have established that the modern climate — rainfall and so forth — can be applied to the ancient period. The elevation of various parts of Palestine is also a constant over time. Elevation can be combined with rainfall, along with some minimal soil information — Cenomanian Limestone has always eroded to *terra rosa* soil, for example. The combinations of these factors define distinct environmental zones, and these zones can be compared with analogous regions that exist today in the world (many of them in South Africa, California, and Chile). Those analogies can fill in the rest of the information needed to decide what subsistence strategies would have been most profitable in each zone, and thus to reconstruct ancient daily life. In rough order from Northwest to Southeast, the 22 regions of the highlands are as follows (Fig. 17). Each zone is here summarized as to probable ancient soil type, rainfall, standing vegetation, and potential economy. The potential agricultural economy will be discussed more fully below. Names of the regions are fairly arbitrary and imply neither assumptions about ancient toponyms nor modern political views.

The northwesternmost of the highland regions is the Ramat Manasseh Plateau, separated from the Carmel Range by the Nahal Tut pass from modern Zichron Yaaqov to Megiddo and Yoqneam. This region had soils of Rendzina, Terra Rosa, and Mediterranean Brown Forest, although the modern presence of the latter two may be the result of erosion (Rabinovitch-Vin 1983:83). Rainfall was (and is) about 28 inches annually. The ancient vegetation was Mixed Tabor Oak Forest Shrublands (Tomaselli 1981:105; Rabinovitch-Vin 1983:77, 83; Harel 1984:70; Dan 1988:116). This shrubland consists of the *Pistacia palestina* species of terebinth, balsam *(Styrax officinalis),* and Mt. Tabor oak *(Quercus ithaburensis).* The thickest growth would be found on north-facing slopes under 600 meters elevation, and on all slopes above that elevation (Steward and Webber 1981:57, 59). The ancient economy could have supported cereals on level

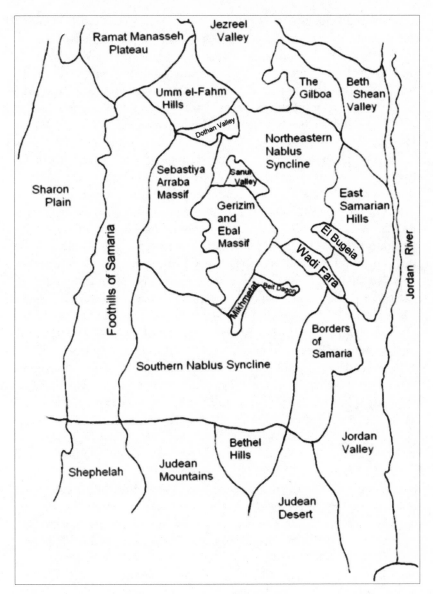

Fig. 17 Regions of the Highlands

and terraced land, especially lentils (both *Lens esculenta* and *L. culinaris*) and alfalfa supplemented by fava beans ("broad beans," *Vicia faba*) and chickpeas *(Cicer arietinum)* (Aschmann 1973:365; Borowski 1987:97). In other, more mountainous cases, goatherding would be prominent (Webley 1972:170). Still other potentially important contributors to the economy would be the export of storax incense (from the balsam trees) and the supply of oak and terebinth timber for the lower regions (G. R. H. Wright 1997:363).

The Sharon Plain itself, as far south as the Philistine coast, lies on the fringe of the study area. Its soils were several, including (Ortho-)Hamra, Brown Hamra, Red and Brown Degrading Sandy Soils, and Husmas — the extent of the latter in antiquity is questionable due to its erosional origin. Rainfall ranges from 20 to 28 inches per annum. The standing vegetation falls into two categories, one north of modern Netanya and one south of this. The northern half was so-called Carob-Lentisk/Carob-Mastic Maquis, "so called" because there was no carob *(Ceratonia)* in Iron I Palestine except for Galilee (Tomaselli 1981:97; Liphschitz 1987-89:151-54). This was a dense thicket of terebinth (both *P. lentiscus* and *P. atlantica*), wild olive *(Olea europaea),*[4] broomtree *(Retama raetam),* ash *(Fraxinus syriaca),* balsam, sycamore *(Ficus sycamoros),* willow *(Salix alba),* wild leeks, wild asparagus, and wormwood *(Artemisia)* on the western and eastern slopes (Zohary 1966-86:1.25, 37; Rabinovitch-Vin 1983:77; Harel 1984:70; Van Zeist 1985:203). The thickest growth would have been where rain was less than 24 inches and on the Hamra soils (Steward and Webber 1981; Rabinovitch-Vin 1983:77). South of Netanya, the stand was Mixed Tabor Oak Forest Shrublands, as on the Ramat Manasseh Plateau, with both Mt. Tabor Oak and Kermesian Oak *(Quercus calliprinos),* particularly on north-facing slopes and on the Brown Degrading soil and Brown Hamra (Steward and Webber 1981:57, 59; Rabinovitch-Vin 1983:83). Thorns would have been ubiquitous. The ancient economy could have supported barley cultivation (both *Hordeum vulgare,* six-rowed barley, and *H. distichon,* two-rowed) on all but the Sandy soils (Zohary 1966-86:2.181). Other crops would have included lentils, millet (both broomcorn millet, *Panicum milaceum,* and Italian pearl millet, *Setaria italica*), alfalfa (Karsena vetch, *Vicia ervilia*), fava beans, peas *(Pisum sativum),* and chickpeas (Zohary

---

4. Its presence is debatable: by pollen count it was extremely rare (Horowitz 1974:409), but it has been found in archaeological contexts (Van Zeist 1985:203).

1966-86:2.200, 222, 301), and flax/linseed *(Linum)* in the swamps (Harel 1984:70). Certainly goats could have grazed here (LeHouerou 1981:502). Both storax and mastic incense (Egyp., *"sntr* from the Retenu route") could have been exported (Goffer 1996:242). Terebinth and oak lumber would not have needed to be imported (G. R. H. Wright 1997:363).

Immediately uphill from the Sharon Plain lay the Foothills of Samaria. The soil is identical to that of the Ramat Manasseh Plateau, and the rainfall is identical to that of the Sharon. This combination supported a three- to five-meter-tall thicket best called Evergreen Oak Forest and Maquis Middle Dense Garrigue Scrub Mattoral (Rabinovitch-Vin 1983:75). Thickest in the southern half of the Foothills of Samaria, and especially on western and eastern slopes where rainfall was less than 24 inches per year and elevation under three hundred meters (Steward and Webber 1981:58-59; Rabinovitch-Vin 1983:77), this consisted of Kermesian and Mt. Tabor oaks, broomtrees, wormwood, wild olives, lilies, wild garlic and leeks, hyacinth, saffron, orchids, myrrh, peonies, and wild asparagus (Quézel 1981:91; Rabinovitch-Vin 1983:83; Harel 1984:70; Dan 1988:118). In the higher altitudes, balsam and terebinth would also have been found (Steward and Webber 1981:57, 59; Dan 1988:118; both *P. lentiscus* and *P. palestina,* remains of which are found at Izbet Sartah; Finkelstein 1985a:154). Horticulture of wine and olives should have been the dominant industry on the lower slopes where rain was under 24 inches (Aschmann 1973:365; Quézel 1981:91; Bornstein 1993:97; note olive remains from Izbet Sartah; Finkelstein 1985a:154). Cultivation is possible for lentils, alfalfa (found at Izbet Sartah, along with barley; Finkelstein 1985a:154), flax/linseed, fava beans, and chickpeas (Harel 1984:70; note sickle blades at Izbet Sartah; Finkelstein 1985a:94). Grazing of goats and cattle, but not sheep, would have contributed to the economy in higher altitudes (Webley 1972:170), and, it seems from the faunal remains of Izbet Sartah, the lower altitudes as well (Finkelstein 1985a, esp. 150). Additional casual sources would include figs *(Ficus carica)* and hunting of red deer *(Cervus elaphus)* and hare *(Lepus sp.),* along with the export of mastic incense and labdanum resin (Goffer 1996:242).

The southernmost portion of the Sharon Plain was bordered on the east by the Shephelah, which continues the east-west width of the Foothills of Samaria south of Wadi esh-Shami and south out of the study area. Unlike the Foothills of Samaria, the Shephelah is less hilly and consists of predominantly Brown Alluvial soil. Its vegetation was the Mixed Tabor Oak

Forest Shrublands of the southern Sharon Plain. The economy would have been based on the cultivation of barley, lentils, alfalfa, peas, flax/linseed, fava beans, and chickpeas (Zohary 1966-86:2.181, 222; Sapin 1968-69:23; Harel 1984:70). Recent landscape archaeology in this area has found that there was no agriculture on the hills in Iron I, only in the wadi valleys. Labdanum resin and storax and mastic incense would have been export-able commodities (S. Gibson and Lass 1997; Goffer 1996:242). Fallow deer (*Dama mesopotamica*) may have been hunted.

Returning to the north, to the southeast of the Ramat Manasseh Pla-teau lay the Umm el-Fahm Hills. The soil is identical to that of the Ramat Manasseh Plateau, but the rainfall drops as low as 20 inches annually. This replicates the conditions of the Foothills of Samaria, except for the eleva-tion. The stand is again Evergreen Oak Forest and Maquis Middle Dense Garrigue Scrub Mattoral. The economy would have been equally divided between olive/vine horticulture and lentil, alfalfa, fava bean, and chickpea cultivation (Aschmann 1973:365). Red deer and hare could have been hunted, and storax and mastic incense exported (Goffer 1996:242). Terebinth and oak timber could also have been exported to the Jezreel Val-ley (G. R. H. Wright 1997:363).

To the south of the Umm el-Fahm Hills is the Dothan Valley. Also re-ceiving 20 to 28 inches of rainfall, its soils were Grumsols, Gley, and Hydromorphic. Natural vegetation was limited to tamarisk (*Tamariscus aphylla* or *T. petandra*), reeds, and thistles (Dan 1988:119). Its economy could have supported either cultivation of lentils, alfalfa, fava beans, chick-peas, and flax/linseed, or caprovid grazing just as easily. Building timber would have to be imported from the higher altitudes.

To the south of the Dothan Valley lies the large Sebastiya Arraba Massif. Its soils were Rendzina and Grumsols, and probably also Terra Rosa and Mediterranean Brown Forest. Rainfall ranged from 20 to 28 inches. The standing vegetation is the same as on the Foothills of Samaria to the west (Evergreen Oak Forest and Maquis Middle Dense Garrigue Scrub Mattoral), with the following exceptions. The Grumsols would not easily support this mattoral scrub, and where rainfall approached 28 inches, terebinth would be rare (Rabinovitch-Vin 1983:75). In any case, at this altitude the *P. lentiscus* variety of terebinth would not occur (Dan 1988:118). Wine could have been the dominant economic factor on the lower slopes of this region, along with fig horticulture (Aschmann 1973:365; Bornstein 1993:97). An equal portion of the economy would come from cereal cultivation on terraced higher slopes — lentils, alfalfa, chickpeas, and fava beans (Borowski 1987:97). Red deer and hare could be hunted, and storax incense and labdanum resin exported (Goffer 1996:242).

Stretching across the center of the highlands from the southern edge of the Sebastiya Arraba Massif south to Wadi esh-Shami, from about the longitude of modern Haris and Deir es-Sudan in the west as far east as the modern Allon Road, is the Southern Nablus Syncline. The soils are the same as those of the Sebastiya Arraba Massif, and rainfall is approximately 28 inches annually. The vegetation was transitional between the Mixed Tabor Oak Forest Shrublands of the Shephelah and the Aleppo Pine Forest (Tomaselli 1981:99). The so-called Aleppo Pine Forest can grow up to ten meters high, but it is highly unlikely that any Aleppo Pines *(Pinus halepensis)* were present: both pollen evidence and dendrochronological evidence show that this species was very rare in Iron I (Horowitz 1974:409; Liphschitz, Biger, and Mendel 1987-89:141-50). The forest of the Southern Nablus Syncline consisted of wild olive, *P. palestina* terebinth in the drier areas, Kermesian oak in drier parts over five hundred meters elevation, Mt. Tabor oak and balsam on all soils except Grumsols above this altitude and on north-facing slopes below, wild garlic, wild leeks, myrrh, broomtree, and boxthorn (Quézel 1981:9; Steward and Webber 1981:57, 59; Rabinovitch-Vin 1983:75, 77). The overall dominant economic factor would have been terrace farming of cereals: wheat (primarily durum wheat, *Triticum durum,* but also emmer, *T. dicoccum,* and *T. vulgare*), barley, lentils, alfalfa, peas, chickpeas, and fava beans (Zohary 1966-86:2.222; Aschmann 1973:365; Rabinovitch-Vin 1983:79). This is confirmed by the presence of wheat, barley, lentils, and alfalfa in the storage silos of Khirbet Seilun (Kislev 1993:356-57). Cereal farming would have been especially dominant in the eastern half of the Southern Nablus Syncline, east of the longitude of modern Nablus. This half would have been free of olive horticulture, which would, however, have played a large role in the economy of the north-central and southwestern areas (Antoun 1972; Harel 1984:70; Bornstein 1993:97). An abundance of raisins from Khirbet Seilun suggests wine viticulture as well (Kislev 1993:356). Caprovid grazing might have been substantial in the southwestern corner as well, and the number of caprovid bones from Khirbet Seilun is confirmation (Hellwing, Sade, and Kishon 1993:311, 325; cattle were also found, but in a profile for cereal production traction; S. Rosen 1993:366). Supplementary strategies include nut and fig horticulture in the north-central area (cf. fig remains from Khirbet Seilun; Kislev 1993:357), hunting of mountain gazelle *(Gazella gazella)* and red and fallow deer (all found at Khirbet Seilun; Hellwing, Sade, and Kishon 1993:311), and export of storax incense and labdanum resin.

South of this zone, extending across most of the same east-west width and south past Jerusalem and out of the study regions, are the Judean mountains. The soils would have been Rendzina, and to an unknown extent Terra Rosa and Mediterranean Brown Forest. Twenty to 28 inches of rain fell annually. The vegetation was High Sparse Chaparral Maquis Brushfields (Tomaselli 1981:99). This consisted of wild olives, both oak varieties, terebinth (both *P. atlantica* and, under three hundred meters elevation, *P. lentiscus*), cypress *(Cupressus sempervirens)*, and wild leeks (Quézel 1981:91; Rabinovitch-Vin 1983:77; Dan 1988:118). A mixed agricultural-horticultural economy consisting of millet, lentils, alfalfa, chickpeas, and fava beans, along with olive and wine viticulture, almonds *(Amygdalus common)*, and walnuts *(Juglans reg.)* on the lower slopes of the north-central and northwestern areas (Zohary 1966-86:2.21, 301; Aschmann 1973:365; Harel 1984:70), is likely here. Red deer and hare could be hunted, and terebinth and oak timber exported to the Judean Desert to the east.

Returning to the northern area of Palestine, the Jezreel Valley portion of the Esdraelon skirts the northern edge of the study zone, and so should be considered. Soils likely by Iron I were already Brown Alluvial Vertisols and Brown Alluvial Grumsols (Stanhill 1978:435). The rainfall was about 20 inches. Willows and wild leeks were common. This was solely a crop-farming region: wheat, barley, lentils, alfalfa, chickpeas, fava beans, peas, and flax/linseed (Zohary 1966-86:2.178, 181, 222; Sapin 1968-69:23; Borowski 1987:89).

Much of the northern part of the hill country falls into the Northeastern Nablus Syncline. The soils were Rendzina, Terra Rosa(?), and Mediterranean Brown Forest(?); rainfall was about 20 inches. Mixed Tabor Oak Shrublands stood here in Iron I — both oak varieties, balsam, all varieties of terebinth (no *P. lentiscus* over three hundred meters altitude), wild leeks, and garlic (Rabinovitch-Vin 1983:77). Although rare today, olives (along with figs) could have been dominant on the lower slopes (Antoun 1972; Aschmann 1973:365; Bornstein 1993:97). Terrace farming — wheat, barley, lentils, alfalfa, peas, chickpeas, fava beans, and onions — was likely dominant elsewhere (Zohary 1966-86:2.222; Rabinovitch-Vin 1983:79; Borowski 1987:97). The mountainous eastern part of the Northeast Nablus Syncline would support goatherding (Webley 1972:170). The timber of oak, fig, and terebinth trees could have been exported to the Jezreel Valley, and storax incense could also have been produced for export. The flint assemblage from Dhahrat et-Tawileh is that of a leather-working industry, indicative of hunting (A. Mazar 1982a:41).

The large Sanur Valley sits on the southwestern edge of this Northeastern Nablus Syncline. This valley of Gley and hydromorphic soils receives 20 to 28 inches of rainfall. Tamarisk, willows, reeds, and leeks were the natural vegetation (Dan 1988:119). Onions, leeks, and garlic may have been the main agricultural element, but both the harvesting of lentils, alfalfa, chickpeas, fava beans, and flax/linseed and caprovid grazing are also possible (Aschmann 1973:365; Bornstein 1993:97).

Rising high above this valley to the south is the Gerizim and Ebal Massif. Here the soils were the same as those of the Northeastern Nablus Syncline, but rainfall was the highest in this part of Palestine — around 28 inches, and even a bit higher, annually. The vegetation was a modified Mixed Tabor Oak Forest Shrubland of oaks (faunal remains of which are found at el-Burnat Sitti Salaamiyeh; Zertal 1986-87:113), balsam, myrrh, wild leeks, and garlic, but only the occasional *P. palestina* terebinth since the rainfall is so high (Quézel 1981:91; Rabinovitch-Vin 1983:77; although it was found at el-Burnat Sitti Salaamiyeh; Horwitz 1986-87). Viticulture was the dominant economy. Olives were found on the lower, south slopes of Mt. Gerizim but rare on Mt. Ebal (although found at el-Burnat Sitti Salaamiyeh; Horwitz 1986-87), and wine throughout (Aschmann 1973:365; Bornstein 1993:97). Pomegranates and figs would also be harvested on the south and west slopes of Gerizim and the west slopes of Ebal (Bornstein 1993:97). Red deer and fallow deer (many remains were found at el-Burnat Sitti Salaamiyeh; Horwitz 1986-87:180; Zertal 1986-87:113), and hare could be hunted (see, e.g., Horwitz 1986-87:175). Remains of caprovids and cattle were also found at el-Burnat Sitti Salaamiyeh (Horwitz 1986-87:174, 177, 179; Zertal 1986-87:113).

On the south of Mt. Gerizim, before the Southern Nablus Syncline, lie the Mikhmetat and Beit Dagon valleys. These were Grumsol valleys with about 20 inches of rain. The natural vegetation consisted of willows, wild leeks and garlic, and thistles. A variety of economies was possible: caprovid grazing, horticulture of olives, pomegranates, and nuts, or farming of lentils, alfalfa, chickpeas, fava beans, and flax/linseed (Aschmann 1973:365; Bornstein 1993:97).

On the northeastern corner of the Judean Mountains are the Bethel Hills. Although identical in soils to the Judean Mountains, the lower altitude and slightly lower rainfall (16-20 inches) make the standing vegetation a blend of the common Mixed Tabor Oak Forest and a Middle Sparse Garrigue Scrub Mattoral. Mt. Tabor Oak and Balsam would have been common only where the rainfall was the highest (Steward and Webber 1981:57, 59; Rabinovitch-Vin 1983:83; Harel 1984:70). Otherwise, the stand would have been cypress, terebinth varieties, myrrh, asphodel, gladiolus, thyme, lavender, and rosemary (Quézel 1981:91). The economy likely equaled out to half horticulture and half crops (Finkelstein, Lederman, and Bunimovitz 1997:66). There was horticulture of wine and olives and farming of lentils, alfalfa, chickpeas, and fava beans (note cereal-producing tools at Khirbet Raddanah; Cooley 1975:9). Additionally, Khirbet Raddanah's excavations found caprovid bones in every household (Hesse 1990:216, 225). The Bethel Hills are another source of timber for the Judean Desert. Storax incense and labdanum resin could be exported.

Another area only tangentially in the study zone is the Beth-Shan Valley and Galilee basin of the Esdraelon, at the northeast extreme of the highlands. This valley is Rendzina soil and receives about 12 inches of rain. Ash, willow, and poplar trees *(Poplarus alba* or *P. euphratica)* were the stand (Van Zeist 1985:200). The dominant crop was wheat, along with barley, lentils, alfalfa, and flax/linseed (Zohary 1966-86:2.178, 181, 200, 258; Antoun 1972:4; Van Zeist 1985:203; Borowski 1987:89).

Perched above the Esdraelon is the Gilboa. This clump of high hills jutting out into the plain contained Terra Rosa(?), Rendzina, and Mediterranean Brown Forest(?) soils, and received 12 to 20 inches of rain. Its natural vegetation was "Type B" High Dense Chaparral Maquis (Tomaselli 1981:98). This consisted of oaks, terebinth (excepting *P. lentiscus*), and true carob (Rabinovitch-Vin 1983:77; Liphschitz 1987-89:151-54).

Two valleys in the southeastern part of the Northeastern Nablus Syncline, although not contiguous, can be considered one region: the El Bugeia and Wadi Fara valleys. Both are Grumsol valleys, with rainfall between 12 and 16 inches annually (Dan 1988). Willows and thistles grew wild here. These intramontane valleys were well suited to caprovid grazing, supplemented by small plots of lentils, alfalfa, and flax/linseed (Zohary 1966-86:2.258; Antoun 1972:4; Van Zeist 1985:203; note a cereal-industry flint assemblage from Khirbet Marah el-Inab, Site #126; Zertal 1996:455-58).

Between the eastern edge of the Northeastern Nablus Syncline and the Jordan River and north of Wadi Fara are the East Samarian Hills. The soils are the same as those of the Northeastern Nablus Syncline, but the rainfall is less than 12 inches annually. Having come full circle, the vegetation here is the same as that of the northern Sharon Plain: the Carob-Lentisk/Carob-Mastic High Dense Chaparral Maquis — oaks and terebinths, wild leeks and garlic (Rabinovitch-Vin 1983:77). Grazing of cattle and goats would have been the dominant economic strategy, although barley, wheat, and lentils could be grown with proper irrigation (Webley 1972:170; Aschmann 1973:365 Rabinovitch-Vin 1983:79).

South of the Wadi Fara, in the Borders of Samaria, this same east-west zone begins to contain Stony Light Brown soils. Here the oaks and terebinth are joined by almonds, summer cypress, lotus, saltwort, seablight, saltbush, glasswort, marigolds, and capers (Rabinovitch-Vin 1983:77; Dan 1988:121-23; Finkelstein, Lederman, and Bunimovitz 1997). The economy, however, would be identical to that of the East Samarian Hills.

To the east of the Judean Mountains and Bethel Hills is the Judean Desert or Jeshimon. The soils here were Loess, Grumic Dark Brown Soils and Vertisols, Stony Light Brown Soils, Stony Serozems, and Brown and Calcareous Lithosols, although rainfall could be up to 20 inches annually (Van Zeist 1985:200; Dan 1988). The halophytic vegetation here included almonds, wormwood, summer cypress, date palms *(Phoenix dactylifera)*, lotus, saltwort, seablight, saltbush, glasswort, marigolds, capers, ryegrass, anabasis, thistles, and thorns (Van Zeist 1985:200; Dan 1988:121-22). Then, as now, the dominant economic factor was caprovid and cattle grazing, especially of sheep (note the abundance of caprovid bones at et-Tell; Callaway 1976:30; 1984:60), although the moderate rainfall would allow lentils, rye, peas, chickpeas, fava beans, and capers to be grown (Zohary 1966-86:2.222; Antoun 1972:4). Salt could be collected in bricks (Akk. $sig_4.mun$) for export (Potts 1997:459). The ashes of desert plants were the only available flux for glassmaking other than Egyptian Natron, and so could have been exported, along with dates and the highly desired date palm roofing (Peltenburg 1997:311; G. R. H. Wright 1997:363).

The Jordan Valley itself, defined here as a broad region south of the latitude of Wadi Fara, receives less than 12 inches of rain. Its soils are Desert Alluvial and Brown Desert Skeletal. Depending on the proximity to the Jordan River, plants are both halophytic and alluvial (Van Zeist

1985:200; Dan 1988:123). These included date palms, balsam, poplar, balm, sycamore, summer cypress, lotus, saltwort, seablight, saltbush, glasswort, marigolds, capers, and anabasis (Dan 1988:121-22; Avi-Yonah 1939:83). Goats could have been dominant, and even wheat, barley, and lentils (Zohary 1966-86:2.178, 181; Borowski 1987:89), but the range of wildlife (including boars [*Sus scrofa*], oryx antelope [*Oryx leucoryx*], gazelles [*Gazella dorcas*], ibex [*Capra nubiana*], and various species of duck) could have made hunting a primary strategy (Webley 1972:170). Other factors include dates, palm roofing, and storax incense.

Immediately several things become evident. One may reflect back on the observation that the Gravity Model–drawn bailiwicks for the Iron I highland settlement span broadly diverse environmental zones. Further expansion of this observation is now possible. The Khirbet Seilun bailiwick, for instance, although roughly contiguous with the Southern Nablus Syncline, has cereal farming, viticulture, and caprovid grazing each in different parts of its administrative network. Although each of these economies could exist totally independently in each part, it is noteworthy that some political and economic unity centered at Khirbet Seilun instead of separate networks for each environmental area. Likewise, the Khirbet Tibne System exploits the western portion of the Southern Nablus Syncline and the Foothills of Samaria, where viticulture would have played an even greater role.

The Tell Balatah System must have handled an immense diversity of ecological strategies, exploiting the Sebastiya Arraba Massif, the Gerizim and Ebal Massif, the Mikhmetat and Beit Dagon valleys, and the Southern Nablus Syncline. Again, managed combinations of viticulture and cereal farming were the strategy. The Tell el-Farah (North) System spans the Northeastern Nablus Syncline, the Wadi Fara and El Bugeia valleys, and the East Samarian Hills, although all these support primarily herding economies. The Tell Dothan System includes parts of the Sebastiya Arraba Massif, the Dothan Valley, the Northeast Nablus Syncline, and the Umm el-Fahm Hills. This area involves every strategy: horticulture, cereals, and herding.

Another important observation that the highland economies were complex. It will not be enough to pull a given site out of the enumerated regions and read that as its subsistence strategy. Within each region there are variations dependent on rainfall, altitude, and position on the hillside (both directional and elevational), requiring *each site* individually to be identified according to these features. This small-scale diversity contradicts an Annales School *longue durée* view of environmental factors and resultant economies being constant.

In those areas where the raising of wheat can provide the main means of subsistence, a full calendric economy can be reconstructed. Where the first- or second-ranked commodities could not be supported, they can be removed from the following scheme without significant changes. This presentation of the highland calendric economy is based on the reconstructed economic strategies just presented, with information drawn from analogy (Turkowski 1969:27-28, 101; Antoun 1972:10-12; Said 1974; Moors 1989:199) and from the Gezer calendar, although the Gezer calendar is again analogy and not primary evidence from the Iron I highlands. The Gezer calendar attests to a wealthy and sedentary community of the coastal plain some two centuries later than the period here in question (S. Rosen 1994:349-50; this fact is ignored by V. Fritz 1996:93).

A schematization can begin in December, when the plowing for legumes begins, a task performed by the men. This plowing begins later in the Jordan Valley. In January men perform the shallow plowing, and both men and women sow the cereals. Sowing of fava beans may begin this early. In February, while sowing of cereals continues, men engage in the second plowing. Sowing lentils and chickpeas at this stage is possible also. In March all the remaining legumes are sown, the olives and vine are dug, and the men plow for green fallow. April sees a continuation of digging olives and vines and plowing for green fallow, with women weeding. Any remaining vegetables (onions and the like) are now planted. In May the harvest begins, with both sexes harvesting lentils, alfalfa, chickpeas, fava beans, and flax/linseed. In June the barley is ready for harvest, the wheat in late June or early July. Men then begin the threshing. Threshing continues into August, when winnowing and vine tending begin. Winnowing and vine tending continue into September. In October both men and women harvest the vines and other fruits, and the olive harvest covers late October and November.

A description of the ancient economy must also take account of hunting. "Judging from the osteological data, hunting played a secondary, but surely not insignificant role in the economic system of the Iron Age I highlands peasant" (S. Rosen 1994:340). Finally, a supplemental source of income could be to hold lowlanders for ransom (*EA* 292:26, 49) or to steal the cattle of the lowlands (1 Chron. 7:21; Redford 1990:558-59).

Temporal Change in the Settlement Pattern

In all of the regions here studied, one might examine temporal change, and one cannot telescope all of Iron I together chronologically. Unfortunately, microceramic distinctions of chronology are simply unavailable, other than to tell the 12th from the 11th century (Finkelstein 1996c:390). For excavated sites, smaller chronological distinctions can be made on the basis of stratigraphy alone (assuming a Wheeler-Kenyon method of excavation), but not for pottery. So for the vast majority of sites of the Iron I highlands, diachronic study is not possible.

The region that was not included in the locational geographic study discussed above, the complex arrangement of sites in the "Benjamin" region, is fertile ground for chronological analysis, however, because of the multiple centers whose several Iron I strata can be correlated. There are several fully excavated sites of large size with multiple destructions and rebuildings during Iron I that can be cross-tabulated with each other and possibly illustrate more of the "cycling" inherent in the complex chiefdom model. The following chronological survey of this subregion illustrates several correlates of the complex chiefdom model.

At the dawn of the Iron Age, several prosperous "cities" existed in this region. Tell el-Ful I was founded (A. Mazar 1994b:76; N. Lapp 1997:346), a 1.35-hectare walled site (N. Lapp 1981:125). Et-Tell "Cobblestone Street Stratum" = Intermediate Stratum IX = Level Ia = Phase II was already in existence, a huge site of 11.0 hectares, although unwalled (Callaway 1965b:40; 1976:30; 1984:53; Stager 1968:8). Its prosperity is attested by bronze items (a chisel from the North Bench House; Callaway 1969b:57), bowls imported from the coast (see above), and uniformly spacious houses: the Pillared House in squares B.XV, XVII, XXII, and XXIV with four hewn-stone pillars and a six-room barn attached (Callaway 1965a:412; 1968a:316; 1969a:59; 1969b:6; 1970a:13-15, 18; n.a. 1969:15); the North Bench House in B.XVII, XVIII, XXI, and XXIII, also piered (Callaway 1970a:13, 16); and the tripartite Southern Bench House in B.V-VI, IX-XI (J. Callaway, draft of "The Iron I Village at Ai [et-Tell]" final excavation report). Beitin Phase 1 was also already in existence (Kelso 1934:417; 1961a:16; 1962:15; Brodsky 1992). It was a walled town with luxury items of iron, Cypriote pottery, marble, and bronze (see above; Kelso 1934:416; 1958:8). Beitin Phase 1 also shows segregation of neighborhoods. The piered masonry house 310/312 (by 1954 season numbering) resembles

Fig. 18 The Site of et-Tell

the houses at et-Tell (H. Weippert 1988:357; Albright and Kelso 1968:32), and House 35 (called Room 3 in the 1934 season) is a three-room house of at least five by six meters (Albright and Kelso 1968:32). These houses are in contrast to the tiny subdwellings made out of the Late Bronze Age palace foundation walls (Kelso 1934:417). Khirbet Raddanah Phase 2 also already existed (Callaway 1984:54). It was a 1.2-hectare, walled town (Callaway and Cooley 1971:12; Cooley 1975:13; G. R. H. Wright 1985:1.75). It, too, had luxury goods like bronze items (Callaway 1970b:231-32; see above) and seals (a black steatite conical seal pendant of a cow, suckling calf, ibex, and the rear of another animal; Denyer 1973:5). Here also there was a residential hierarchy: the central, hewn-pillared, three-room pier house in Site S has taller pillars and more storage and is bigger (16 × 5 m.) than the 14 or so houses in Site R or the houses in Site T (Callaway 1970b:231; Cooley 1975:8; Callaway 1984:54). El-Jib Period I = "Pre-Fortress Period I" was founded, a walled city of 11.0 hectares (Pritchard 1960a:8; 1961:22; 1962a:63, 102; 1962b:122; 1963:7, 10; 1964a:37, 39; H. Weippert 1988:403). It also contained items of bronze (e.g., bronze needle #915; "No. 2 Notebook," p. 1148). Residential hierarchy is here evidenced by the large house in Area 10, square

L-5 (10-L-5), a hewn-pillared house like those of Beitin and et-Tell, larger than the other houses of the site (Pritchard 1963:12). Tell en-Nasbeh Stratum 4 was also founded, likely a small, insignificant village (Graham 1981:33; Zorn 1993:4).

The situation at the start of Iron I, then, is one of multiple centers. Et-Tell and el-Jib are much larger than the others, but the absence of a city wall at et-Tell militates against its being the A-level center, and it is unlikely that el-Jib controlled so many large sites far to its east. Possibly all these sites were centers, leaving them as independent simple chiefdoms.

In ca. 1175, Beitin Phase 1 was destroyed (Albright and Kelso 1968:33). It was immediately replaced by a poorer, cruder town in Beitin 2: buildings had no foundations and were made of mixtures of stones and bricks (Albright 1934:11; H. Weippert 1988:399). Still, bronze objects, scarabs, and iron objects were found (all listed above and below under imports and weaponry).

The first regional change, however, occurred in ca. 1150. Tell el-Ful Level I was destroyed and abandoned (Albright 1933:7; Sinclair 1960:6; P. Lapp 1965:4; Stager 1968:9; Graham 1981:30; A. Mazar 1994b:76; N. Lapp 1997:346). So was et-Tell (Callaway 1976:30). At the same time, Khirbet Raddanah was remodeled as Phase 3, an overcrowded city of poor houses, some haphazardly thrown up over hastily covered silo pits (Callaway and Cooley 1971:11; Cooley 1975:10). Some prosperous areas existed, too, such as in Site R, Area R.III, which in a mud, brick-paved room contained the Anatolian-style krater (see above) and an inscribed jar handle (see Chapter 8, below). There were also many iron and bronze objects from this phase (Cooley 1975:11-12; Waldbaum 1978:25; see above). The site of Khirbet ed-Dawwara was founded at this moment, a town only 0.5 hectares in size but with a city wall and bronze and Iron items, likely a sort of hill-fort (Finkelstein 1987:20; 1988c:79; 1990a:163, 168-69, 196-97; V. Fritz 1995:56-57). Within two decades, et-Tell was rebuilt as the "Silo Granary Stratum" = Level Ib (Callaway 1976). It was still unwalled, but had become suddenly overcrowded like Khirbet Raddanah, with new houses springing up and old ones being subdivided (Callaway 1965a:412). Although the North Bench House was not rebuilt and lay in ruins, the South Bench House continued to be occupied, and in fact it was renovated, with stone floors replacing the beaten earth ones (Callaway 1965b:26-27; 1968a:316; Stager 1968:8). Farther east a high wall was built in a semicircle, using pieces of the Early Bronze wall, to isolate two house-compounds (Callaway

1976:22-23). This is all in contrast to the crude two- and three-room dwellings on the edge of Site C (Shiloh 1978:45). These huts included House 152 (with Room 150), 13.5 by 5.1 meters; House 189 (with Rooms 190, 183, 184, and 208), 13.5 by 6 meters; and House 207 (with Room 206). Even poorer were the squatters who moved into large Room A of the Early Bronze Age palace on Site D, put a divider across the middle, and built their fires right on the palace floor (Marquet-Krause 1935:339; Callaway 1965b:38-39; 1984: 54). They did the same in the palace's Hallway B (Marquet-Krause 1935:339).

Something serious had clearly happened in the region. Whatever destroyed Tell el-Ful and et-Tell resulted in the overcrowding of Khirbet Raddanah, and of et-Tell after it was rebuilt. But why was it rebuilt and Tell el-Ful not (and would not be for a hundred years)? Perhaps the destruction of Beitin in 1175 was somehow connected with this event. What of the site of Khirbet ed-Dawwara? When everything is taking a downturn, a new site is founded here, which is a walled hill-fort despite its small size (a "borough" in the strict definition of the term as a fortified cluster of houses).

In 1100, Beitin Phase 2 was destroyed (Kelso 1934:417; 1956:40; Albright and Kelso 1968:32-33). Its successor, Phase 3, is even poorer, with cob walls all of an irregular mix of bricks and stones (Kelso 1934). The entire site looks like the poorer parts of Khirbet Raddanah and et-Tell, but even here there are bronze items (pin #298, slug #285 = #2.0185 at the Pittsburgh Theological Seminary), and, for the first time, Philistine pottery (Kelso 1934:417). The situation in "Benjamin" then remained unchanged until 1050.

In 1050, Khirbet Raddanah Phase 3 was destroyed and abandoned forever (Cooley 1997b:402). Within two decades, Tell el-Ful was rebuilt as Level II, with its monumental keep at the center (see discussion below; Graham 1981:37; N. Lapp 1981:xvii). The site was well over two hectares at this point, as the residential quarters of the city extended down the lower east slope, all the way into Wadi Zimri, where Area E of Shimon Gibson's 1996 excavation produced massive amounts of Iron I pottery in fills (S. Gibson 1996). Imported items such as coastal bowls (see above), Cypriote White Painted ware I, and iron were present (Kurinsky 1991:119; A. Mazar 1994b:51, 78). At the same time, Beitin Phase 3 was destroyed, and rebuilt as Phase 4a with fine masonry of dressed piers, burnished and other new pottery forms, basalt items, and scarabs (see above; Albright 1934:11; Albright and Kelso 1968:34-35, 63).

Tell el-Ful became the center for the region. Whatever its cause was, the destruction of Khirbet Raddanah had a positive effect on the neighboring cities, facilitating the renaissance of Tell el-Ful and the renovation of Beitin. That for as long as Khirbet Raddanah 3 existed, no Tell el-Ful could, might suggest that Khirbet Raddanah had in fact taken some of Tell el-Ful's center duties in 1150, and the center returned to Tell el-Ful a hundred years later. The question is: Why does et-Tell not improve in 1025? It is the largest site of all, and had been in much the same state as Khirbet Raddanah. Yet it is neither destroyed nor renovated. It is wrong to suggest that Tell el-Ful II was a Philistine garrison, and that the Philistines took control of the region around 1050 (as per Singer 1994:323). This seems to be based directly on the biblical text and is not supported by archaeology. There is no Philistine pottery at Tell el-Ful II (Albright 1933:8; Brug 1985:96), and it is in fact at this point that Philistine pottery *disappears* from Beitin (Kelso 1955:7). Only at Tell en-Nasbeh could one reconstruct a Philistine garrison (given the on-site manufacture of Philistine pottery), and there only an unfortified one!

The end of Iron I saw a sweeping wave of destructions. In 1000, Tell el-Ful II was destroyed in a sizable blaze (Graham 1981:23). Et-Tell was destroyed in a destruction layer thick enough to merit its own level number (Level II = Phase XI; Callaway 1965b:38; 1969b:7). Tell en-Nasbeh Stratum 4 was destroyed (Zorn 1993:112). El-Jib I was destroyed (Pritchard 1964a:37, 50-51). One must ask who destroyed all these sites while leaving Beitin, the one site that was destroyed the most often in Iron I.

Some other questions also need addressing. Why is it that occupation at el-Jib is continuous throughout this period? It may be because Pritchard excavated by the Reisner-Fisher Method of following architectural elements down and not the Wheeler-Kenyon Method of reading strata in the debris, and so he missed the individual layers. However, destruction layers are hard to miss. If el-Jib was walled and so large, how could it stay out of whatever politics and military activity affected the rest of the region?

The role of Tell en-Nasbeh also raises questions. No houses can be reconstructed for Iron I (Zorn 1993:106), except maybe one in R.17. They may have been wooden structures (Zorn 1993:106). Some people were living in the caves of the site, including Cave 193 and Cave 243 (Zorn 1993:361, 404, 416). The first question, already posed, is what the people living in these tents and caves were doing with Phoenician globular jugs, making their own Philistine Bichrome. Another issue regards the function of the site. There were about two hundred silos, mostly plastered, hollowed out of the bedrock, and concentrated in squares AG-AM.20-25, AA-AB.14, AE.17, T.21, T.14, V-W.13, and N-R.16-18, where they are so concentrated that there are eight silos per 100 m^2 (N. Lapp 1981:61; Zorn 1993:107, 239). The silos average a capacity of 2.4 m^3, and the smallest ones are the oldest ones (Zorn 1993:104). Now even if the silos were kept at only 70 percent capacity, and another 30 percent of that was lost to pests or saved as seed, that still equals 179,000 kilograms of grain, or enough to feed between five hundred and a thousand people (a 1.7–3.4-ha. city) for a year, depending on what consumption figure is used (Zorn 1993:248). Tell en-Nasbeh must have been a regional storage facility for a larger surrounding area, although this still does not explain the presence of the Philistine pottery and the imports.

Mortuary Evidence

There are other facets of the complex chiefdom model that do not require the settlement pattern to be mapped. One of these facets is the analysis of the remains of the dead. The catalogue of mortuary evidence from the Iron I highland settlement is meager. There are no cases where it can be determined if distinctions of sex, age, or rank are made by including different kinds of objects. Typically, there are only meager amounts of data about the Iron I tombs. Often all that exists is the tomb itself and the pottery used to date it, which provides only tomb type and location, and often even these details are not mentioned in publication. At Iraq et-Tayyih (#C3), there are Iron I tombs about which nothing more is known (Campbell 1991:20). The same is true for the three Iron I tombs at Faria el-Jiftlik (#C2; Mellaart 1962:154; although this tomb belongs to the Deir Allah System), the tomb at Iraq Burin (#C4; Bull and Campbell 1968:38; Jaroš and Deckert 1977:33), Tomb 2 at Tell Dothan (Cooley and Pratico 1995:160), and the three at Deir el-ʿAzer (Site #407; Cooke 1925:115). There is an Iron I tomb at Khirbet Birzeit (Site #37) on the south slope (Abel 1928:50; "1996 Site Survey"). Near the site of Tell Marjame (Site #6), there is a single Iron I tomb at a distance to the north, between Khirbet Samiyya, Dhahr el-Mirzbaneh, and Khirbet el-Aqibat, in the midst of a group of 27 Late Bronze I tombs (n.a. 1971:23). At an Iron I tomb at Khirbet Majdal (#C1), lamps with closed wick holes were found, but no other information is available (Yannai 1995:279), and it is really off the western edge of the study area.

In other cases, the assignment of an Iron I date is questionable. At Tell el-Farah (North), Tomb 5 has been published as 11th century, with re-use in the 10th (Chambon 1984:67). Yet it is impossible to disentangle this "reuse" if there even was one: all indications of 11th-century use may be merely deposit of residual materials or heirlooms. Items such as Samarian jars, incised tablets, and imitation Cypriote bilbils ("1947 Catalogue of Objects," items #F884-F1764) are more at home in the Iron II context.

What remains of mortuary evidence from the highlands after removing the empty tombs and those of questionable dating is a mere eight graves, each published idiosyncratically. These are Tell en-Nasbeh Tomb 54 (McCown and Wampler 1947:82-83); Tell en-Nasbeh Tomb 29 (McCown and Wampler 1947:84, 88-93); Jelamet ʿAmer (Zertal 1996:215); Taiyiba (Yannai 1995:279), although this is almost off the west edge of the study area; Khirbet Nisya Tomb 65 (Byers 1994; 1995); Tell Dothan Tomb 1, Level 1 (Free 1962:120; Cooley and Pratico 1994:152) and Tomb 3 (Cooley and Pratico 1995:160); and Khirbet en-Namleh (Zertal 1984:110; 1992:140). The latter is also likely a cemetery for Tell Dothan, but it may be mixed: although Zertal calls the site 100 percent Iron I (1984:110; 1992:140), he then shows in his illustrations an Iron II cooking pot (1992:140) and mentions other Iron II pottery in passing (1984:188). Tell en-Nasbeh Tomb 29 does contain Iron II pottery, but nothing that could not be also 11th century, and no long-stepped dromos tombs of its type have ever been found for Iron II (Loffreda 1968:263; McClellan 1985:284-86).

It is not necessary to include full descriptions of these tombs and their contents here, but rather to systematize the accumulated data. Whenever possible, details on the body treatment, the grave itself, its contents, and any biological information from the body have been collated together. From these summaries, it is useful to emphasize "form" since it is possibly most indicative of ranking (Binford 1972:21; Wason 1994:53). As all these graves are disturbed contexts, quantitative analysis of attributes is not possible (Brown 1981:29; Feinman and Neitzel 1984:75; Hedeager 1992:103; Bard 1994:102). For disturbed graves, rather, combination qualitative analysis is used (Hedeager 1992:101). This method tags each grave for the presence or absence of selected burial attributes: specific goods (here imported pottery has been used), esoteric minerals, body rituals, expensive weapons, local symbols, grave type and location, pottery only, and "Number of Artifact Types" (NAT) — the count of types found, each type being tallied as "one" whatever the number of objects of that type found (Hedeager 1992:103). This tabulation for the eight graves allows the graves to be grouped into sets by combinations of attributes (Goldstein 1980:110). One attribute that is not used here for this grouping is tomb type, because this varies by region and ethnicity in Iron I (Wenning and Zenger 1986; Bloch-Smith 1992:29, 39, 137).

The tombs fall, then, into two groups: pottery-only graves and others. Tell en-Nasbeh Tomb 29, Jelamet 'Amer, Taiyiba, and Tell Dothan's Khirbet en-Namleh cemetery all have nothing but pottery. The others have many additional types of grave goods. There is nearly a double correlation of this division with tomb location, an attribute especially indicative of ranking (Brown 1981:29; Feinman and Neitzel 1984:75; Bard 1994:102). All of the pottery-only tombs are at some distance from the nearest inhabited site, except for Tell en-Nasbeh Tomb 29. The graves with multiple types of goods (higher NATs) are attached to sites.

Some additional things are evident. First is the scarcity of imported pottery in mortuary contexts. Only at Taiyiba and Tell Dothan Tomb 1 is there any foreign pottery, and only one piece each (a Cypriote Black-on-Red vessel at Taiyiba and a Phoenician stand [#T1.2010.P966; "Dothan Archaeological Expedition Spring 1964 Notebook," "Objects from Tomb 1 (1964 Season) Notebook," and "1960 Notebook"] at Tell Dothan). This absence of foreign pottery is notable, given the presence of many non-ceramic imports: Mediterranean cowry shells (Khirbet Nisya Tomb 65; Byers 1994; 1995), ivory (both at Tell Dothan Tomb 1: a pendant and a scarab [#K32 in the Rockefeller Museum, "1964 Photograph A"] and Khirbet Nisya Tomb 65; Byers 1994; 1995), and alabaster (two spindle whorls [#T1M4 and T1M8; same reference as the stand above] and a burnishing stone [#T1M7] from Tell Dothan Tomb 1).

Second, Tomb 1 at Tell Dothan is anomalous (Fig. 19). Its NAT is 23, compared with the next highest figure of 12 for Khirbet Nisya Tomb 65. Its contents contain many items not found in the other tombs: items of alabaster and ivory, animal bones (some in a jug, some in a krater; Cooley and Pratico 1994 plus above notebooks). Also, it is unusual when compared with a much simpler, contemporary tomb at the same site, Tomb 3, which, nevertheless, is not pottery-only (and Tomb 2 could also not have compared with Tomb 1). This oddity may be due to the Tell Dothan System be-

Fig. 19 Tell Dothan Tomb 1

ing the northernmost system, and the influence of the lowland cultures to the north. But it should not suggest that Tell Dothan was part of that culture, as contemporary tombs from Afula are all single primary supine graves with north-south orientation, and in fact *they* are pottery-only (M. Dothan 1955:47-49).

As for indications of ascriptive rank, there is no way to correlate grave goods or any of the attributes with sex and age. The only tomb with body information at all is Khirbet Nisya Tomb 65, with a standard sex distribution of fifty individuals aged fifty to sixty years (Byers 1994). As the arrangement of bones and grave goods was disturbed, correlating the two is not possible. As to the dichotomy between pottery-only isolate tombs and higher-NAT city graves, there could be any number of reasons: ethnic, social, and the like. It is tempting to see in the city graves' many imports and luxury items something relevant to rank. Seals and scarabs were uniform grave-good markers of whatever distinction this was — two seals (#M2650 and #M2547 = object registry #35.3138 = photo #1498) and two scarabs (#M2649 = object registry #35.3139 = "X number" 287 and #M2639 = object registry #35.3130 = X#276) from Tell en-Nasbeh Tomb 54, one seal from Khirbet Nisya Tomb 65 (Byers 1994; 1995), four scarabs from Tell

72

Dothan Tomb 1 (e.g., #T1M1) — and in "Benjamin" iron objects acted similarly — 25 rings and two arrowheads from Tell en-Nasbeh Tomb 54 (McCown and Wampler 1947:83), and a ring and two bracelets from Khirbet Nisya Tomb 65 (Byers 1994; 1995).

The obvious question is: Where was everyone else buried? Can we suppose some bizarre circumstance under which the elites were buried in the towns and the poor in the country? This hardly seems the case, given the Cypriote Black-on-Red ware from the isolated pottery-only grave at Taiyiba (Site #C5), although this site is really off the western edge of the study area. Tell en-Nasbeh still poses a problem with pottery-only Tomb 29 beside NAT = 8 Tomb 54. Yet with no bodies to correlate, telling achieved rank from ascribed is not possible.[5] All of the tombs were communal (it is not possible to tell for Jelamet 'Amer, Taiyiba, and Khirbet en-Namleh), and it has been suggested that communal burial implies either ascriptive rank or no ranking, but never achieved rank (Wason 1994:90-91). This is flimsy evidence, however, from which to argue for complex chiefdoms, and the mortuary evidence must remain equivocal. Nevertheless, such continuity of residential hierarchy through multiple phases and therefore multiple generations (as House 10-L-5 at el-Jib with four living surfaces and the South Bench House at et-Tell, which lasts through the rebuildings of the city) can be used as indications of ascriptive rank.

Other Archaeological Correlates

Besides the notations of residential hierarchy already described for the "Benjamin" region, indications of difference in scale and wealth in the "built environment" can be more broadly based on size, decor, materials, furnishings, and location (Feinman and Neitzel 1984:75; Jamieson-Drake 1991:81-106 catalogues such for the southern highlands). A hierarchy of construction materials can be seen. Rubble stone houses would have been doomed to collapse in the earthquake-ridden regions of the north-central Palestinian highlands. Historically, only the poorest dwellings have been of rubble-and-clay constructions (Canaan 1933:31). Most intermediate qual-

---

5. The bones from the Tell en-Nasbeh tombs were, in fact, collected and taken by Theodore McCown, the son of Chester McCown, to Berkeley. But he never presented any results, and his notes and the bones have been lost (J. Zorn, personal communication).

ity houses were therefore of mud bricks, using a few courses of stones to keep water from washing away the mud and to keep osmosis from bringing water up (Canaan 1933:31). Additionally, the prevailing winds come from the northwest, making a house in the northwest quarter of a site the ideal, and most expensive, location (Pritchard 1957:25).

Other than Benjamin, described in detail above, examples from the highland settlement of residence hierarchy include Tell Balatah Level XI. In Field I, near the east city gate (loci 178-79), the houses are poor — in fact, the old east gate was converted into a two-room house (Fig. 20) — and other flats were built on top of the Late Bronze wall and guardhouse in this field (G. E. Wright 1957:22; Campbell 1966:7; Bull and Campbell 1968:4; Toombs 1992). This "squatters' neighborhood" is in contrast with Field IX, where a large house from the Late Bronze Age with a courtyard was rebuilt along its same plan (Phase 11; Campbell and G. E. Wright 1965:416-17). The rebuilding of the same house from the Late Bronze era might indicate ascriptive rank: continuity of status generation to generation. It was, in fact, in this house that the Cypriote imports mentioned earlier were found (G. R. H. Wright 1967:55).

A few other items from the systemization of Peebles and Kus remain to be considered. These include location of sites near good sustenance, evidence of conscripted labor of no more than one season, evidence of warfare or defense, and regional storage (besides the foregoing discussion of Tell en-Nasbeh).

To illustrate the proximity of sites to sustenance, a bit of clarification is needed. If by sustenance one means arable land, then all of the erosion difficulties described above are encountered. It is quite simple, however, to use water resources as "proximity to sustenance." For the regions mapped for settlement patterns, there are good data for the distance of each site to the nearest source of water (drinking or irrigation or both). The Tell el-Farah (North), Tell Dothan, and Attil systems can be treated together, and the Tell Balatah System on its own, and the average distance from site to nearest water source computed.[6] For the northern systems, the mean distance to water is 2.8 kilometers, with a standard deviation (population = 47) of 2.24. For the Tell Balatah area, the mean distance is 1.34 kilometers,

6. Older cisterns were reused and new ones constructed in Iron I. But since the entire study area lies over the same chalk/limestone rock, the chance for cistern use is fairly uniform and cisterns can be removed as a variable.

Fig. 20 Makeshift Dwellings in the East Gate of Tell Balatah

with a standard deviation (population = 42) of 1.30. The Tell Balatah System is more in line with Peebles and Kus's criterion of proximity to sustenance, based on water resources, than those systems to its north.

Evidence of both defense and conscripted labor includes the city wall at el-Jib. This is the so-called "Inner Wall" (Pritchard 1960a:8; 1961:22; 1963:7; H. Weippert 1988:403). Exposed in Areas 8-10 in the northwest of the site, it can be seen from the exposure in 10-L-5 that it was between 1.6 and 3.4 meters wide and likely covered a circuit of 1010.4 meters (Pritchard 1960a:8; 1962a:102; 1962b:122; 1963:10; 1964a:33). Other evidence of conscripted labor at el-Jib is the water system. The consensus is that the "pool" was from the Iron I system (Hallote 1997:403). The "pool" is a cylindrical cut into the bedrock 11.8 meters in diameter and 10.8 meters deep. There is a spiral staircase along the north and east sides that at the bottom continues into a tunnel to a spring room 13.6 meters below the pool floor. The construction of this pool required the quarrying of some 3,000 tons of rock, a matter of conscripted labor. Caution should be exercised here, however, as some have suggested that the only basis for dating this pool to Iron I was the biblical account of the "Pool of Gibeon" in 2 Samuel 2 (A. Mazar 1990:478-81, 527n.15). Others, constructing a typology of water systems, date the pool to the 7th century B.C. (Galling 1965:243; Shiloh 1987:212). In fact, there is some evidence that the excavators initially saw the stratigraphic relationship between the pool and the nearby 9th-century stepped tunnel such that the pool was the later of the two (Pritchard 1961:4-8). So too much weight should not be placed on the pool.

Other defensive indications in this southern region come from Khirbet Raddanah. Here, in Phase 2, the houses were lined up along the perimeter of the site and the spaces between them filled with limestone rubble to create a curtain wall (G. R. H. Wright 1985:1.75). The result was a wall about one meter thick (Callaway and Cooley 1971:12). This combines with weaponry finds from Phase 2, including a bronze battle axe and a bronze section of armor (Callaway 1970b:231-32). Bronze knives, coats of mail, daggers, and spear and javelin points were also found in Phase 3 (Cooley 1975:11-12).

There was also a city wall at Khirbet ed-Dawwara (Finkelstein 1985b:20). This was a solid oval perimeter enclosure wall 1.65 to 3 meters thick, made of fieldstones (Finkelstein 1988c:79; 1990a:168-69; V. Fritz 1995:56). Again, this was for defense and probably built by conscripted/contributed labor.

In Phase 1 of Beitin, the Middle Bronze city walls were repaired on the west edge of the site (Kelso 1934:416; "1960 Report to the Jordanian Department of Antiquities"), while in Area I (by the 1934 labeling scheme), the Late Bronze city walls were reused (Kelso 1958:8). From the various Iron I strata, many weapons were found: an iron arrowhead (#1079) from House 310/312 in Phase 1 ("1954 Daybook 1," "1954 Daybook 2," "1954 Object Cards," "1954 Record Book"), bronze socketed spearheads (e.g., #613) from loci 146-48 in Phase 2 (Albright and Kelso 1968:85), sling stones (e.g., #1042; "1954 Daybook 1," "1954 Daybook 2," "1954 Object Cards," "1954 Record Book"), iron (e.g., #2134; "1957 Room Cards," "1957 Daybooks," "1957 Artifact Book 1," "1957 Artifact Book 2"), bronze, copper, and flint arrowheads (e.g., #3065a = Pittsburgh Theological Seminary #2-3060 from Southwest Room Pit 5 in Area P East Garden), iron and flint javelin heads, a limestone dagger pommel (#1090) from the northwest corner of Room 313 (called Room 24 in an earlier numbering scheme; "1954 Daybook 1," "1954 Daybook 2," "1954 Object Cards," "1954 Record Book").

Et-Tell also produced many weapons, primarily from the "Silo Granary" Stratum (= Level Ib). From here came an iron lance head and iron dagger from Sites D and G (Waldbaum 1978:25), an iron spear-butt from elsewhere on the site (Meron 1985:25), and 16 sling stones from Site B ("1964 Objects Registry").

The abundance of sling stones at Tell en-Nasbeh is further evidence of warfare or defense (McCown 1947:262).

The most impressive fortifications of the "Benjamin" region are at Tell el-Ful. In Level I, a city wall was uncovered in Areas XVII and VII on the west side of the tell, and revetment fortifications in Area I on the south side (N. Lapp 1981:125). With Level II, though, the fortifications are massive. Following the liberal interpretation of the remains, the structure in question is a fortress (G. E. Wright 1941:38; Graham 1981:23-25; H. Weippert 1988:404). Fortress I was exposed in Areas XIII (the northwest and west sides of the fort), II (the north side), VII, and XVII (the latter two south walls; N. Lapp 1981:125-26). It was built of half each, hard *mizzi* stones and *nari* stones, and had beams of pine and cypress, indicative of a second story (Albright 1924b:7-8; Sinclair 1960:14; Borowski 1987:132). These preserved sections reveal the southwesternmost of four corner towers 11.6 by 17.8 meters, built of rubble walls 2.15 meters thick (Sinclair 1960:11-12; A. Mazar 1994b:77). Using this tower and other wall sections (contra A. Mazar 1994b:77, it is not a single segment), one can reconstruct the four-towered citadel as 57 by 62 meters, with non-casemate walls 1.5 meters wide connecting the towers (Graham 1981:23-25; H. Weippert 1988:404).

There is also a more conservative interpretation that argues that since the tower is preserved to a height of two meters (Albright 1924b; Sinclair 1960:11), one must wonder why none of the other three towers was preserved at all (A. Mazar 1994b:78). It is possible that the tower stood alone, as a sort of keep, similar to the Ammonite towers west of Amman (G. R. H. Wright 1985:77, 210). Even then, the keep is evidence of defensive architecture, and of public building on a scale to require conscripted labor.

Moving north, Khirbet Seilun also has a city wall, again evidence of defense and likely conscripted labor (Finkelstein, Bunimovitz, and Lederman 1993). Further evidence of contributed labor is the construction in Area C (squares D-F.37-44 on the west slope). Here the entire Middle Bronze glacis was torn down to build pillared buildings 312 and 335 on terraces with retaining walls (Finkelstein 1983b:99; Finkelstein et al. 1985:131; Bunimovitz 1993:21, 23). These buildings may also be evidence of regional storage (Finkelstein 1993c:386). Building 312, a four-room structure, is in fact a two-story building. Hall 306 is its basement (Bunimovitz 1993: 29-30). This basement contained 15 collared-rim pithoi lined up in rows on the south, east, and west walls (Finkelstein 1985a:137; Bunimovitz 1993:29). Building 335 was similarly packed with storage pithoi (Finkelstein 1993c:384). The assemblage here is of 76 percent storage vessels to 23 percent kitchenware. Yet the nature of these buildings is more complicated. In construction, 312 has dressed interior walls and some floors paved with slab stones (Bunimovitz 1993:21). Room 335 has a central compacted-chalk courtyard and dressed interior walls (Bunimovitz 1993:23). It was from these rooms that the aforementioned hematite weight was found, along with various pots with zoomorphic reliefs (lions, rams, horses, leopards; Bunimovitz 1993:27). The exact function of these structures remains elusive.

From settlement geography, the site of Izbet Sartah (#351) deserves much less attention than it has received (e.g., n.a. 1978; Kochavi and Demsky 1978; Finkelstein 1985a; 1992b; 1994:51; Dever 1991a; Watkins 1997). It is a small, Class B-sized site with one supporting village on the western fringe of the highland settlement beyond the Khirbet Tibne System. Yet there is evidence for conscripted labor, in that the buildings of Late Bronze Level III were cleared at one time to build a central, four-room pillared house (Finkelstein 1985a:14, 173). This house with stone-drum pillars, built of mud bricks on a stone foundation, with a flagstone floor, is made of Rooms 106b, 108b, 109b, 112b, and 119b, and has therefore been variously called "House 109b" and "House 112b" (Finkelstein 1985a:14, 17-18). It was 12 by 16 meters in size with 1.4 meters thick walls (Finkelstein 1992b). A fifth, annex room was added to bring it to 12 by 20 meters, not counting its plastered courtyard (locus 514; Finkelstein 1985a:14, 17). For an example of residential hierarchy, this house in the center of the site was surrounded by 43 stone-lined pits, and then around these were 20 crude, simple houses. Examples of these simple houses are #310, a tiny (6 × 7 m.) four-room house in Area D including Rooms 310, 302, 306, 308, and 309, with a flagstone floor (Finkelstein 1985a:22); #533 (including Room 532) in the north; #905, possibly a four-room house (Finkelstein 1985a:23); 916, another tiny four-room house (about 80 m²) in Area E in the east, including Rooms 936, 912, 902, and 919 (Finkelstein 1985a:22); #2018 in Area D (Finkelstein 1985a:21) and #2008, including 2015, 2003, and 2001 — both in the northwest; #3003; and #3005. Unfortunately, no remains were found in the central house in this period (Finkelstein 1985a:42). Fourteen Philistine sherds were found on the site as a whole, including one in Room 916 of House 916 (#9097/1), another in House 310, one in House 533, and two in Houses 3003 and 3005 (Finkelstein 1985a:62, 66, 68, 70, 91-92). Although these are hardly evidence of foreign trade, given that the Philistines were living within a kilometer, it is interesting that there was Philistine pottery in the poorer houses. More importantly, House 905 also produced a 20th-Dynasty scarab (#9111) of a seated lion with a Ma'at feather and uraeus over the lion (Finkelstein 1985a:104). Here an Egyptian item is found in a supposedly poor house. Evidence of warfare consists only of a single bronze arrowhead in House 905 (Finkelstein 1985a:136, 154).

In the Tell Balatah System, the B-level site administering the southeast, Khirbet Urma, shows fortification as evidence of defense. The Middle Bronze and Late Bronze walls were reused as defensive walls, beyond their function as retaining walls and buttressing (Campbell 1991:50-51). Even if the refurbishment of these walls did not require conscription of labor, it is possible that the Khirbet Urma water system did. Several huge cisterns were hewn, one measuring 1800kL (Bull and Campbell 1968; Campbell 1991:52-53). Some of these may have been Middle Bronze, but not all. Also in this system, at the site of el-Burnat Sitti Salaamiyeh (#135), which although it is size Class C2 has no subordinate villages, there was a 110 meter-long, thick enclosure wall (W29-W75), 1.5 meters high, enclosing a pale of 3,500 m² (Zertal 1985; the site's supposed cultic nature will not be explored here). In Area B, this wall has a gate (locus 220) seven meters wide with three steps leading to a paved courtyard platform (Zertal 1985:34; 1986-87:119-20). This wall is too small to be evidence of defense, really more of a close, but it was likely built by conscripted labor, as was the 250-meter-long, 1.7–2.5-meter-wide retaining wall built to the west and downslope from the enclosure wall (Zertal 1986-87:108).

The fortifications at the center of Tell Balatah are more complicated. It is certain that the Late Bronze wall went out of use. It has already been mentioned that the old Late Bronze east gate became squatters' homes. Nevertheless, apparently the Late Bronze fortification lines remained standing undestroyed in parts of Field I (G. E. Wright 1957:22). In other parts of Field I, the fortification line was moved back 10 to 11.1 meters to the east of the Late Bronze wall, roughly onto the remains of the Middle Bronze Age wall (Campbell 1966:7). Thus, the east side of the city was walled. In the north, however, it is not as clear what defended the city. Again the gate was converted into small houses, rendering it unusable as a gate, but here a new fortification line could not be found (Sellin and Steckeweh 1941). As for evidence of the mustering of labor, there was the temple in Field V. "Migdal Temple 2a" of the temenos Phase 9 was reno-vated, with a stone altar installed outside it and some sort of columns in-side (Fig. 21; Jaroš 1976:39; Toombs 1992). The architectural nature of the Phase 9 temenos, however, is poorly understood, and therefore not much more can be said (Boraas 1986).

In the Tell el-Farah (North) system, the B-level center of Khirbet Fuqaha (Site #217) was fortified somehow (Zertal 1983a:44), as was the only B-level center of the Attil System, Tel Ze'evim (Site #264; Ne'eman 1990:34*, 41-42).

Additionally, an obvious indication of warfare is the presence of de-struction layers. So, on a quick run through the region, most of Khirbet Raddanah Phase 3 was destroyed in 1050 (Cooley 1997b:402). Beitin was destroyed several times: in 1175 after Phase 1, noting ash layers in Sub32, Sub50, 301, 302, 308, and 310; after Phase 2 in 1100, as evidenced by very se-vere fire in Sub32; and likely after Phase 3 in 1030 (Kelso 1934:417; 1956:40; Albright and Kelso 1968:32-33, 35). Stratum 4 of Tell en-Nasbeh, such as it was, was destroyed at the end of the 11th century (Zorn 1993:112). The "Cobblestone Street" Stratum of et-Tell was destroyed around 1150, and the "Silo Granary" Stratum was destroyed at the end of the 11th century, its de-struction layer so thick as to qualify as its own "stratum," Level II/Phase XI (Callaway 1965b:38; 1969b:7; 1976:30). Khirbet Seilun Level V was destroyed around 1050, the destruction being most intense in Area C and in Danish House A (Stager 1968:7; Finkelstein 1985a:168-69; Bunimovitz 1993:21). This destruction does not date to the 8th century, as the Danish excavators maintained (Buhl and Holm-Nielsen 1969). Tell Balatah Level XI was de-stroyed around 1125 (Campbell 1993:601; Seger 1997:22).

Finally, it not possible to label exactly objects that act as symbols of hierarchy (as desired by Earle 1987a:69-70), although undoubtedly the weapons and other items in tombs were as much political symbols as func-tional weapons. To the extent that such illustrate trade and access to for-eign goods, this has already been considered. No caches or hoards have been found in the Iron I archaeological record.

Fig. 21 Migdal Temple of Temenos Phase 9, Tell Balatah

Summary: Israelite Complex Chiefdoms?

Looking at the cumulative information in support of the complex chiefdom model and the multiplicity of interrelating variables, two systems can be immediately dropped. Neither the Attil System nor the Khirbet Tibne System has sufficient levels of hierarchy: Attil is not bimodal in its site-size distribution, and Khirbet Tibne's settlement pattern is wrong. They were likely simple chiefdoms that were still part of the larger Israelite bloc. Additionally, Izbet Sartah can be eliminated because, although it has residential hierarchy, conscripted labor, and imports, it is not a system at all but an isolated village with one daughter.

At the other extreme, the Tell Balatah System was most surely a complex chiefdom. Its settlement pattern follows the prediction of Steponaitis. Its site-size distribution is bimodal. It shows evidence of imports in the center (although awkwardly also in some smaller sites) as well as of cycling of centers, of residential hierarchy, of defense, and of conscripted labor. The sites of the system are found close to easy (water) sustenance.

It is also most likely that the "Benjamin" region was one or more

81

complex chiefdoms. The cycling is most clear here. All of the centers except Khirbet ed-Dawwara have imports. All of them except Khirbet Raddanah indicate possible contributed labor. All of them show evidence of defense, and most of residential hierarchy.

The rest of the systems are more equivocal. The Khirbet Seilun System does have imports in the center, defense, and conscripted labor. The Tell Dothan System shows bimodal site-size distribution and imports in the center, although its settlement pattern is too much like Central Place Theory. The Tell el-Farah (North) System follows the Steponaitis settlement pattern, but imports are found in both the center and the villages. Some of these may have been "dimorphic" chiefdoms, such as a complex chiefdom with a city-state at its head (the analogies are the Marri, Bugti, and Brahui "tribes" under the city-state of Kalat), where the city-state's king (Iranian *sirdar*) may or may not be the same individual as the chiefdom's paramount leader (Iranian *Khan;* Rowton 1973:212, 215; 1976:221-22, 243).

In summary, I am tentatively suggesting that Tell Balatah, "Benjamin," and likely Khirbet Seilun were complex chiefdoms but that the systems to the north are questionable. The evidence shows that not all of Israel was of the same type of society simultaneously.

Boundaries of the Highland Settlement

Often the Theissen Polygon "boundaries" are not between highland systems but between Israel and the "outside world." Here the issues of ethnicity again emerge. It is in fact an issue of territoriality that is beyond ethnicity (Saks 1986:19). It involves group assertion, will, and communication, and does not necessarily imply a *defended* territory (Saks 1986:19-21, 32). The boundaries are not as important as the territories they define, and thus the Israelites' relations with others would have ranged from symbiosis to conflict (Machinist 1994:48; Portugali 1994:217). Boundaries imply incompatibilities between types of social units (Hodder 1985:142). As discussed above, these cultural boundaries or frontiers also become visible in stylistic differences (Hodder 1985:156).

If these frontiers separate incompatible types of social units, then it is important to use shared variables in comparing two units to see if they are incompatible. This is the nature of Gloria London's critique of many studies attempting to draw this frontier (1987). She points out that comparing the highlands with the lowlands often involves comparing the urban lowlands with the rural highlands, and that the rural lowlands ought to be the comparand in order to limit the variables compared (1987:42). It is of great import, however, that there really *are* no urban highlands — nothing like Tel Miqne/*Ekron* VIIIa-VII of the 12th century, a 20-hectare site with fortifications more than three meters thick (Gitin and T. Dothan 1987:199; T. Dothan 1989:9; 1990:27; T. Dothan and Gitin 1993:1053), nothing like the Iron I tablet from Taanach (Tell Taanek, for 12th-century Levels IA-IB or Level II, depending on which terminology is used, a 4.5-hectare city mentioned as *Takhnaka* in Thutmose III's Pylon VI Karnak list) written in Northwest Semitic, a receipt for a grain shipment (TT433; Glock 1993:1432). Furthermore, London's own exploration of rural-rural comparison is weak. She concludes without evidence that all the differences are due to the rural-vs.-urban dichotomy, and that collared-rim pithoi and four-roomed houses are characteristic phenomena of rural villages everywhere (1987:43, 47). Yet her comparisons are often from Cyprus; she never did look at the rural Palestinian lowlands. There are many sites she could have examined, such as rural "Amorite" villages around Belameh and Taanach: Khirbet Abu Ghannam (Site #292), Beit Qad (Site #253), er-Requq (Site #144), or Jebel Haniyeh, or Philistine villages like Mesubbim, Farwaha, or En ha-Yadid; Dever has, in fact, suggested such a comparison of lowland villages with those of the highlands (1997a:43).

For the purposes of this study it does not really matter "who" was over those boundaries, except to say that the highland society was bounded by several different "incompatible social units." Good discussions of the changing situation outside the highlands in Iron I, and the accompanying problematic issues, are provided by Müller-Karpe (1977), Weinstein (1992:148), Lesko (1992:153), Bikai (1992:134-37), Dever (1992b: 100), Bunimovitz (1994:195), and Kuhrt (1995:328).

By Theissen polygons, the frontier of highland Israel is defined as those areas beyond the economic systems illustrated by the Gravity Model. The location of these marches can be supported by other evidence. It can be shown that those sites in the polygons of lowland sites rather than highland also possess lowland material culture. Further, often the Theissen boundaries fall just along natural landforms.

One of the systems bordering the highlands on the northeast is that of

Beth-Shan.[7] Sites that fall in the Beth-Shan system by the Gravity Model, such as Tel Amal Level 4 (Tell el-ʿAsi; Site #112, unless this is to be redated to Iron II as per McClellan 1975:216, 220), Tel Teomim, Tel Shukah (esh-Shuk), and Tel Shalem (Tell Radgha), all turn out to have Philistine pottery (S. Levy 1962:147; Zori 1962:163-64, 175, 185; S. Levy and Edelstein 1972:337-38). This leads one to trust the similar gravity alignment for Tel Malqokh (Tell Maqhuz) and Tel Terumot (Khirbet El-Khomrah), which do not (Zori 1962:174-75). Cisjordanian Tell el-Mazar (Site #205) gravitates to the system of Deir Allah, a site of five hectares with 12th-century Levels A and B being followed by a possible Sea People occupation in 11th-century Levels C and D, and in fact shows the supposed Sea Peoples' ceramic forms (Peterson 1977:272-73).

Occasionally, researchers have not determined specifically which center a site gravitates to once it has been established that it is *not* to a highland center. Thus, Tel Shalwim (Tell el-Firr) and Har Saul (Tell el-Kulilah; Site #249) are drawn to either the Beth-Shan System or to Afula[8] or Shunem/Solem.[9] This is supported by bichrome pottery at both Tel Shalwim and Har Saul (Zori 1977:6-8, 83). Its absence at Tell esh-Sheikh Hasan (Tel Yosef HaYashnah) is not a problem (Zori 1971:18; 1977:26-27). Tel Mevorakh (Tell Mubarak; Site #325) inclines toward 25-hectare Dor, likely inhabited by the Tjekker (Sikila) Sea People, and Mevorakh's Phoenician forms support this (E. Stern 1978:67; Bikai 1992:132; Singer 1994:296). In the Philistine area, Tel Malot Level 4 (Tell el-Malat; *Gebath* of 10th-Dynasty lists) gravitates to either Tel Miqne or Gezer.[10] Nahal Mazor gravitates to Azor,[11] Aphek,[12] or Tel Qana, and Kfar Qasim to Tel Qana. In

7. Egyptian *Bitsanu*. Levels VIIB-A were Egyptian under its governor Userkhepesh, but no longer Egyptian in the 11th-century Upper Level VI (Hebrew University stratum S2) and Lower Level V (Hebrew University stratum S1; Weinstein 1992:143). It is unclear whether the occupants of the latter levels were Sea Peoples or Amorites, but it does not matter for purposes of this study (Negbi 1991).

8. 12th-century Level IIIB occupation characterized by many Cypriote imports (M. Dothan 1955:46). It is unclear whether the 11th-century Level IIIA is a Sea People occupation (M. Dothan 1955:35-43, 48; Raban 1991:19; Gal 1994:46).

9. *š-n-m/š-n-m-iჳ* of Thutmose III's Karnak List 1 and the *Šunama* of the Amarna Letters (Zori 1977:55-56).

10. Egyptian *Gazru* — a seven-hectare city in 12th-century Level XIV and 11th-century Levels XIIII-XI (A. Mazar 1985:125; Singer 1985:116; Dever 1992b:100).

11. Two hectares in both centuries, the 12th century characterized by "Hittite" burials and the 11th by Philistine burials (Kempinski 1979).

12. The site is already post-Egyptian by the 12th-century Level X_{11}. Although its eth-

each case, Tel Malot, Nahal Mazor, and Kfar Qasim, there is also Philistine pottery at the site (respectively, Shavit 1993; Kochavi and Beit-Arieh 1994:63*, 226; and Kochavi and Beit-Arieh 1994:24*-25*; n.a. 1975:15). Gimzo is a case where the Philistine pottery is absent (Finkelstein 1996f:237-38).

Looking at topography, all the sites that gravitate to the Beth-Shan system (Figs. 22-25) fall below a hundred meters elevation, and in fact this is a steep drop from an elevation of over two hundred meters for the highland settlement to below sea level for all of the Beth-Shan System except Jelamet Hamul (Site #308). Deir Allah exploits only Cisjordanian sites below sea level, entirely from the valley where Wadi Farah empties into the Jordan. In the northwest, the Umm el-Fahm Hills are largely without sites, Tell Dothan's northern frontier stopping at their southern foot. Dor, Megiddo,[13] Tel Kedesh (Tell Abu Qudeis),[14] and Taanach exploit only sites below two hundred meters elevation or north of the pass that modern Route 65 follows. South of this, the Tell Balatah System does not extend below three hundred meters elevation except for Ras el-Burj (Site #128).

The most problematic frontier is the southern march, delimiting highland "Benjamin" from the Gezer System in the west, the Jerusalem *burgh* in the center,[15] and the extension of the southern highlands up to Tell es-Sultan in the east.[16] Since it has not been possible to employ the Gravity Model in the southern "Benjamin" area, and therefore not possible to draw the polygons, detecting the southern frontier might seem impossible unless one were to revert to a site-by-site "pots = people" "identification" of sites. Again we should emphasize that this is to be avoided (see

---

nicity is unknown, its resemblance to Tell Abu Hawwam suggests Amorite (Singer 1994:297). This is followed by Philistine Level X_{10} (Singer 1994:297, 316).

13. Egyptian *Magidda*. 12th-century Megiddo VIB reverts from Egyptian to local control in the 11th century as Level VIA (Singer 1994:319).

14. Level VII covers both centuries (Zori 1977:50-51; Stern and Beit-Arieh 1979).

15. Jerusalem was already post-Egyptian by the 12th century (Redford 1990:32), and it continued as some sort of four-hectare Hittito-Hurrian city under its *ewri-na* king into the 11th century (Kempinski 1979).

16. An Iron I occupation can now be established at Tell es-Sultan/Tel Jericho (Weippert and Weippert 1976:131, 137). The ceramic forms here are mainly "highland" but very southern, and not comparable to those of the study region — parallels are from Lachish VI, Tell el-Farah South, Beth Shemesh, and Sahab (Weippert and Weippert 1976:119, 122, 128). The Iron I cremation burial of Pit Tomb 11 (Garstang 1933:36) also does not resemble anything in the north-central highlands.

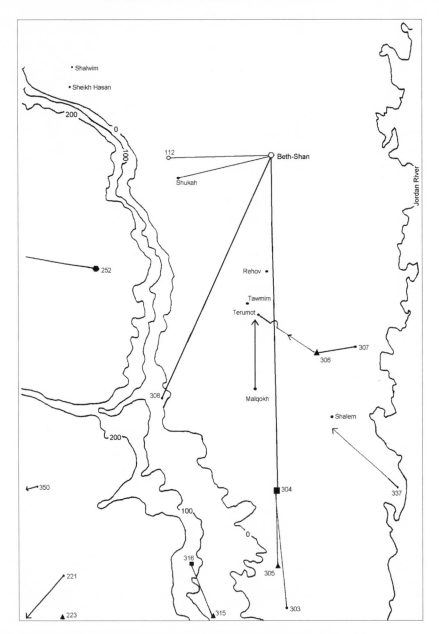

Fig. 22 Northeastern Frontier of the Highland Settlement

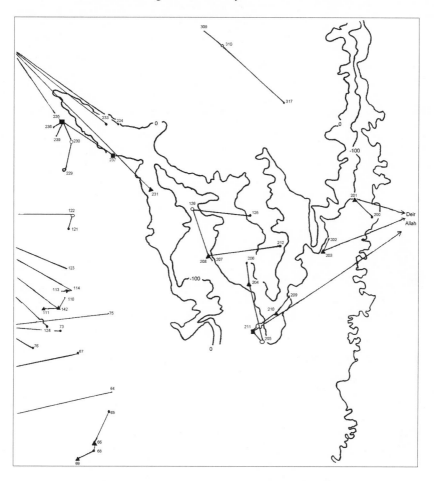

Fig. 23 Eastern Frontier of Tell el-Farah (North) and Tell Balatah

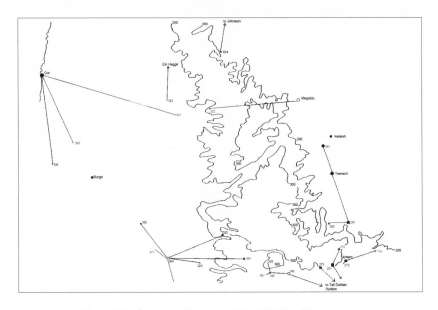

Fig. 24 Northwestern Frontier of the Highland Settlement

Fig. 25 West-central Frontier of the Highland Settlement

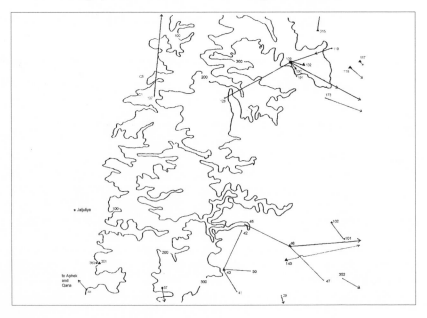

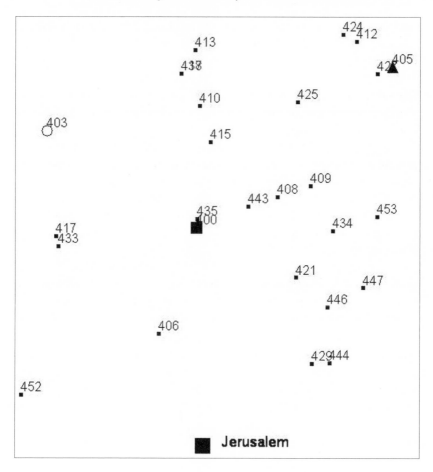

Fig. 26. Southern Portion of the Sites of "Benjamin"

Bunimovitz 1990:210-13). Sites and pots cannot be "Canaanite" or "Israel-ite" any more than they can be "female" or "male."

Fortunately, the identification of the south frontier is aided by voids in the settlement pattern (see Fig. 26). In the east, there are no sites any-where near Tell es-Sultan and its satellite at Khirbet el-Mefjir (Site #79). Near Jerusalem, there is an almost total gap west of Tell el-Ful, with no sites between Tell el-Ful's latitude and Jerusalem. The two exceptions to this gap are Sanhedria (Site #406), which is no more than a single lamp, and Mispe Har Nof (Site #452), which cannot be eliminated. To the east of the longitude of Tell el-Ful, the array of Iron I sites does encroach closer to Jerusalem, but only slightly so, except for three sites: Ras Tammim (#445), the unnamed site at 176.133 (#444), and the unnamed site at 177.135 (#447). The only one of these sites to fall south of the latitude of Mispe Har Nof is Site #447, and even this is more than four kilometers from Jerusalem. The Jerusalem *burgh* thus drawn roughly matches Jerusalem's Late Bronze Age borders (Na'aman 1992:284).

In the west, where there is no gap, gravity modeling has drawn Yalu[17] and Bir el-Hilu[18] west to the Gezer system, along with el-Burj (Site #256), Horvat Tittorah (Site #257), and er-Ras (Site #258). Sites such as Nebi Annir (Site #32), Khirbet esh-Shuna (West; Site #33), Beit 'Ur et-Tahta (Site #450), and Khirbet el-Kafireh (Site #414), on the other hand, gravitate to the east. The sites of the Gezer System are all below three hundred meters elevation.

What this shows, then, is that the ethnic distinction of the highland settlement, which has been supported in Chapter 1 by the Merneptah Stele and by the continuity with Iron II archaeologically, and earlier in this chapter for stylistic reasons, is further supported by economic reasons. That is, the Theissen Polygons define the trade networks of the centers in question, and they are clearly disconnected from the lowlands. The location of the polygon boundaries has been further supported by their correspondence with topographic features and with occurrences of ceramic markers.

17. Site #259 — the *Ayyaluna* of *EA* 273 and 287 and the *'yrn* of 22nd-Dynasty texts (Albright 1924a:10; Finkelstein 1996f:239).

18. Site #261; the *Rubute* of *EA* 289:11 and 290:5 and the *rbt* of Shishak's list, with Philistine pottery (Aharoni 1969:140; Finkelstein 1996f:237).

CHAPTER 6

Ancient Near Eastern Sources for the Highland Settlement

Another source for independent information about the 12th- and 11th-century highland settlement is contemporary ancient Near Eastern records. Such sources would not be merely descriptions of the ancient Near Eastern context within which the Israelite society existed in the hills, but sources that can provide evidence about what was going on in the highlands.

Beginning bluntly, there is next to nothing relevant to this period of the highlands (Singer 1994:283). There are at least four possible explanations why there are no documents in ancient Near Eastern sources about the Iron I hill country (Schäfer-Lichtenberger 1996:79). The first explanation, that there was "no one up there," has been disproved by the foregoing archaeological analysis. The second explanation is that the only hegemonic power capable of extending its claim to power into that region, Egypt, was in fact incapable. Egyptian control in the highlands collapsed even before the end of the reign of Rameses III, and surely had by the end of Rameses IV (1134 B.C.; Singer 1985:117; Kuhrt 1995:209). Only a few items from times later than Rameses IV have surfaced in Palestine, all of them north of the study area (Weinstein 1992:146). "As is the case with empires forced to retreat from their colonies, Egypt did not document its withdrawal from Canaan" (Singer 1994:283). A third explanation is that papyrus Egyptian records, contracts, and the like have not survived, and the fourth is that records survived but have not been found.

Lacking any direct records, several options still remain open. One might be tempted to modify the Egyptian description of the Late Bronze

Age II highlands of Palestine and apply it to Iron I (as done by Smelik 1992:25). The Amarna Letters in particular attest to a diplomatic interchange between Egypt and highland Palestine. The situation involves rival city-state kings, in the highlands, Shechem,[1] Jerusalem (*EA* 286, 287, 288, 289, 290), Hebron further south (*EA* 280), and so on, although reduced to the status of Egyptian vassals (e.g., *ḫazannūti;* Redford 1990:29). Additionally, there were urban centers that were Egyptian garrisons, filled with military foreign service corps and *Medjay* Nubian police officers (Redford 1992). Although one can reconstruct a general picture of social disintegration, particularly in the letters of ʿAbduhepa of Jerusalem (*EA* 286-90), the texts attest to fully functioning city-states, with subject territories (Egyp. *mat;* Redford 1990:68), fortifications (*EA* 244.15-19), and royally administered commerce (*EA* 31.125-36).

As we have shown from the Iron I archaeological reconstruction, this cannot be the proper picture for Iron I. This degree of state complexity had collapsed by the 12th century. So although it is wonderful to have a text like Papyrus Anastasi I (*ANET* 475-79) whose authors know Palestinian geography well (note Papyrus Anastasi I XVIII.21.6-8), it cannot be used as a description of the Iron I highlands.

Another temptation is to look at the Egyptian picture of coastal and southern Palestine, which is more comprehensive for Iron I, and interpolate for the highlands. Papyrus Anastasi 3 shows that during the reign of Rameses III (until 1152 B.C.), Egypt held a powerful grip on parts of Palestine in response to the Hittite conquest of Syria, particularly in the southern part of the country, the Jezreel Valley, and the Jordan Valley (Weinstein 1992:142; Kuhrt 1995:328). Palestine supplied Egypt with grain, wine, oil, slaves, and horses (Kuhrt 1995:328-29). For the post-1150s, there is the text of Wen-Amun (*ANET* 25 = P. Moscow 120; dated early 11th century; Goedicke 1975:9; Kuhrt 1995:210). It has an extensive, and seemingly accurate, portrayal of Dor (*ANET* 25:9ff.; Goedicke 1975:4-5). Nevertheless, we have already shown that the conditions on the coast and plains were not similar to those of the hill country. A text like Wen-Amun cannot, therefore, be used to describe the highland settlement.

1. Egyptian *Sakmim(i)* or *Ša/ikmu* of Sesostris III's Khu-Sebek text #1-2, Late Group Execration Text #6, Rameses II's Papyrus Anastasi 1 XVIII.21.6, Turin Ostracon 6693.2, *EA* 245, 250, 252, 254, 280, and 289; = Tell Balatah; it was quite powerful at the time of its invidious ruler Labʿayu (*EA* 245, 250, 280; Ahlström 1993:244).

As we have already discussed, one text that does deal with the Iron I highlands is the Merneptah Stele. The previous discussion of this inscription concerned using the name "Israel." Perhaps one can draw more *about* this "Israel" from the stele. Three types of attempts have been made with this aim. One relies on structural analysis of the "Israel coda," another on analysis of the determinative used for "Israel," and the third on a connection with reliefs found at Karnak. To begin with the structural analysis, it is useful to present the coda without punctuation. This is *not* a fresh translation of the text or a critical assessment of previous translations, since such are not germane to the study:

> Now that Libya [*Tjehenu*] has come to ruin
> Hatti is pacified
> The Canaan has been plundered into every sort of woe
> Ashkelon has been overcome
> Gezer has been captured
> Yenoam is made nonexistent
> Israel is laid waste and his seed is not
> Hurru is become a widow because of Egypt

Many scholars have attempted a sort of metrical structural analysis of this pericope (e.g., Fecht and Hornung 1983; Ahlström and Edelman 1985; Ahlström 1993:284-85). If the place names in the pericope are subject to such features as chiasmus, inclusios, and parallelism, then one can parallel "Israel" with "Canaan," seeing them either as two names for the same entity or as two portions of a larger whole (Ahlström and Edelman 1985; Ahlström 1993:385). Alternatively, "Israel" parallels structurally with "Hurru," making it a broad geographic term or implying that Israel was much more extensive in the time of Merneptah than simply the highlands. The problem is that there is no reason to assume that the scribe responsible was concerned with symmetry or structure at all, even if the modern reader can discern such structure or, here, several structures (Huddlestun 1991:4). More thorough study of the production of such texts in Egypt is called for before one can treat an Egyptian victory stele as one would a psalm.

Extensive arguments have been made from the determinative used for "Israel" (e.g., Ahlström 1991b:22; 1993:285). The name "Israel" carries the determinative indicative of an enemy people (throw stick + two hu-

man figures + three plural strokes), in contrast to the other three toponyms, Ashkelon, Gezer, and Yenoam, all of which are followed by the determinative indicative of an enemy territory or city-state (throw-stick +
hill-country). No one disputes this, but what it means is much debated.
The sequence of three city-states followed by a people is crucial to Yurco's
(1986) discussion to be examined below. Others have used the determinative to indicate that Israel was loosely organized, or egalitarian, or nomadic, and more (Stager 1985b:59*, 61*; Hess 1993:134). A thorough examination of Egyptian scribal practice, however, shows the use of the
determinative to be almost completely arbitrary. Even restricting the examination to texts dating from Merneptah's reign, Huddlestun's (1991) catalogue finds no consistency in the use of the determinative (see also
Yoyotte 1990:112). Within the Merneptah Stele itself, in lines 4-5 the
Meshwesh, who are definitely a people, have the city-state determinative;
in line 5 and line 10 the Libyan people *(rbw)* have the city-state determinative; and in lines 11 and 21 Libya (*Tjehenu* [*thnw*]) has *both* the people determinative and the city-state determinative. The determinatives should
not be overread for "what they say about Israel."

Using the determinatives, Frank Yurco has argued that the four battle
scenes at Karnak flanking the wall stele of Rameses II's Hittite Treaty are
not to be dated to Rameses II but to Merneptah, and furthermore that they
depict the battles of the end of the Israel Stele (Yurco 1986; followed by
many, e.g., Yoyotte 1990:114-17 and Ahlström 1993:287). Yurco then
matches each scene with one of the place names in the stele, and suddenly
a picture, literally, of Iron I Israel is presented in the fourth battle relief of
the upper course. Now scholars can "see" that the Israelites look just like
the Canaanites in the city fortresses!

The first problem is that some scholars remain unconvinced of the
dating of the reliefs to Merneptah instead of Rameses II (Redford
1992:275n.85). Even if they are from Merneptah, and even if they are the "illustrations" of the Israel Stele, it remains questionable whether Yurco has
"matched" the pictures with the correct toponyms. If, for example, the second battle relief is Israel, then the individuals pictured there look nothing
like the Canaanites, but like Shasu (see below). Yurco starts with Ashkelon
and reads the four scenes clockwise, but this is only one of many options:
compare the efforts to correlate the Palestinian reliefs of Seti I at Karnak
with the relevant texts, which show that some must be read downward,
others upward (Broadhurst 1989; Huddlestun 1991:5). Yurco's response is

that he can use the stele to order the reliefs (so replying to Anson Rainey in *BAR* 17/6[1991]:61)! Furthermore, it is unlikely that, even if the pictures do match the toponyms precisely as Yurco suggests, much information can be gained from looking at the reliefs. Such reliefs are stylized; thus if Battle Scene 3 really is Yenoam, it is odd that it looks nothing like the fortress with the name Yenoam carved on it in the reliefs of Seti I at Karnak (Huddlestun 1991:6). Either Yurco's scene three is not Yenoam, or the drawings cannot be used as accurate depictions of the places shown (or both).

The most that can be drawn from the Merneptah Stele, apart from the sound datum of the name "Israel" in its proper geographic location (see Chapter 1), is that the Egyptian scribe saw fit to mention this people or place in such a small list intended to represent Egypt's enemies in the Levant (Redford 1992:266). The name must have acquired some type of importance by the end of the 13th century to warrant this inclusion. This fact is more provocative than anything drawn from the structural or determinative examination had suggested, and has yet to be adequately explained.

A final avenue to learn about the Iron I highlands has been to identify the inhabitants, that is, the Israelites, with the "Shasu" of Egyptian records, and apply what is said about the Shasu to Israel (Redford 1990:73, 279). The Shasu were Semitic-speaking pastoral cattle-nomads of both the Late Bronze and the early Iron Ages (Giveon 1971:240; Redford 1992:276). The late-13th century Papyrus Anastasi 1 (XIX.23.8-11) shows them acting as brigands around the Jezreel Valley, and they were as far southwest at the time of Rameses II as to threaten Ashkelon (Giveon 1971:236-37; Redford 1990:72). They were organized in clans (Egyp. *mhwt wb*), ruled by what in anthropological terms would be called "big men" (C_3), making them "tribes" (Braun and Plog 1982). If the Shasu are Israel, then here is quite a bit of detail about them sociologically.

The first problem is that if Yurco is correct about the Karnak reliefs, the Israelites do not look like the Shasu. For then the Israelites, like the Canaanites, would have long hair tied with a sweat band or would be bald with full beards and mustaches and wear robes with capes, whereas Shasu have goatee beards and wear berets and kilts.[2] Yurco may have the pictures lined up wrong. The second criticism of the Shasu = Israel equation is that the Egyptians continue to call all the Shasu, even those in the highlands,

2. However striking the idea of kilt-wearing highland clan chieftains might be.

"Shasu," after they begin to call Israel "Israel." In Papyrus Anastasi 6 (*ANET* 259; lines 54-56), which dates to the 20th Dynasty and therefore well after the Merneptah Stele, the Shasu are still "Shasu"; they have not "become" Israel (Caminos 1954:76-77). The most serious criticism of any attempt to learn about the Iron I highlands from accounts of the Shasu is that the Shasu bear no resemblance to the archaeological picture of the Iron I highlands. The highlands were most definitely not inhabited by anthropological tribes of pastoral transhumant cattle-nomads. The accounts of the Shasu cannot be used as a substitute for Egyptian records of highland Israel.

CHAPTER 7

A Social History of
Highland Palestine, 1200–1000 B.C.

We can now gather up the archaeological data discussed above and extract the conclusions they point to for a social history. To write a social history of highland Palestine involves the construction of a narrative. As we have discussed above (see Chapter 2), this is the act of a choice from among various possible narratives that could describe the period. It is a choice both of content and of form. A social history, as discussed in Chapter 2, isolates the ideas of the period from the conditions of their production and in fact discards them (Chartier 1982; cf. Chapter 10, below). Here, then, is a collective, systematic, and structural reconstruction of a whole society (Chartier 1982; LaCapra 1982; Hunt 1989; Darnton 1990) — something decried in Chapter 2, but a step toward a cultural history (see Chapter 10). This narrative may in fact be providing information about historical patterns that may not even have been discernible to the people living when those patterns existed (Tuchman 1994:311).

This reconstruction is drawn from the archaeological data presented in Chapter 5, as interpreted and expanded by the complex chiefdom model described in Chapters 3 and 4 in places where this has been proven applicable in the course of Chapters 4 and 5. For this reason, and to emphasize the narrative nature of this history, we have kept citations to a minimum, and we will not endlessly repeat the phrase "as the discussion above has shown." Also, to avoid preempting the discussion in Chapter 9, we will give the sites their ancient names in cases where these are known apart from the biblical text, and otherwise their modern names.

Society in the 12th- and 11th-century highlands of Palestine was village based. Small villages exploited economic niches variously of herding, cereal agriculture, and vine and olive horticulture. Although most of the local villages were self-sufficient, they presented tribute in cash crops or conscripted labor to higher levels of economic centers, although without specialized administrative control apparatus.

These villages were on the hilltops — even the larger ones had a population of only about four hundred people. They usually did not have walls, simply clustering the houses together. They also did not have domesticated horses or camels, nor much iron. And they were using flint and bronze tools and weapons, especially slings — all in contrast to the lowland inhabitants.

They lived in nuclear families, but often in clusters of houses around a common courtyard with their relatives. The average nuclear family had two or three children that survived infancy. The houses had three or four rooms, and likely sleeping quarters on the roof or a covered roof loft. The house of a moderately prosperous family might have had a second story of wood — tamarisk or poplar or palm. One of the first-floor rooms was a court for the animals. The people did raise animals — sheep and goats, mostly, not cattle — and for dairy products, not meat. The herders would take the animals out in the morning up to ten or fifteen kilometers away from the village. But the hills were then heavily vegetated with a thick scrub — evergreen shrubs with short pine and oak and pistachio trees — no more than four meters high, with orchids and peonies and lilies and crocuses, and so animals were always secondary. Instead, the people would burn off some of the brush and then terrace the hillsides and farm about an hour's walk around the town. And they did have orchards on these terraces. Olives grew wild and were easily domesticated, and so olives and grapes were prevalent.

These little villages were partly self-sufficient, but not autarkic: there was a sharing of risks and responsibilities to cope with local environmental constraints and labor needs. They were not egalitarian. Each larger town had its rich and poor. In the larger towns, there were likely town elders belonging to one family, or a single chief and his noble family. These were legally the owners of all the land, although in practice the average person farmed what his own family managed without really being a tenant farmer. But these elite families did exist. They had separate neighborhoods in the town; their houses were larger, maybe with walled yards and paved courts, but not palaces. They likely wore distinctive clothing, and they intermarried with members of their own extended family or with families of other towns' elders.

Five main polities controlled the north-central highlands: Tell Dothan, Tirzah, Sakmim, Khirbet Seilun, and a complex network of cities to the south. These five polities were of a single ethnicity, and economic interchange was prevalent, although the mobilization of goods in each was independent. From the archaeology, one cannot support any sort of amphictyony. This has been clear to archaeologists since de Vaux (1971; 1973:19-36), and more recently detailed by many scholars (e.g., Mayes 1974; de Geus 1976; Lemche 1985:301). Nor can one conclude that these Israelite polities never fought each other (as per Mendenhall 1976:157). These polities engaged in friendly trade relations with neighboring Amorite and Philistine powers, this trade being managed exclusively by the top levels of highland society.

If one were to have entered the hill country from the north along the Watershed Route from the Amorite plain cities of Takhnaka and Yabla'amu, the shire of Tell Dothan would have been the first encountered. The city of Tell Dothan (Fig. 27) lay on the heath of the Dothan valley, with its nine subordinate administrative centers far off into the surrounding thicket and shrublands. Beyond its control to the west, smaller polities of highlanders inhabited the thicket.

Across the Marj Sanur heath, the shrublands to the southwest were the domain of Tirzah. The chieftain at Tirzah traded with foreign groups for their finished fancy goods, importing silver, iron, basalt, Phoenician pottery, and the like to redistribute to his subchiefs (such as the powerful one at Khirbet Einun) to build and maintain political support. In this way, the chief could demonstrate his power both by possession of these goods as marks of exceptionality and through the act of accumulation, as the fountainhead of the society's prosperity. This Tirzah domain was a polity primarily of herders, those of the high shrublands and thicket to the east, and of the Wadi Farah and el-Bugeia valleys. Relations with foreign powers were at times more direct than for Tell Dothan's polity, for although mountains barred the frontier with Beth-Shan in the north, control of the Wadi Farah Valley was contested with the municipal principality of Deir Allah across the Jordan jungle. Sites like Khirbet Marah el-Inab were valuable prizes.

Across the Jebel el-Kabir lay the chiefdom of Sakmim. This complex chiefdom had a paramount at the fortified city of Sakmim, and nine

Fig. 27 Tell Dothan

subchiefs in smaller centers, the most powerful ones at Tell Sofar, Ras Zeid, and Khirbet el-Urma. The villages of this extensive chiefdom, built in cleared sections of the thicket and shrublands, could largely support themselves with cereal farming. The main crop was wheat. Everything else was secondary. From wheat they would make bread, animal fodder, pastas, beer, mulch for gardens, and straw for baskets and mats. They ate additional foods from other crops that they grew: they would grind up lentils, chickpeas, and broad beans and make them into falafel; barley and millet were grown primarily to brew beer.

Olive oil, flax, and other cash crops were moved as tribute from the villages of the thickets, shrublands, and downs of the valleys at the southern edge of the chiefdom to the subchiefs and from the subchiefs to the paramount, a portion being reserved at each stage. Often the paramount only symbolically received all this produce, and actually took only what he needed to live, although conspicuous consumption to the excess by the chief could be a demonstration of his social distinctiveness and economic authority.

The economic prosperity of the paramount chieftain and his subchiefs was not shared by all segments of society. For while the chief lived in his house with its courtyard in central Sakmim, just to the northeast the poor dwelt in huts at the old East Gate.

Sometime in the mid-12th century, the limits of production were nearing. The production of locally made sumptuary goods such as storax incense and labdanum resin, which were only part-time crafts, ceased, so that more time could be devoted to production of sustenance. This gave the paramount less opportunity to trade with foreign powers for their luxuries, and therefore fewer sumptuary goods to distribute to his subchiefs. By 1125 a rebellion resulted, the chieftain was overthrown, and Sakmim destroyed.

A two-level decentralized system, without a paramount chief and with little external exchange, was the result. Sakmim remained unoccupied, and each subchief ruled his portion. Although each subchief received exotic craft goods like incense and useful tribute like oil from his subjects and gave them fancy finished goods, it was in much smaller amounts than in the centralized stage. None of the subchiefs or their children could assume the status of paramount after the conflict was resolved; the chiefdom fragmented into smaller units for the remainder of the early Iron Age.

To the south of the Mikhmetat and Beit Dagon downs was the modest chiefdom of Khirbet Seilun. The paramount chieftain at the walled capital administered a chiefdom of a smaller size than Sakmim's, with only two subchiefs, one at Tell Marjame who administered the entire eastern steppe and one with a dual capital at Khirbet Sur (B) and Khirbet Bir el-Kharayib. Much of the rest of the forest was administered directly from Khirbet Seilun.

The people of the villages of this chiefdom were variously farmers, herders, and hunters. They supported the chieftains with oil, wine, and enough grain or meat to live on, and provided items such as incense and resin for trade for alabaster, Philistine pottery, and other items. Such trade was extensive enough for the chiefdom to be using the Egyptian gold standard of weight. Another means of tribute was the conscription of labor, the likes of which built the wall of Khirbet Seilun and the pillared buildings on the west side of the city.

The relation among the elites of the highland chiefdoms resulted in the city of Khirbet Seilun importing most of its non-everyday ware pottery — jars, bowls, and lamps — from the Tirzah chiefdom. About the time Sakmim was destroyed, Khirbet Seilun switched to importing these from one or more of the resultant simple chiefdoms of the Sakmim region. Presumably, since this region was closer, it was more economical to do so, although the quality of pottery was inferior to the Tirzah products. Hostile relations with the centralized Sakmim chiefdom might previously have prevented import from Sakmim, although one cannot go as far as to say Sakmim was non-Israelite (as do Orlinsky 1962:94; Reviv 1966; B. Mazar 1982:45; and Würthwein 1994).

In the middle of the 11th century, an invader apparently attacked the chiefdom of Khirbet Seilun and destroyed it. The most severe destruction occurred at the pillared buildings on the west side of the city.

In the fells and brushfields to the south of the Khirbet Seilun chiefdom, there were several prosperous cities at the dawn of the Iron Age, an assortment of simple chiefdoms: one was from the walled brushfield city of Tell el-Ful I; one ruled from the huge, but unwalled, city of Et-Tell, its authority extending a bit into the eastern desert; one around the walled town of *Rd* in the fells, where the chief's line lived on the north side of town and the poor lived on the ruins of earlier buildings; one at Khirbet Raddanah, a small, walled town in the brushfields where the chief also lived on the north side of the city; and one from the large, walled brushfield city of *Gbʿn/Qbʿn*, where the chief lived beside the city wall. All these chieftains traded resin and incense for scarabs, Cypriote pottery, marble, iron, and copper from Wadi Arabah, in the latter case also offering in trade oak and terebinth timber. Their interrelations were cordial. Many of them shared the regional storage facility at Tell en-Nasbeh, where guards were stationed in caves and wooden huts.[1]

In the middle of the 12th century, *Rd*, Tell el-Ful, and et-Tell were destroyed. Refugees poured into and impoverished Khirbet Raddanah and eventually into rebuilt *Rd* and et-Tell. The elite of these cities continued to prosper, however, such as in the southeast neighborhood of Khirbet Raddanah and the east side of et-Tell. North-central and southwest et-Tell were the depressed neighborhoods. Since much of its territory was swallowed up by Khirbet Raddanah, Tell el-Ful was not rebuilt, its chiefs' line presumably gone. A fortified borough appeared at Khirbet ed-Dawwara, however, on the desert's edge. In 1100 *Rd* was again destroyed and rebuilt in an even poorer condition. The entire site looked like the poorer parts of Khirbet Raddanah and et-Tell. The situation then remained unchanged until the middle of the 11th century.

Around 1050 Khirbet Raddanah was destroyed and abandoned forever, and *Rd* was again destroyed. Because it had either taken advantage of

1. An adequate explanation for the Philistine pottery, especially the locally made material, remains elusive.

the situation or helped to bring it about, Tell el-Ful was rebuilt and became the capital of a complex chiefdom spanning much of the region. Its chieftain had a keep in the center of the city, and was able again to import iron and Cypriote and coastal pottery. *Rd* was rebuilt as a prosperous city. Only et-Tell remained unchanged, neither destroyed nor renovated. It remained a segregated, unwalled city with a serious demographic problem.

Gbʿn/Qbʿn remained unaffected by these circumstances. Securely ruling the western brushfields, it escaped all of the destructions and population displacements of the 12th and 11th centuries. It did not, however, escape the destructions that marked the end of the 11th century. Tell el-Ful, et-Tell, Tell en-Nasbeh, and *Gbʿn/Qbʿn* were all destroyed.

CHAPTER 8

The Hebrew Bible as Source for the Highland Settlement

On the basis of archaeology, we have provided a reconstruction for the highlands of Palestine in the 12th and 11th centuries. This reconstructed society has been shown to fit well with the complex chiefdom model, at least in the regions of Tell Balatah and farther south, and possibly to the north as well. We have used the anthropological model to provide the details missing from material culture remains, presenting a reconstruction of Israelite society in Iron I.

This model can be expanded further. It can be extended to describe how such a society textualizes sociopolitical reality, if at all. A useful metaphor here is "taphonomy" (for extensive discussion, see Schiffer 1976; also, Rossignol 1992:6). For the archaeologist, taphonomy refers to the process by which items go from active use in an ancient culture to modern archaeological artifacts. The taphonomic process thus includes such things as breakage, discard, recycling, reuse, curation, litter collection, burial, deposition, erosion, and so on. To make good sense of any archaeological artifact, the archaeologist must construct a taphonomic model, which is his or her proposal about how the object came to be where and as it was found. The model begins with the proposed sketch of the ancient use and discontinuation of use of the object, and proceeds temporally to the present.

A useful way to look at textualization in a society, then, would be to view textualization as "textual deposition," and the resultant texts present today as "textual artifacts" (Buccellati 1988:134). If the biblical text is a "textual artifact," it cannot be understood without a taphonomic model of its "deposition." Our goal in this chapter, then, is to construct a taphonomic model from event to text that can be added to the complex chiefdom model: to learn where and how a memory of the past would have been preserved and then describe the depositional process of that textualization. In fact, such a model is indispensable for any historical criticism of the biblical text.

Our goal is not to look at texts about the Settlement period (as do Ishida 1973; Halpern 1983:105-261; Flanagan 1988:86; and Portugali 1994:212, 214-15), but texts "from" the Settlement period. However, locating "texts from the period" does not mean engaging in a source-, form-, or traditions-critical search for 13th- and 12-century texts, as proposed by Townsend, who calls that "the first step back toward finding out about the time of the Judges" (1972:24). This has always been the standard method, as seen, among others, in the works of Sellin (1922), Richter (1963), Schunck (1963), Smend (1970), V. Fritz (1982; 1996:122-36, 179-91), Hecke (1985: 25-57), Couturier (1989:218), Briend (1990), Smelik (1992:23-24), Cazelles (1993), Neef (1995), Edelman (1996:150, 156), Kallai (1997), and even Thompson (1987), although Lemche points out that it has never been successful (1992:528; cf. Dever 1997d:291-94). When one says "texts from the Settlement period," the emphasis needs to be on the *"from"*; the process of getting "from" that period is a taphonomic one.[1]

One way or another, the ethos of a society and the events that it endures will be encoded (Derrida 1970:249). There is evidence that writing was known in the Iron I highlands and was an available medium for this encoding. Even from small sites writing has been found, such as the tiny village of Khirbet Tannin (Site #285) in the Tell el-Farah (North) System, which produced a 58-by-61-by-9-millimeter potsherd inscribed either *ŠMN* ("oil"?), or, if read left-to-right, *nimiš*, "wasp" (Lemaire 1985:14).

From Khirbet Raddanah, in the Site R room that produced the "Anatolian" kernos krater, a jar handle was found inscribed with the letters *'HL* or *'HR* (Cross and Freedman 1971:20). If the former reading is correct, it may be a diminutive of the personal name "Ahilud," "Ahilah." It could also be "Ahlay," perhaps a diminutive of "Ahiram," which happens to be the name of a Benjaminite clan in Num. 26:38 (Aharoni 1971:130-31; Cross and

---

1. Consciously left aside here is the case of the "Song of Deborah" (Judges 5), which many hold to be an Iron I composition. Its analysis involves a different set of questions. Although this poem and others embedded within the Primary History might have great bearing on the social history of Iron I Israel, they have been bypassed here as beyond the scope of this study.

Freedman 1971:22). Stratigraphically, the inscription comes from Phase 3, but epigraphically it has been dated to the 13th or 12th centuries (Aharoni 1971:132; Cross and Freedman 1971:20-22; Callaway 1973). In this case, since there is no 13th-century occupation at Khirbet Raddanah (only an Early Bronze I occupation precedes the Iron I), it would have been manufactured in Phase 2 (Callaway and Cooley 1971:15; Cooley 1975:12). Also from Khirbet Raddanah Phase 3 came a bronze dagger with writing on it, never deciphered (Cooley 1975:12; the inscribed dagger is never again mentioned and could not be located).

At Izbet Sartah Level II, inside Silo 605, archaeologists found a supposed abecedary inscribed on a wheeled storage jar (Kochavi and Demsky 1978:23-25). It consisted of five lines of eighty-three letters total, written left-to-right. It is epigraphically dated to the 12th-11th centuries (Kochavi 1977:4, 6; Garbini 1978:289). Anything beyond this information may be conjectural. The consensus is that this is simply an abecedary, written in proto-Phoenician (Garbini 1978:294), or, according to Naveh, some sort of "Philistine" Greco-Canaanite (Naveh 1978:35).[2]

It is difficult to see how any of these "texts" can be seen as "textualization of history." They merely establish that writing was at least minimally known and available in Iron I Israel (Jamieson-Drake 1991:136-59). More substantial texts must be found to develop the taphonomic model.

One potential way to begin to construct this textual taphonomic model would be to use the morphologically analogous cultures identified by the complex chiefdom model, in ancient Hither Asia and elsewhere, and examine how these cultures recorded their own histories and attempted to

---

2. Dotan (1981) challenges the view that it is an abecedary and gives a translation by rearranging the lines:

1. 'Arip son of Khag (= Khaggi of Gen. 46:16 and Safaitic) brought to Hod (= Ugaritic [*UT*, 389 #749], Amarna) a wineskin for the hungry one.
2. Tt (cf. Phoen. *Pt-ben-Tt* [*KAI* 1.12 #52, 3; 2.70]) brought garments of animal leather to Adoniba'al (cf. Phoen.).
3. Pure wool
4. [PN] brought to [PN].

If this is an accurate translation, it presumes an extremely defective text, with no *matres lectionis* (Dotan 1981:169), which makes sense for this period. Dotan argues that it has to be "Hebrew," given the presence of words that do not occur in other Canaanite languages: *'B, 'BM, R'BM, SMR,* and *'R* (Dotan 1981:170). Nevertheless, no one other than Dotan has accepted that this is anything more than an abecedary.

preserve a memory of their pasts, orally or textually. Others, for example, Gottwald (1993:169), have called for such a methodology, and some rough attempts have been made at taphonomic modeling of the biblical text in the past, notably by Whitelam (1989). The latter, however, used no control over ethnographic analogy and borrowed, arbitrarily, textual deposition processes from tribal groups in Africa and empires of the Incas and Aztecs. Similarly problematic, as Jamieson-Drake has shown (1991:153), are attempts to use state- and empire-level societies of Egypt and Mesopotamia as analogies for "deposition" of the complex chiefdoms of Iron I (as per Tertel 1994). Analogous societies need to be identified. The first option should be to look elsewhere in the Iron I Near East.

Scholars have made extensive study of "textualization" in Mesopotamia, Hatti, and Egypt (e.g., Vanstiphout 1995), but the most likely candidates for morphologically analogous secondary complex chiefdoms are the early Iron Age communities of Transjordan. One cannot simply jump, however, to adopt analogies from Ammon and Moab without control (as does Dearman 1992a:28). Here several different situations were in existence. Beginning in the south, that area south of modern Wadi el-Hesa (the ancient Zered River) may be called, for lack of a better term, Edom. This is in no way meant to suggest that a kingdom of Edom was in this location in Iron I. The region of Edom unfortunately shows virtually *no* Iron I settlement before the 8th century B.C., especially in its northern portions, at which point it jumps to statehood because of external influences (Bienkowski 1992:6; 1995:41, 46; Hart 1992:93, 96-97; Knauf 1992:53). Northern Edom in Iron I was probably the home of nomadic groups organized at a "tribal" level, possibly analogous to the Iron I highlands south of Jerusalem, but not to those north (Bartlett 1989:74).

In far southern Edom, however, extending into Cisjordan at the southern end of the Negeb, Egyptian influence led to a more complex society. Thus in the Wadi Rumman area, around Aqaba and Timna, Egyptian exploitation of the resources may have artificially produced a sedentary, chiefdom society (Bartlett 1989:81). This did not extend north into the Negeb (Beit-Arieh 1995:33). However, since this was an artificial circumstance, more than just a matter of secondary chiefdoms, it is also an open question whether an analogy with the northern Cisjordanian highlands can be drawn.

Following Nelson Glueck, other archaeologists have argued that an Iron I settlement did exist in Transjordanian Edom (MacKay 1983:18-28;

Finkelstein 1995c: 127-37; 1996d). From this they have reconstructed chiefdom societies (Knauf-Belleri 1995:108-9). This is hotly contested by archaeologists such as Bienkowski (1992; 1995) and Hart (1992), but since *no* substantial texts have been found from Iron I Edom anyway, the issue is moot now (Knauf-Belleri 1995; Vanderhooft 1995).

The next region to the north, conveniently called Moab, includes the area from Wadi el-Hesa up to the Madeba Plateau, either to Wadi el-Mawjib (the ancient Arnon River), or as far as Wadi Hesban. In Iron I, the region of cultural continuity extended about as far north as modern Madeba (Younker 1998). Aside from an absence of Iron I on the southern Kerak Plateau and Edom-like underdevelopment on the Dhiban Plateau, the settlement pattern of this region, as seen from recent surveys of the area from Wadi el-Mawjib to Madeba, farther south on the East Kerak Plateau, and in the Ghor at the south end of the Dead Sea, reveals systems (perhaps three of them) with one center about ten hectares, two of about one hectare, all three walled, and an abundance of small villages under half a hectare (Dearman 1992b:70). This is the condition for all of Iron I Moab, and in the Ghor it continues into Iron II. This is exactly the complex chiefdom situation of the north-central highland study region. Here, then, is an ideal analogous society for constructing the textual taphonomic model.

Unfortunately, there is only one inscription from this society, and it is not usable. This is the Baluʻah Stele. Most likely it was originally written in the Early Bronze Age, in a script that has now become unreadable, and was reused in Iron I for reliefs only (Van Zyl 1960:32). Although it is an interesting item, showing some Egyptian influence and individuals who look like Shasu, it has no text (Bartlett 1989:70).[3] Actually, a nonwritten stele is an important analogy. One might conclude that Iron I Israel would have produced similar methods of "textualization," that is, nonverbal ones (Redford 1992:275). In any case, one cannot use the Mesha Stele as an analogy, as by the time of Mesha Moab had become a full-fledged state society (Orlinsky 1962:18).

North of Madeba is the region conveniently called Ammon. This extends as far north as the Yarmouk River. There is no reason to create any border at the Nahr ez-Zarqa (ancient Jabbok). This area contains many

---

3. That is, unless, as MacDonald (1994:14) has suggested, it was actually *written* in Iron I, although the text is so far eroded that this is difficult to prove.

fortified sites of more than ten hectares (e.g., Amman, Umeiri) and a complex settlement system of roads, irrigation, monumental art, glass technology, and royal seals indicative of a state (Braemer 1987:192-93, 197; Knauf 1992:53; Younker 1998).[4] It would not, then, be comparable to the Iron I Cisjordanian highlands and thus useful as an analogy in helping to define the textual taphonomic process. Accordingly, the 9th-century Amman Citadel Inscription dialogue text, a product of a state society, is not useful in this effort (Aufrecht 1989:#59).

As for the region north of the Yarmouk River, conveniently called Bashan, the survey data are too fragmentary to be of use, and no texts survive.

The next possibility, besides Transjordan, in seeking analogies to the textual taphonomic process, is to look at other complex chiefdoms throughout history and around the globe. The case in most of these societies is just as one might begin to expect for highland Israel from the archaeology of Iron I there and in Moab: societies capable of writing, but whose literature was oral. In Samoa's secondary complex chiefdoms, for example, literature was oral even among the literate (Keesing and Keesing 1956:168). The same thing was true for the Cuna native Americans, for whom writing was reserved for a ritual function (Sherzer 1990:9, 123), as perhaps for the "Oil" or "Wasp" inscription from Tell Tannin described above. Oral and written literature do not exist in dichotomy, but often side-by-side (Niditch 1993:8; Rabinowitz 1993:32; Foley 1994, who cites ethnographic examples from Old Latin to Native American).

The actual "literature" of complex chiefdoms, by analogy, probably resembles the Tahitian complex chiefdoms' dramas (Oliver 1981:208), long family traditions (Rofé 1982; Berge 1994:201 and analogies cited therein), and the like. One need not distinguish among these genres, or among sagas and myths and legends; the term "lore" can contain everything from folktales and oral histories to jokes and games to quilt designs (Kirkpatrick 1988; Niditch 1993:3). Possibly the ancient Israelite traditionists did not make such distinctions (Niditch 1993:11).

If the textualization was oral, that should not eliminate the possibility of coming up with a taphonomic model for the text. The study of oral

---

4. LaBianca and Younker (1994), after amassing all these data, then conclude, largely under the influence of the biblical text, that Ammon was "tribal." Ottosson (1994:221-22) sees Iron I Ammon as identical to the Iron I north-central highlands.

tradition has a long history in biblical studies. However, contrary to most such studies (e.g., Alt, Von Rad, the "Uppsala School," Townsend 1972: 41-45; V. Fritz 1996:191-202), beginning with the written biblical text and finding the material in it that is of oral origin is impossible (B. Long 1976:195-96; Kirkpatrick 1988; Thompson 1992:94; Niditch 1993:6-7; Foley 1994). Instead, one must look at how oral lore becomes text, continuing the model of the "deposition." Oral traditions can and do survive into text, as Anglo-Saxon poetry shows (Foley 1994). Vansina (1985:57-58) groups the ways in which this can happen into two classes: one is through "accidental" mention in a separate, almost unrelated text; the other is via the conscious effort of a later ancient "researcher" (see Chapter 9).

The first case, the "accidental" mention, can preserve such things from the composition of the oral lore as dialect, vocabulary, personal names, geographic names, genealogy, possibly a little cultic information, and possibly a little military technology, although, unfortunately for the present study, *not* stories of events (Kirkpatrick 1988; Vermeule 1972:309-12 provides case studies). This contention runs against the oral tradition theories of Gunkel and Gressmann (Kirkpatrick 1988), who saw strong preservation of narrative history. Narrative can perdure, but traditions of conduct (ethos) and ritual last longer (Shils 1981). Nevertheless, oral lore is not by nature "ahistorical" and devoid of any elements from its time of origin (Dowden 1992:35-36).

"Remembering and recording history, we cannot forget, is never a neutral enterprise" (Machinist 1994:46). This means that the taphonomic process is not as simple as how a sherd gets buried (although that is not really a simple process either); there is human initiative at every stage, choices about content, perceptions about writing and the nature of words (Rabinowitz 1993:1, 27).[5] Put bluntly, how is it possible to handle the biblical text historically without a taphonomic model from event to text, and how is it possible to write such a model — or even to suggest a connection from the oral encoding to the biblical text — without having a historical reconstruction of *every* period in between? The obstacle seems insurmountable. Combine this obstacle with the fact that at one end there are no written analogies to Iron I highland texts (the Baluʻah Stele excepted),

---

5. On the latter, Rabinowitz (1993) proposes to use references to words in surviving literary texts (1993:2) to arrive at such perceptions, but in the end he spends most of his effort exploring the perceptions of the *terms* for "word" and "writing."

and unfortunately writing a taphonomic model for text is not yet possible. This is an issue for further study. Other possible analogies for the textual taphonomic process are possible, including known cases of complex chiefdoms such as southwestern Iran of the 5th millennium B.C. and what may be found by a further search for ancient Near Eastern secondary chiefdoms — on the fringes of Anatolia, in southwestern Arabia, and so forth. The search ought to continue, but as with any archaeological taphonomic model, one should not jump to write the model without an ethnographic analogy.

CHAPTER 9

Highland Israel in the Hebrew Bible

I have mentioned that there is another way in which oral lore becomes written text: through active "research" by an ancient "scholar" later than the period of the orally "recorded" topic. This is not a taphonomic process, but one of "excavation." Rather than follow the chronological sequence from event and ethos to oral "deposition" to textualization to text, examination of this second avenue deals with a process that begins in the middle.

The previous chapter showed that to compose a taphonomic model would require knowledge about every stage and *Trägerkreis* of the process, but that the process remains a black box. If, however, there is a "researcher" somewhere in the past who sought to write a "history" about, say, the Iron I period, then one does not have to reconstruct the forward movement of the "textual (oral or written) artifact," because at some point in the process, another individual has reversed the direction and sought the past (and it does not even really matter how or why).[1]

The society of the Iron I highlands has been reconstructed from the archaeological record interpreted through the anthropological model in Chapter 6. At the same time we have the biblical text, which purports to be relevant in some way to this society. The previous chapter attempted to model how a text would come from the society as reconstructed to the text as it stands. Such a model could not be drawn from the cases considered.

---

1. One of the best newer studies of "how" and "why" is Mullen (1993:121-215). There is still an element of "forward movement" in the process from the "researcher's" time to our reception of his work.

However, if the text as it stands is itself historiographical, if it is the product of conscious effort to write about a previous past (argued effectively by J. M. Miller 1987:54; Polzin 1989:227n.58; Mullen 1993:8; Lemche 1996d: 104-105n.25), then an alternate way to explore the relationship of the text to Iron I society would be to compare directly the archaeological reconstruction of the society and the text's reconstruction.

This is *not* the same as "good, old-fashioned" historical criticism. A taphonomic process surely did take place. The ancient "researcher" is an interruption in that process, in a crude sense not unlike a Hellenistic mouse digging up an Early Bronze potsherd and putting it in a Hellenistic context. We are not arguing that the ancient "researcher" was some sort of "first historian" who somehow obtained an accurate reconstruction of Iron I (as per Halpern 1983:8; or Chaney 1986:61, 63; or Schloen 1993, who assumes *a priori* that Judges 5 *and* the tribal allotments are accurate). The "researcher's" reconstruction is likely not even a combination of the conditions of Iron I with those of his or her own time, but probably includes all sorts of elements from times in between because of inaccurate "research" and an archaizing desire (see, among others, Albright 1966:11; Lemche 1988:56; Redford 1992:276-77; Hutton 1994:45-46). Nevertheless, "to an extent" one can find history in textualized oral lore; Dowden (1992:72, 79) has shown the degree to which the textualized forms of the oral lore (i.e., ancient accounts) of the complex chiefdoms of Late Bronze Age Greece correspond with the history of that period as reconstructed by modern scholars. The ancient "researcher" did do some real research: he or she is not some nuisance the modern scholar must try to remove. In fact, that "researcher" is the only means for determining how the particular writers of Israel itself reconstructed Iron I. If one abandons naive definitions of history (like those of Smelik 1992:15) and stops looking for an ancient von Ranke (as do Lemche 1984b:106 and Thompson 1992:373, 377) or, worse, an ancient, orderly, right-thinking version of oneself, the Israelite "researcher" can be very helpful (cf. Darnton 1986:227).[2] Ancient Israelite "researchers," although not annalists, likely did have sources, and probably did distinguish primary and secondary sources, although they kept such — to their minds — unimportant details to themselves (Veyne 1988; Rabinowitz 1993:94-109; Van Seters 1995).

2. Even worse, some scholars manipulate their definition of history writing based on whether they want to prove or disprove that the Israelite writer was a historian.

But if one begins with anything other than the final form of the text, say, from source criticism (as do Smelik 1992:23-24; P. K. McCarter in H. Shanks 1997:32) or from tradition history (as does Moenikes 1995: 133-59), one is required to reconstruct some stage inside the black box. If one speaks of the Deuteronomistic Historian's (yet alone his *Grundlage's*) reconstruction of Iron I (as per Van Seters 1983), then one must reconstruct the world of the Deuteronomistic Historian (as does Whitley 1957). That would be a worthy goal, but scholars' results have differed extensively, and some have argued that there was no Deuteronomistic Historian at all (Knauf 1996). Or perhaps snipping out the Deuteronomistic Historian from the extant text is simply not possible (Gooding 1982:70*-72*; Licht 1983:108; Thompson 1987; Peckham 1995:371, 377). Some reconstructions such as the Deuteronomistic Historian have achieved the status of canons of the field when perhaps they are little more than folk traditions among scholars, anthropologically speaking (Thompson 1992:94; Lemche 1998:158).

Additionally, if one compares one reconstruction (like DtrH) with another reconstruction (like the complex chiefdoms of Iron I), the whole enterprise approaches a house of cards. Justifying the DtrH is well beyond the scope of this study, while the complex chiefdom reconstruction has been extensively justified here. If one wishes to compare this reconstruction with something that has concrete existence, only the final form of the text can be used (leaving aside all the text-critical issues of defining that final form), not a coherent pre-text that is supposedly cleaner than the real text (Flanagan 1987:29; Polzin 1989:14-15; Mullen 1993:7; Knauf 1996; Lemche 1998:160). And it is the text itself that must be used, not the scholars' reconstruction of what it means (as does Brandfon 1987:34-38).

One metaphor of the "Paris School" of the study of textualized oral lore (see Chapter 8) is that of a painting (Dowden 1992:36-38). Textualized oral lore paints a picture of the world it describes. The ancient Israelite "researcher" painted such a picture of Iron I.[3] That he or she did this is in fact irrelevant:[4] the point is that the biblical text *is* such a painted picture

---

3. For discussion of other "paintings" of the same Iron I scene, see Tadmor (1987:15-27). The only biblical scholar, to my knowledge, to have used this painting analogy is V. Philips Long (1994:66).

4. The analogy is used by V. Philips Long (1994:67), but to explore why the "painting" was undertaken. There are also different "styles" of painting found in the biblical text, some more "realistic" and others more "abstract," so that for a study like Long's, the eye/mind of the painter remains an important element to consider. An understanding of "why" the

of its "period of the Judges." To define this metaphor better, consider a Renaissance painting of the assassination of Julius Caesar. The dress and the architecture may be Renaissance. There may be elements in the painting that are Romanesque, or from other periods between the Roman and Renaissance, which the artist included, knowing merely that they were "past." This does not mean that Caesar's assassination is fictitious. If a historian studying Roman history, who had explored the issues of Caesar's assassination, were to look at the painting, he or she could pick out details related to the "actual" events — or rather, to the events as that historian had reconstructed them (Snodgrass 1971:302-59). For such subjects as the history of Rome, such a thing is never done; historians of ancient Denmark, for example, do not look at Shakespeare's "Hamlet" to see what relates to their own reconstructions. Yet this is exactly what biblical scholars are always doing, since many circumstances have compelled this particular painting, the biblical text's historical-literary epics, to be examined by those dealing with the history of Israel, with what the painting depicts (Walton 1989:112). Although one could easily just ignore the painting as irrelevant and write a history of ancient Palestine from other sources (as, e.g., does Finkelstein 1996b:200), it can be examined. In this case, one can "confront the information in the OT [the painting] with the results of archaeological excavations in Palestine" (Lemche 1992:529; also W. Dever in H. Shanks 1997:32). We are actually confronting it with the scholars' interpretation of those results (another kind of painting), an interpretation always present and here explicit with the anthropological model. Picking out the "authentic" features of the painting is "text archaeology" (T. Thompson in H. Shanks 1997:32). And, contrary to the attestations of some (e.g., Thompson 1991:90; 1996:34; Davies 1992:31-32), I will show here that some features of the painting do match the archaeological painting of Iron I.

In this chapter I will compare some of the "paintings" of Iron I found in the biblical text with the reconstruction presented in this study. The goal here is not to exhaust all the biblical texts that might correlate with Iron I. To cover all such cases, many of which must surely be scattered throughout the entire Hebrew Bible, is well beyond the scope of this study. The point is to show some examples of how this can be done.

---

painting of Iron I found in the so-called Deuteronomistic History was undertaken is the aim of Mullen (1993:5, 32-47).

The examples that are illustrated here are really three. Since the principal conclusions of the archaeologically reconstructed history are geographic ones, the first of these examples will be a historical geographical dialogue with the text. The second example, taken from Judges 9, is directly suggested by that historical geographical discussion. The third sample, from 1 Samuel 2, is the passage supposedly "depicting" Iron I that best resonates with the complex chiefdom model. Such is the principle of selection, albeit arbitrary.

The aim here is not to reverse course, discard all the methodological boundaries set in Chapter 2, and begin with an analysis of these texts that purport to deal with Iron I. The procedure is to begin with the archaeological reconstruction presented in Chapter 6 and then approach the final form of some texts that are suggested by the archaeological reconstruction and look for places of correspondence. It is beyond the scope of this study to examine why or how these correspondences exist, although I will make some further statements on this matter at the end of the chapter.

On the one side, scholars of oral tradition have discovered from case studies of Late Bronze Age Greece and Armenia that textualized oral lore often preserves place names (Vermeule 1972:309-12; Grosby 1997:25). Historical geographers have likewise noted the extremely long durability of place names through history (Baker 1991:236; Kallai 1996b; McQuillan 1996:5). These two observations yield the postulate — and it is just that, it is not here "proven" — that the biblical text does preserve ancient place names, and the corollary is that modern historical geography can identify these place names.

Historical geography is an entire discipline in itself, although it has become unfashionable. In recent decades, archaeologists have found it necessary to provide identifications for every site they excavate, and often these are given on very little basis (cf. the bases used for the identification of Izbet Sartah as Ebenezer or Tell Marjame as Baal-Shalishah; respectively, Finkelstein 1992d; Kallai 1971). Proper historical geography depends on more than occupations from the proper periods. It involves full knowledge of the topography, analysis of relevant Egyptian lists, examination of later ancient identifications of the site (e.g., Josephus or Jerome), etymological derivation of the modern Arabic name(s) of the site, and periods of occupation. It is really a specialized field or subfield of the history of ancient Israel, and it is not a footnote job for the archaeologist, or for the biblical scholar simply trying to find a site to match a biblical story (see the discussions of the location of Bethel by Livingston [1971-72; 1990; 1994; also Blizzard 1973-74]).

So, in cases where thorough historical geography has been undertaken, with all of the techniques just mentioned, we will assume that the historical geographers have done their jobs accurately. The extension of the historical geography postulate is that the generally accepted site identifications are accurate and do not require individual treatment here. To discuss the identification of each of these sites is not only beyond the scope of this study but it would also be a monumental task worth several books. I will follow the consensus here. Where historical geographers have disagreed on the identification of a site, I will take no position, and the site will be left with its modern name. Similarly, when an ancient place name has been identified with more than one site, I will give *none* of those sites an identification other than the modern name.

Some of the most thorough historical geographies include those of Borée (1930), Simons (1937; 1959), Ahituv (1979; 1984), and Rainey (1984). Other important essays include Guthe (1915), Elliger (1930; 1937; 1938; 1970); Kallai (1954; 1956; 1958; 1971; 1986a; 1996b), B. Mazar (1954; 1975), Jenni (1958), Kuschke (1962), Schunck (1962), Kappus (1968), Aharoni (1969), Knierim (1969), Monson (1983), Harel (1984), Naʿaman (1985; 1986a:145-46, 153-58; 1996b), and Rubin (1989). From these, we can replace many site names in the reconstruction of the society with "ancient" names. What we have said about these ancient places in Chapter 6 can then simply be restated with the ancient names, and the "paintings" then brought in for comparison.

Given the major historical geographical studies listed above, the five main polities become, therefore, Dothan, Tirzah, Shechem, Shiloh, and the Benjaminite area. Within Benjamin, the identifications become el-Jib = Gibeon, Tell el-Ful = Gibeah, Tell en-Nasbeh = Mizpah, Beitin = Bethel, and et-Tell = ʿAi. Khirbet Raddanah remains unnamed, since the proposed identification by Aharoni (1971) as Ataroth(-addar) is weak. Similarly, many B-level and lower centers also gain names.

Instantly, interesting correlations with the biblical text appear, along with some contradictions. Shiloh, Shechem, and the centers of Benjamin just listed that were important in Iron I are presented as such in the books of Judges and 1 Samuel (admittedly the issues are complex, but here the point is merely to note this fact). Dothan and Tirzah, on the other hand, are not presented as such. No identification has been adequately provided for Khirbet Raddanah, as just noted, though the site was very important in Iron I. There is nothing in the identification of Tell en-Nasbeh with Mizpah to explain its unusual nature: nothing in the stories about Mizpah that relates to the Philistine issues discussed in Chapter 5. The importance of Khirbet Tibne in the highlands may be echoed in Timnath-Serah's attribution as the home and burial place of Joshua (Josh. 19:49-50; 24:30). Most of the cities that the writer of Judges 1 believed had remained in the hands of the Canaanites in Iron I turn out, as has been shown in Chapters 1 and 5, probably to have been non-Israelite: Jerusalem, Beth-Shan, Taanach, Dor, Ibleam (Khirbet Belameh), Megiddo, Gezer, and Aijalon (Judg. 1:21, 27-29, 34).

If one rewrites the narrative history presented in Chapter 6 above with the "ancient names," more interesting things appear. Beginning in the south, the important events in the history of Benjamin and their attendant questions take a new form. Around 1150, something serious happened. The destruction of Gibeah, and perhaps the destruction of Bethel a few decades earlier, affected the entire region, possibly resulting in the overcrowding of ʿAi and of Khirbet Raddanah. Whatever this event was, perhaps something of it is echoed in Judges 20, in the Israelite civil war against Gibeah and Benjamin (also Hos. 9:9; 10:9). There is no archaeological evidence for the destroyers of Gibeah being Israelite, and the entire population of Benjamin was not destroyed in 1150. One might propose (or conclude) that Israel knew its own history only in a shadowy way. There may be no connection at all between 1125 B.C. and Judges 20, but the possible connection is worth musing upon.

About 1025, the destruction of Khirbet Raddanah by an unknown assailant facilitated the renaissance of Gibeah, which became the capital. Perhaps this event is reflected in 1 Samuel, with the rise of Saul (1 Samuel 8–31), with Gibeah his capital (1 Sam. 11:4). Again, although there is no "proof" of the biblical story in the archaeology, that is not at all what is here sought. But if the Saul story reflects something of 1025 B.C., if Judges 20 reflects something of 1125 B.C., they have the potential of providing something that archaeology and anthropological model cannot: not mere hierarchies and economies but ideological content of the social structures and symbols not otherwise accessible.

To continue, Gibeon remained removed from and immune to all these events. Perhaps this is preserved in the biblical text's ethnic identification of Gibeon as non-Israelite. The material culture of Gibeon is identical to that of the rest of Benjamin, but for some reason the events of Benjamin did not concern or affect Gibeon. The devastation of Benjamin in 1125 and the resuscitation of Benjamin in 1025 did not deal with Gibeon. Note that we are not arguing here that this was *because* Gibeon was non-Israelite, as the biblical text says; perhaps it was the other way around: that the biblical text says Gibeon was non-Israelite because it was not part of Iron I Benjamin. And perhaps both are true, but it is impossible to tell.

Gibeon was included, however, in the general destruction of 1000. Gibeon, Gibeah, 'Ai, and Mizpah were all destroyed, and if by the same agent, then by someone who made no distinction between Gibeon and Benjamin. Perhaps this is echoed in the Philistine advance portrayed at the end of the reign of Saul (1 Samuel 28; 2 Sam. 5:17-25). Again, many details in the biblical narrative are not corroborated by the archaeology, but with this painting metaphor that does not matter. Perhaps what happened in 1000 is behind some of these stories.

Moving north, we come to the Shiloh chiefdom. Despite its relatively small territory, Shiloh is the only chiefdom capital with evidence of large-scale interaction with other Israelite chiefdoms: the import of pottery from the chiefdom of Tirzah and later from the chiefdom of Shechem. The biblical text holds to the view that Shiloh was somehow central to all of Israel (Josh. 18:1, 8-10; 19:51; 21:2; 22:9, 12; 1 Samuel 1–4; Jer. 7:12, 14; 26:6, 9; Ps. 78:60). Without in any way suggesting that archaeology establishes that Shiloh was the amphictyonic center or even the pan-Israelite cult center, perhaps the archaeological evidence does attest to something that is also reflected in the biblical text's view of Shiloh (as per Lemaire 1990:283-84). The destruction of Shiloh in 1050 may be reflected in Jer. 7:12, 14; 26:6; and Ps. 78:60, which place a destruction of Shiloh on the heels of the defeat by the Philistines at Ebenezer (1 Samuel 4).[5]

The chiefdom to the north, that of Shechem, was, as has been shown, quite substantial. There were nine subchief centers. Because of the inherent features of complex chiefdoms, there was a successful rebellion in 1125, undertaken by one or more of the subchiefs. The only subchiefs powerful enough to succeed in such a rebellion would have been the ones at Tell

---

5. In fact, the presence of this tradition in the nonhistorical texts is even more important: it is a case of the other, "accidental mention" way in which oral lore is textualized ("accidental" in the technical sense described in Chapter 8). One can see from Jer. 26:6-8 that it is the mention of Shiloh that strikes such a nerve with the priests and prophets that they demand his death. (I wish to thank Jack Lundbom for sharing this insight with me.)

Sofar, Ras Zeid, and Khirbet el-Urma, the latter of which can now be identified with Arumah (Campbell 1991:105-6). These three were the ones with the most strategic economic positions themselves and the most subordinate C-level sites and villages of their own. Now the only one of these subchief capitals that was fortified was Arumah, making it the most likely to have led the rebellion of 1125.

One must think of Judges 9 (Campbell 1983; 1991:105-6). According to the biblical story, Arumah was the city of Abimelech (Judg. 9:41). The text establishes that he is not a Shechemite. In Judg. 9:28, Gaal ben-Ebed asks, "Who is Abimelech — and who is Shechem — that we should serve him." "Who is Shechem?" can be repointed as "Who is [a] Shechemite?" or one can use the Septuagint's "Who is a son of Shechem?" (Alexandrinus) or "Who is the son of Shechem?" (Vaticanus). It does not matter that elsewhere the Shechemites are called the "lords" of Shechem and not the "sons"; in this verse the issue is not citizenship but ethnicity (Boling 1963:480), as in the use in *EA* 59:2 of the "sons of Tunip" for its citizens. "*The* son of Shechem" does not indicate Zebul (as per Boling 1963:481); it refers to Gaal ben-Ebed and the others who are with him in 9:27.

Verse 28 goes on to clarify that not only was Abimelech not Shechemite, but he "served" the "men of Hamor," presumably the Hamorite chiefs of Shechem. This makes him a subchief. In some sort of bid to rule Shechem or rule from Shechem, with the support of others of the chiefdom, Abimelech ends up destroying Shechem (Judg. 9:45-49). Yet this would-be paramount does not turn Arumah into the new capital. Judg. 9:53-54 tells us that he is killed.

There are obvious inconsistencies. The biblical narrative presents Abimelech as king of Shechem (Judg. 9:6) well before the battle that results in its destruction. It is also not clear what the text is picking up on by making Abimelech "king" of Shechem, but over Israel (all of it?) his activity is described in v. 22 by the verb ŚRR. The meaning of this verb is elsewhere to rule as a prince (Isa. 32:1), as the master of a house (Esth. 1:22), or generically as a ruler (Prov. 8:16). The Septuagint has *herxen*, the aorist indicative active of *arxō*, "to be foremost." What the character of Gaal ben-Ebed alludes to is also not clear. And there is no logical reason for Abimelech to follow the destruction of Shechem with an expedition in Judg. 9:50 (par. 2 Sam. 11:21) against a low-level site in the Tirzah system, which is what Thebez is whether it is Khirbet Fuqaha (Site #217; Zertal 1983a:44; 1996:196-97) or Khirbet edh-Dhuq (Site #229; Elliger 1930; 1938; Jenni 1958).

120

Some of these details may reflect matters of a much later time than 1125, and the Israelite "researcher" has put them together. It is even possible that they contain reflections of events *earlier* than 1125, and the "researcher" has conflated them. The Israelites did not know their own history. Still, there is also the possibility that details are accurate in the Abimelech story that could not be verified by archaeology alone.

All of this depends on the historical geographic postulate. However, kernels of accuracy can be seen in the painting without historical geography, and here sample texts can be examined. Consider the following translation of 1 Sam. 2:13-16, which is that of the New Revised Standard Version, except where italicized. The italicized emendations will be dealt with in turn.

> 13The *correct custom* of the priests *with* the people had been: whenever anyone would offer his sacrifice, the assistant of the priest would come, while the meat cooked, with a three-pronged fork in his hand. 14He would put it forward into the pot, kettle, cauldron, or jar. Everything the fork would bring up, the priest would take for himself. This they did to all of Israel coming there to Shiloh. 15*But now,* however, even before they burned the fat, the assistant would come and say to the man sacrificing, "Give the priest meat to roast, because he won't accept boiled meat from you — only raw." 16The man *would say* to him, "Let the fat be burned *as usual,* and then take for yourself what you want." He would say to him, "You will give it now! Otherwise, I will take it by force!"

In v. 13, the phrase translated here (and in other modern versions, e.g., the Jerusalem Bible) as "correct custom" is *mišpaṭ*. Many modern translators render this as "the custom" or something similar, maintaining that there is no dichotomy between the activity of vv. 13-14 and those of vv. 15-16. This makes all these activities condemnable. But there is a contrast between the acts of vv. 13-14 and those of vv. 15-16, and this first depends on the legitimacy of the former activities. The word *mišpaṭ* almost always has a legal connotation; the single case where it refers to an illicit practice is 1 Kings 17:34 in reference to the Samaritans. But the weight of the lexical evidence is to translate "correct custom," following 1 Kings 5:8 and 1 Sam. 27:11, or the phrase *mišpaṭ hakōhănîm* as "the priests' due," following Deut. 18:3; 21:7. The Septuagint's *dikaiōma* also has the attested meaning of "just claim/due" from Thucydides (1.141) in the 5th century B.C. to Plutarch

(*Demetrius* 18) in the 2nd century A.D. The particle *'et* has been translated here as the custom "with" the people (as in the older RSV); cf. Gen. 14:2, 8, 9; 17:3; 42:40; Num. 20:13; 1 Kings 8:15; Jer. 1:16; 4:12; 5:5; 12:1; Ezek. 2:1; 3:22, 24, 27; 14:4; 44:5; Isa. 30:8; 45:9; 50:8; 66:14; Ps. 35:1; 67:2; 78:8; Prov. 23:11. The alternate to "with" is "from," following the Septuagint's *para tou*, the Syriac, Naples Latin Codex 1, the Targum, and Deut. 18:3, but the meaning is nearly the same.

The other key to drawing a contrast between the two activities of the priests, the habitual ones of vv. 13-14 and the aberration of vv. 15-16, is the first words of v. 15, *gam bĕṭerem*. This is to be translated, "But now, however, even before. . . ." This use of *gam* in the adversative sense, indicating a contradiction with previous phrases, is well attested: Jer. 6:15–8:12; Ezek. 20:23; Neh. 6:1; Ps. 95:9; 129:2; Eccl. 4:8, 16; 5:18. The meaning "even before" for *bĕṭerem* can be found in Exod. 12:34; Num. 11:33; Josh. 3:1; Ruth 3:14a; Isa. 65:24; Hag. 2:15; and Ps. 119:67, and for the Septuagint's *prin* in Tob. 2:4. In v. 16, the sacrificer emphasizes that the practice has changed, asking that things be done "as usual," *kayyôm*. This word should not be translated as "now" as in 1 Sam. 9:27 and many other texts, but as "as usual," as in 1 Sam. 18:10, the Syriac, and 4QSam[a], or "as formerly" following Gen. 25:21, 33; 1 Kings 1:51. "As formerly" can also be the meaning of the Septuagint *prōton*, or *proteron* in several minuscules of the Proto-Lucianic recension. The "as formerly" meaning is attested in the *Iliad* 21.405; Josephus, *Antiquities* 19.201; 20.173; 2 Cor. 1:15; Eph. 4:22; and *2 Clement* 13:1.

The only other change from NRSV is the attribution of an imperfective aspect to *wayyō'mer* at the start of v. 16. It is difficult to make this Hebrew verb form anything other than preterite/past perfective, but one could argue that the *wayyō'mer* follows the priestly assistant's question and is meant to answer it, thus the *waw* shows the sequence of question and answer, and since the question comes in a context of habitual activity, the answer does too. This is supported by the Greek, which is here imperfect (*elegen;* the verb is omitted in Codex Alexandrinus).

This passage, even by the traditional translation, has always been interpreted in a cultic sense (Stolz 1981:33). This has only met with difficulty. Nevertheless, rituals and protocols of conduct are supposed to be among the longest-lasting of traditions (Shils 1981); so this feature of the painting may be old. Comparison with the complex chiefdom reconstruction supports this, as follows.

In the complex chiefdom model, which has been shown to apply to

Shiloh, we noted that useful tribute is brought by the people to the chieftain. We also noted that the chieftain does not actually take all of the food, but rather symbolically receives it, and then it is returned to the people (see Chapter 3, above; and Earle 1977:225 and Peebles and Kus 1977:425-26 for the ethnographic parallel of the Hawaiian *Makihiki* ritual).

This is exactly what is happening in 1 Samuel 2, according to the present translation. The "chieftain" Eli's[6] usual practice was to take only a token of the useful tribute brought to Shiloh (vv. 14, 16), but his sons were keeping *all* of the tribute food (v. 15), and thus angering the populace. In v. 17 the *'ănāšîm* who treated the offering of Yahweh with contempt are not the assistants or Eli's sons, who are always called *nă'ārîm*, but the sacrificers themselves, the *'îš* of vv. 13 and 15. The sacrificers' response was to hold the offering in contempt, that is, stop bringing it at all. It is not a problem that the text calls it the "offering of Yahweh." The chieftain is fed for his sacred powers and activities, such as intercession (Drucker 1951:257-58; E. Wolf 1966:52; Peebles and Kus 1977:426-27; Steponaitis 1978:420; Kristiansen 1982:245; Earle 1987b:298; Pauketat 1991:24). Eli's relation to Yahweh gives him a sacred legitimacy, which makes his support obligatory for the people (Helms 1979:71; Spencer 1987:376; Earle 1987a:71; Maisels 1990:244).

The punishment Eli and his house receive can also be read within the complex chiefdom model. The curse against Eli in 1 Sam. 2:32b reads, *wělō'- yihyeh zāqēn běbêtkā kāl-hayyāmîm.* The NRSV confusingly renders this as, "There shall not be an old man in your house forever." Now H. Reviv has described the role of what he calls "the elders" (Heb. *zāqēn*). Although he may overplay their importance, he argues that these elders were likely the subchiefs under the paramount chief (Heb. *nāśî*), whom he terms the "head" (Reviv 1989:18). So if the Hebrew word *zāqēn* is translated with the meaning "chieftain" or "subchief," then the phrase reads, "There will not be a (sub)chief from your family ever again." Furthermore, in v. 33 the NRSV translates, "All the increase of your house shall die by the sword of men," using the Septuagint and 4QSam[a] addition of "by sword." The Hebrew is *wěkol-marěbbît bêtkā yāmûtû 'ănāšîm.* A suggested reading

---

6. An entire study could be devoted to the biblical text's description of Eli's roles, as well as to the entire biblical description of leadership in the "period of the Judges" overall, and these descriptions could then be compared with the complex chiefdom model. Such a study would, however, involve a very different approach to the biblical text than that which is explicit here. The present example alone is sufficient to call Eli a "chief."

would refer to the future progeny (Heb. *marĕbbît*) of Eli's house who will die "as" *'ănāšîm,* which has the attested meaning "soldiers," especially in 1 Samuel (1 Sam 4:9; 17:4; 18:27; 23:3-4; 24:3; 25:13; 1 Kings 2:2), as well as "men." Then it would allow the phrase to say that Eli's descendants will die as "common soldiers" as opposed to elite subchiefs (*'ănāšîm* also has the "common" connotation; Deut. 3:11).

Other correlations from some later period will fit with this story, as well — details that reflect things of a much later time, which the Israelite "researcher" has put together, both because the Israelites did not know their own history and because of the influence on the "researcher" of aspects of rhetoric and persuasion. Still, there is also the possibility that details in the Eli story are accurate that could not be seen from the archaeology alone.

This is a sample of features of the textual painting that bear a direct resemblance to the archaeological-anthropological painting of the Iron I highlands. There are many other elements of the painting that *could* fit with Iron I, although there is no way to argue that they do. It is probably the case that at least some of the resemblances outlined here are too close to be coincidence. But to go beyond this remark to posit the "how" and "why" of the connections would require another study as long as this one. A thorough exploration of the mechanism by which the "painter" arrived at these would involve a number of issues: In what period were these relevant portions of the biblical narrative written? Why were they written (Mullen 1993:5, 32-47)? Is the biblical writer primarily a copyist, a tradent, a novelist, or a researcher (Veyne 1988)? If a novelist or researcher, to what extent were his own rhetorical interests, situation, and audience influencing his writing (Hutton 1994:45-46)? In that case, what was the nature of the society in which he was writing (Whitley 1957)? If copyist or researcher, just how did earlier sources come to be included in his work (Albright 1966:11; Halpern 1983:19; Lemche 1988:56; Redford 1992:276-77; Rabinowitz 1993:94-109)? What were the societies involved in the composition of such earlier sources? From when, ultimately, did the sources come — from Iron I? From earlier times? From times between Iron I and the author's own? Is it possible that the very places of correspondence outlined in this chapter could have their origin in one of these many other periods (i.e., from any time in history up to the author's own)? A full evaluation of the means by which the "connections" here illustrated came about cannot be written without tackling all of these issues (McNutt 1999:5). Such a project would be a worthy complement to this one.

CHAPTER 10

Conclusions:
Toward a Cultural History of Early Israel

In this study I have ascertained the sociopolitical nature of Israelite society for the period immediately before the rise of the Monarchy at the end of the 11th century B.C. This involved applying the anthropological model of complex chiefdom to describe the systemic structure of society. I have also treated current presentations of this model, examining its various versions as it is presented by anthropologists.

I applied the complex chiefdom model to the realia of 12th- and 11th-centuries highland Palestine. The archaeological information from the Iron I hill country provided a basis for evaluating the complex chiefdom model and for fine-tuning it to describe the social history of the Iron I Israelite community. Unfortunately, because of problems inherent in the data set, for the most part I could not use statistical methods. The dearth of ancient Near Eastern sources dealing with the 12th- and 11th-centuries highland settlement quickly exhausted that avenue for gaining further details.

I used the archaeologically based reconstruction of highland Israel to identify morphologically analogous cultures elsewhere in the ancient Near East and beyond. Unfortunately, it was not possible to examine how these cultures recorded their own histories in "textual artifact." But I did use the archaeologically based reconstruction of highland Israel as a sounding board for the biblical text. I compared some examples from the biblical text with the reconstruction and explored several areas of correspondence, noting also places of contradiction.

There are, however, areas that are neither contradictory nor correspondent. Those are the things that the biblical literature is most about, "relatively few, highly complex and ambiguity-ridden concepts around which the social organization of a culture revolves and the emotional and intellectual energy of its members is largely spent" (Polanyi 1981:99). Moreover, only such concepts can move a history beyond the social history of economics and politics into a more ("new") cultural history.

The text might provide information about such concepts from Iron I; it would be most difficult to prove that it does not. However, such information is inextricably bound with thick cultural concepts, intentions, concerns of the author's own period, and concerns of many others before his or her time (Dever 1997d:298). The text cannot be used as a direct source for reconstructing the cultural concepts. Archaeology, on the other hand, is unsuited for uncovering such things. It is not that archaeology does not find "culture." Just in iconography, there is an immense collection of items from the Iron I highland settlement. In fact, all artifacts have a symbolic, ideological side — and ideology does not exist independently of material culture (Bard 1992:3-4). Nevertheless, archaeology is unsuited to "reading" the material culture as text, for understanding that ideological side of artifacts (Hodder 1991; but cf. Flannery and Marcus 1993; Hodder 1993; Peebles 1993; and Renfrew 1993), and even the iconography can be read only by the questionable connection with iconographic vocabularies of other ancient Near Eastern cultures (Lamberg-Karlovsky 1993:288). Lastly, an anthropological model like the complex chiefdom model is also ill-equipped to write a cultural history, since ideology is relegated to merely one aspect among many elements of the system.

In this study I have eliminated ideology as peripheral, have not even granted it any role in the reconstruction presented in Chapter 6, and that is probably a deficiency. Surely ideology played an immense role in human decisions at all levels: where to place a settlement, acceptable modes of production, motives for supporting chieftains, ranking of society, preservation of history, textualization of that preservation, and so forth. Some method must be arrived at for retrieving these "highly complex and ambiguity-ridden concepts around which the social organization of a culture revolves and the emotional and intellectual energy of its members is largely spent" (Polanyi 1981:99) for Iron I before a cultural history of highland Israel can be written for the 12th and 11th centuries B.C. Such a method might even involve discarding the complex chiefdom model so meticulously constructed here. The maxim for that endeavor is that of Northrop Frye (1983:107), "All these answers are true as far as they go, so we shall ignore their truth in order to get a little farther."

Key to Iron I Sites in Figures

For full descriptions, see R. Miller 2002b.

1. Kh. (Khirbet) Seilun
2. Jebel Dhahrat ez-Zaban
3. unnamed site at M.R. 183.150
4. Kh. en-Najama East
5. unnamed site at M.R. 180.160
6. Tell Marjame
7. unnamed site at M.R. 181.161
8. Tell esh-Shuna Center
9. Kh. en-Najama West
10. Tell Dawara
11. Kh. Dhiyab
12. Tell Balatah
13. Kh. esh-Sheikh Nasrallah
14. unnamed site at M.R. 173.165
15. Wadi el-Hammam
16. Tell Mneitra
17. unnamed site at M.R. 170.154
18. Kh. Tarafein
19. Tell er-Ras
20. Kh. en-Nebi
21. Kh. es-Sur A
22. Tell Sofar
23. Kuma

24. Jebel Ajram
25. Kh. Bir el-Kharayib
26. unnamed site at M.R. 171.169
27. unnamed site at M.R. 172.166
28. unnamed site at M.R. 167.158
29. Bir et-Tell
30. Farkha
31. Arura
32. Nebi Annir
33. Kh. esh-Shuna West
34. Sheikh Issa
35. Kh. Sarsara
36. Kaubar
37. Kh. Birzeit
38. Kh. Tibne
39. unnamed site at M.R. 158.154
40. unnamed site at M.R. 157.160
41. Kh. Fassa
42. unnamed site at M.R. 160.172
43. Kh. et-Tell (M.R. 158.168)
44. Qurnat Haramiya
45. Izbet Abu Halil
46. unnamed site at M.R. 164.170
47. Kh. esh-Shajara
48. Ras Zeid
49. Kh. Hamad
50. Kh. el-Burak
51. Beit Rima
52. Klia
53. Deir Ghassana
54. unnamed site at M.R. 158.159
55. Kh. Burraish
56. Deir el-Mir
57. Deir Qassis
58. Deir Daqla
59. Kh. ed-Duwwar
60. Kh. Ali
61. Kh. Banat Barr

62. unnamed site at M.R. 168.157
63. Jurish
64. unnamed site at M.R. 187.169
65. unnamed site at M.R. 187.168
66. es-Siyar
67. Jarayish
68. Kh. Bani Fadil
69. Sheikh Mazar
70. Kh. Jibit
71. unnamed site at M.R. 181.167
72. unnamed site at M.R. 185.161
73. Kh. en-Nebi Nun
74. Kh. Urma
75. Kh. Tana et-Tahta
76. el-Kurum
77. Kh. el-Qariq
78. Ukasha
79. Kh. el-Mefjir
80. Tell es-Sultan
81. Tell ʿAish
82. Kh. el-Auja el-Foqa
83. Rafid
84. Kh. Najmat Khuneifis
85. Ghuraba
86. Kh. es-Sur B
87. Kh. Alyata
88. Kh. et-Tell (M.R. 175.159)
89. ʿAtara
90. et-Taiyibeh South
91. Kh. Kulesan
92. Kh. Marajim
93. Rahaya
94. Tell el-Qarqafa
95. Sheikh Hatim
96. Qabalan
97. Tell esh-Sheikh Abu Zarad
98. Kh. ʿAtarud
99. Einabus

100. Kh. Rujan
101. Jamma'in
102. Kh. el-Khaush
103. unnamed site at M.R. 176.162
104. unnamed site at M.R. 180.162
105. unnamed site at M.R. 182.155
106. Rujeib
107. unnamed site at M.R. 177.163
108. unnamed site at M.R. 146.165
109. Nahal Shillo
110. unnamed site at M.R. 184.174
111. Kh. Ghannam
112. Tel Amal — J8
113. unnamed site at M.R. 185.174
114. Qasr Fara
115. Kh. Shureim
116. el-Kurrum A
117. Ijenisiniyah
118. Kh. Miyamas
119. Sebastiya
120. Hannun
121. Ras ed-Diyar
122. Kh. Shuweiha
123. Kh. Tana el-Foqa
124. Yanun
125. Wadi Abd el-Al
126. Kh. Marah el-Inab
127. Bir el-Hadab
128. Ras el-Burj
129. Qarqaf
130. et-Tuweilat
131. Kh. ed-Duweir
132. Kh. el-Qebubah
133. Qusin
134. Kafr Kuz
135. el-Burnat Sitti Salaamiyeh (Mt. Ebal)
136. Asira esh-Shamaliyya A
137. Asira Shamaliyya B

138. el-Aqabe
139. Jebel el-Batin
140. Kh. et-Tell (M.R. 164.169)
141. Kh. Matwi
142. Kh. Yanun
143. Kh. en-Namleh
144. er-Requq
145. Kh. Saben
146-199. Unassigned site numbers
200. Tell Abu Sidra
201. Kh. es-Salih
202. Wadi Abu Sidra
203. Iraq Matar
204. Kaziye er-Ratrut
205. Tell el-Mazar (Cisjordan)
206. Wadi Ras Kharubeh el-Marah
207. Bab ed-Daiyq
208. Qasr el-Asbah
209. Ras el-Kharubeh 6
210. Ras el-Kharubeh 7
211. Waqf es-Samadi
212. Kh. Ras el-Kharubeh
213. es-Sirtassa
214. Ras el-'Ain
215. Ras el-A'war
216. Salhab
217. Kh. Fuqaha
218. Kh. Janzar
219. Tell Dothan
220. el-Khirbe Mahrun
221. Tayasir
222. Tell el-Farah North
223. Tughrah
224. Kh. Einun
225. es-Skhra
226. Kh. ed-Deir East
227. Iraq Rajjah
228. Ras Jadir

229. Kh. edh-Dhuq (Kh. el-Fukhar)
230. Kh. Ein Farr
231. Iraq el-Hamra
232. el-Muntar A
233. Maqbarah
234. Maqabar
235. Tell el-Unuq
236. Khallet Shuk
237. Tell el-Miski
238. Kh. Beit Farr A
239. Dhahrat es-Senobar
240. Kh. Nib
241. Kh. el-Minuniyye
242. Kh. Sabattah
243. Yasid
244. Qaadat es-Seiyad
245. el-Mamaleh
246. Kh. Kheibar
247. Sanur
248. Kh. Mayyase
249. Har Saul
250. Givat Jonathan
251. Nuris
252. Jalbun
253. Beit Qad
254. En Jezreel
255. Horvat Mazrim
256. el-Burj
257. Horvat Tittorah
258. Kh. er-Ras SW
259. Yalu
260. Unassigned site number
261. Bir el-Hilu
262. Deir Ammar
263. Tell esh-Sheikh Sobar
264. Tel Ze'evim
265. Tell el-Abeidah
266. Khrab

267. Kh. Masaod
268. Kh. Rujjam
269. es-Salah
270. Batn Umm-Nari
271. el-Qureinat
272. el-Khirbeh Ra'y
273. Joret el-Ward
274. Tell el-Muhaffar
275. Joret 'Amer
276. Tall
277. Khallet Seif
278. Burqin
279. Kh. Abu Kahut
280. Kh. Ibn Amr
281. el-Batn es-Sama
282. Zebabida
283. el-Kebarra
284. Kh. ed-Deir NE
285. Kh. Tannin
286. Kh. Za'atara
287. Kh. Umm el-Butm
288. Kh. Anahum
289. Sheikh Safiriyyan
290. Dhahrat et-Tawileh (Bull Site)
291. Marah el-Khararib
292. Kh. Abu Ghannam
293. 'Ajje
294. Kheir-Allah
295. er-Rame
296. Kharaiyeq en-Natsarah
297. Jaba North
298. Sanur el-Khirbe
299. Jebel Qurein (Wadi Abu Nar)
300. Attil
301. Abu Rish
302. Kh. Wasil
303. Kh. Tell el-Hilu
304. Tell el-Hamme

305. Muntar esh-Shaq
306. Keren Zeitim
307. Kfar Qaraim
308. Jelamet Hamul
309. Khallet esh-Sharde
310. Yusuf
311. Khallet Nakhleh
312. Kh. el-Khrebat A
313. Yerzah
314. Ras Mrah el-Wawiyat
315. el-Bird
316. Mhallal
317. Khallet Mak-hul
318. Suweida
319. Hamamat
320. Kh. Umm el-Alaq
321. Kh. Abu Shuqeir
322. unnamed site at M.R. 159.221
323. unnamed site at M.R. 155.221
324. Tel Parus
325. Tel Mevorakh
326. Tel Esur
327. Kh. en-Nasriya
328. Kh. Bartaa
329. Kh. Abu Rujman
330. Zebubah
331. Kh. el-Farisiyye
332. Kom el-Ghaby
333. el-Hish
334. er-Ras North
335. Jebel Illan
336. el-Mustah
337. Tell Abu es-Sus
338-349. Unassigned site numbers
350. Ras Salmeh
351. Izbet Sartah
352. Kh. Ras Qurra
353-399. Unassigned site numbers

400. Tell el-Ful
401. Et-Tell
402. Kh. Raddanah
403. El-Jib
404. Tell en-Nasbeh
405. Kh. ed-Dawwara
406. Sanhedria
407. Deir el-ʿAzer
408. Ras Dhukeir
409. Hizma
410. Er-Ram
411. Kh. Nisya
412. Mukhmas
413. Kh. Kafr Tas
414. Kh. el-Kafireh/Tell Kefira
415. Kh. Irha
416. Ein Umm esh-Sharayit
417. Kh. el-Burj
418. Kh. Bir el-Hamam
419. Beitin
420. Wadi el-ʿAsas/Qurnat Shahtura
421. ʿAnata
422. Kh. Badd Abu Muammar/Kh. el-ʿUneiziyeh
423. Kh. Tell el-Askar
424. Kh. el-Hara el-Foqa
425. Jaba
426. Kh. el-Mukhatir/Kh. el-Maqatir
427. Kh. el-Qubbe
428. Rammun/Kh. Umm el-Rammin
429. Ras et-Tahuneh
430. Sheikh ʿAkrallah
431. unnamed site at M.R. 168.144
432. unnamed site at M.R. 174.147
433. Kh. el-Kurus
434. Kh. ʿAlmit
435. unnamed site at M.R. 172.137
436. Kh. Ghureitis
437. Khallet esh-Shih

438. unnamed site at M.R. 168.145
439. Kh. el-Hafi
440. unnamed site at M.R. 178.144
441. unnamed site at M.R. 174.147
442. Surrey Hill
443. Kh. Ras et-Tawil
444. unnamed site at M.R. 176.133
445. Ras Tammim/Ras Tumeim
446. Eth-Thughra
447. unnamed site at M.R. 177.135
448. unnamed site at M.R. 181.149
449. Beit 'Ur el-Foqa
450. Beit 'Ur et-Tahta
451. Beit Iweis
452. Mispe Har Nof/Deir Yassin
453. Kh. Abu Musarrah/Ein Fara/Tel Fara

Burials

C1. Kh. Majdal
C2. Faria el-Jiftlik
C3. Iraq et-Tayyih
C4. Iraq Burin
C5. et-Taiyiba West
C6. Jelamet Amer

Bibliography

Abel, F.-M.

1928.   Notes sur les environs de Bir-Zeit. *JPOS* 8:49-55.

Aharoni, Y.

1969.   Rubute and Ginti-Kirmil. *VT* 19:137-45.

1971.   Khirbet Raddana and Its Inscription. *IEJ* 21:130-35.

Ahituv, S.

1979.   *The Egyptian Topographical Lists Relating to the History of Palestine in the Biblical Period.* Diss., Hebrew University. Jerusalem. In Hebrew.

1984.   *Canaanite Toponyms in Ancient Egyptian Documents.* Jerusalem: Magnes Press.

Ahlström, G.

1980.   Review of de Geus, 1976. *JNES* 39:322-35.

1982.   Where Did the Israelites Live? *JNES* 41:133-38.

1986.   *Who Were the Israelites?* Winona Lake: Eisenbrauns.

1991a.   The Role of Archaeological and Literary Remains in Reconstructing Israel's History. Pp. 116-42 in Edelman, 1991a.

1991b.   The Origin of Israel in Palestine. Pp. 19-34 in Edelman, 1991b.

1993.   *The History of Ancient Palestine.* JSOTSup 146. Sheffield: Sheffield Academic Press.

1995.   Administration of the State in Canaan and Ancient Israel. Vol. 1, pp. 587-604 in *Civilizations of the Ancient Near East,* ed. J. M. Sasson. New York: Charles Scribner's Sons.

Ahlström, G., and Edelman, D. V.

1985.   Merneptah's Israel. *JNES* 44:59-61.

n.a.

1971.   Ain Samiya. *HA* 37:23. In Hebrew.

Albright, W. F.

1923.   The Ephraim of the Old and New Testaments. *JPOS* 3:36-40.

1924a.   Researches of the School in Western Judaea. *BASOR* 15:2-11.

1924b.   *Excavations and Results at Tell el-Ful.* AASOR 4. New Haven: Yale University Press.

1924c.   The Excavations at Gibeah of Saul. *Qobets* 1:53-60.

1926.   The Topography of the Tribe of Issachar. *ZAW* 44:225-36.

1929.   New Israelite and Pre-Israelite Sites. *BASOR* 35:1-14.

1933.   A New Campaign of Excavations at Gibeah of Saul. *BASOR* 52:6-12.

1934.   The Kyle Memorial Excavation at Bethel. *BASOR* 56:2-15.

1935.   Observations on the Bethel Report. *BASOR* 57:27-30.

1940.   *From Stone Age to Christianity.* Baltimore: Johns Hopkins University Press.

1946.   The Late Bronze Town at Modern Djett. *BASOR* 104:25-26.

1951.   The Eastern Mediterranean about 1060 BC. Pp. 223-31 in *Studies Presented to David Moore Robinson,* ed. G. E. Mylonas. 2 vols. St. Louis: Washington University Press.

1956.   *Archaeology and Religion of Israel.* 4th ed. Baltimore: Johns Hopkins University Press.

1964a.   *History, Archaeology, and Christian Humanism.* New York: McGraw-Hill.

1964b.   Introduction to H. Gunkel, *The Legends of Genesis.* New York: Schocken.

1966.   *Archaeology, Historical Analogy, and Early Biblical Tradition.* Rockwell Lectures 6. Baton Rouge: Louisiana State University Press.

Albright, W. F., and Kelso, J.

1968.   *The Excavations at Bethel.* AASOR 39. Cambridge, MA: American Schools of Oriental Research.

Allen, M. W.

1980.   A Synthetic Reconstruction of the Religion of Iron Age Ai and Raddanah. Unpublished term paper for Southern Baptist Theological Seminary, Louisville.

Amitai, J., ed.

1985.   *Biblical Archaeology Today.* Jerusalem: Israel Exploration Society.

Anbar, M.

1991.   *Les tribus amurrites de Mari.* OBO 108. Diss., Tel Aviv. Göttingen: Vandenhoeck & Ruprecht.

Anderson, D. G.

1990.   *Political Change in Chiefdom Societies.* Diss., University of Michigan.

Bibliography

Antoun, R. T.

1972.   *Arab Village*. Bloomington: Indiana University Press.

Aschmann, H.

1973.   Man's Impact on the Several Regions with Mediterranean Climates. Pp. 363-71 in di Castri and Mooney, 1973.

Aston, M.

1985.   *Interpreting the Landscape*. London: B. T. Batsford.

Astour, M. C.

1968.   Mesopotamian and Transtigridian Place Names in the Medinet Habu Lists of Ramses III. *JAOS* 88:733-52.

1995.   Overland Trade Routes in Ancient Western Asia. *Civilizations of the Ancient Near East* 3:1401-20.

Aufrecht, W. E.

1989.   *A Corpus of Ammonite Inscriptions*. Ancient Near Eastern Texts and Studies 4. Lewiston, ON: Edwin Mellon.

Aviram, J., ed.

1973.   *Eretz Shomron: The 30th Archaeological Convention, September 1972*. Jerusalem: Israel Exploration Society. In Hebrew.

Avi-Yonah, M.

1939.   Middle East's Economic Past. *Palestine & Middle East* 11:82-87.

Badé, W. F.

1927.   Excavation of Tell en-Nasbeh. *BASOR* 26:1-7.

1928.   *Excavations at Tell en-Nasbeh*. Palestine Institute Publications 1. Berkeley: Palestine Institute.

1929.   Tell en-Nasbeh in 1929. *Bulletin of the Pacific School of Religion* 8(3):3-12. = The Tell en-Nasbeh Excavations of 1929. Pp. 483-94 in *Smithsonian Report for 1930*. Washington, DC: Smithsonian Institute. = The Tell en-Nasbeh Excavations of 1929. *PEFQSt* 1930:8-19.

1936.   New Discoveries at Tell en-Nasbeh. Pp. 30-36 in *Werden und Wesen des Altes Testaments*, ed. P. Volz, F. Stummer, and J. Hembel. BZAW 66. Berlin: Alfred Töpelmann.

Banning, E. B.

1996.   Highlands and Lowlands: Problems and Survey Frameworks for Rural Archaeology in the Near East. *BASOR* 301:25-46.

Bard, K. A.

1992.   Toward an Interpretation of the Role of Ideology in the Evolution of Complex Society in Egypt. *Journal of Anthropological Archaeology* 11:1-24.

1994.   *From Farmers to Pharaohs: Mortuary Evidence for the Rise of Complex Society in Egypt.* Monographs on Mediterranean Archaeology 2. Sheffield: Sheffield Academic Press.

Barth, F.

1961.   *Nomads of South Persia.* Boston: Little, Brown.

Bartlett, J. R.

1989.   *Edom and the Edomites.* JSOTSup 77. Sheffield: Sheffield Academic Press.

Beck, L. A., ed.

1995.   *Regional Approaches to Mortuary Analysis.* New York: Plenum Press.

Beit-Arieh, I.

1995.   The Edomites in Cisjordan. Pp. 33-40 in Edelman, 1995.

Bendor, S.

1996.   *The Social Structure of Ancient Israel.* Jerusalem Biblical Studies 7. Jerusalem: Simor.

Berge, K.

1994.   "Comments" to Lemche, 1994. SJOT 8:198-205.

Bernbeck, R.

1994.   *Die Auflösung des häuswirtlichen Produktionsweise.* Berliner Beiträge zum Vorderen Orient 14. Berlin.

Berry, B. J. L.

1968.   Approaches to Regional Analysis. Pp. 24-34 in *Spatial Analysis,* ed. B. J. L. Berry and D. F. Marble. Englewood Cliffs, NJ: Prentice-Hall.

Bienkowski, P.

1992.   The Beginning of the Iron Age in Southern Jordan. Pp. 1-12 in Bienkowski, 1992.

1995.   The Edomites: The Archaeological Evidence from Transjordan. Pp. 41-92 in Edelman, 1995.

Bienkowski, P., ed.

1992.   *Early Edom and Moab.* Sheffield Archaeological Monographs 7. Sheffield: J. R. Collis.

Bikai, P. M.

1992.   The Phoenicians. Pp. 132-41 in Ward and Joukowsky, 1992.

Binford, L. R.

1964.   A Consideration of Archaeological Research Design. *American Antiquity* 29:425-41.

Blakely, J. A.

1996.   Toward the Study of Economics at Caesarea Maritima. Pp. 327-45 in

Caesarea Maritima, ed. A. Raban and K. G. Holum. DMOA 21. Leiden: E. J. Brill.

1997. Resurrecting a Dead Tell: Tell el-Hesi. Seminar presented at the W. F. Albright Institute of Archaeological Research, Jerusalem.

Blizzard, R. B., Jr.

1973-74. Intensive Systematic Surface Collection at Livingston's Proposed Site for Biblical Ai. *Westminster Theological Journal* 36:221-30.

Bloch-Smith, E.

1992. *Judahite Burial Practices and Beliefs about the Dead.* JSOTSup 123. JSOT/ASOR Monograph Series 7. Sheffield: JSOT Press.

Böhl, F. M. T.

1960?. The Excavations of Shechem. In Horn, 1960?. = E.T. of *Die Ausgrabung von Sichem.* Ziest: G. J. A. Ruys, 1927.

Boling, R. G.

1963. "And who is Š-K-M?" (Judges XI 28). *VT* 13:479-82.

Boraas, R. S.

1986. Iron IA Ceramics at Tell Balatah. Pp. 249-64 in *The Archaeology of Jordan and Other Studies,* ed. L. T. Geraty and L. T. Herr. Berrien Springs: Andrews University Press.

Borée, W.

1930. *Die alten Orstnamen Palastinas.* Leipzig: Eduard Pfeiffer.

Bornstein, A.

1993. Precious Things of Heaven — Ancient Agriculture in Samaria. Vol. 3, pp. 87-115 in *Judea and Samaria Research Studies,* ed. Z. H. Erlich and Y. Eshel. Kedumim-Ariel: The College of Judea and Samaria Research Institute.

Borowski, O.

1987. *Agriculture in Iron Age Israel.* Winona Lake: Eisenbrauns.

Bradford, M. G., and Kent, W. A.

1977. *Human Geography.* Oxford: Oxford University Press.

Braemer, C.

1987. Occupation du sol dans la région de Jérash aux périodes du Bronze Récent et du Fer. *Studies in the History and Archaeology of Jordan* 4:191-98.

Brandfon, F. R.

1987. Kinship, Culture, and "Longue Durée." *JSOT* 39:30-38.

Brandl, B.
1993.   Scarabs and Other Glyptic Finds. Pp. 203-22 in Finkelstein, Bunimovitz, and Lederman, 1993.

Briend, J.
1990.   Israël et les Gabaonites. Pp. 121-82 in Laperrousaz, 1990.

Briese, C.
1985.   Früheisenzeitliche Bemalte Phönizische Kannen von Fundplätzen der Levanteküste. *Hamburger Beiträge zur Archaeologie* 12:7-118.

Broadhurst, C.
1989.   An Artistic Interpretation of Seti I's War Reliefs. *JEA* 75:229-34.

Brown, J. A.
1981.   The Search for Rank in Prehistoric Burials. Pp. 25-37 in *The Archaeology of Death*, ed. R. Chapman, I. Kinnes, and K. Randsborg. New Directions in Archaeology. Cambridge: Cambridge University Press.

Brug, J. F.
1985.   *A Literary and Archaeological Study of the Philistines.* BARInt 265. Oxford: British Archaeological Reports.

Brumfiel, E.
1976.   Regional Growth in the Eastern Valley of Mexico. Pp. 234-49 in *The Early Mesoamerican Village*, ed. K. Flannery. New York: Academic Press.
1992.   Distinguished Lecture in Archeology: Breaking and Entering the Ecosystem. *American Anthropologist* 94:551-67.

Brumfiel, E. M., and Earle, T. K.
1987.   Specialization, Exchange, and Complex Societies. Pp. 1-9 in Brumfiel and Earle, 1987.

Brumfiel, E. M., and Earle, T. K., eds.
1987.   *Specialization, Exchange, and Complex Societies.* Cambridge: Cambridge University Press.

Buccellati, G.
1988.   Archaeology and Biblical Archaeology. Vol. 3, pp. 125-36 in Shaath, 1985-88.

Bull, R. J.
1960.   A Re-examination of the Shechem Temple. *BA* 23:110-19.

Bull, R. J., and Campbell, E. F., Jr.
1968.   The Sixth Campaign at Balatah (Shechem). *BASOR* 190:2-41.

Bunimovitz, S.
1990.   Problems in the "Ethnic" Identification of the Philistine Material Culture. *TA* 17:210-22.

1993.   Area C. Pp. 15-34 in Finkelstein, Bunimovitz, and Lederman, 1993.

1994.   Socio-Political Transformations in the Central Hill Country in the Late Bronze-Iron I Transition. Pp. 179-202 in Finkelstein and Na'aman, 1994.

Bunimovitz, S., and Finkelstein, I.

1993.   Pottery. Pp. 81-196 in Finkelstein, Bunimovitz, and Lederman, 1993.

Cahill, J. M., Tarler, D., and Lipton (Lipovich), G.

1989.   Tell el-Hammeh in the 10th Century BCE. *Qadmoniot* 22:33-38.

Callaway, J. A.

1964.   Excavations at Ai (et-Tell). *ASOR Newsletter* 1964-65(1):3-8.

1965a.   Ai. *RB* 72:409-15.

1965b.   The 1964 'Ai Excavations. *BASOR* 178:13-40.

1966.   The 1966 'Ai Excavations. *ASOR Newsletter* 1966-67(2):2-4.

1968a.   Evidence on the Conquest of 'Ai. *JBL* 87:312-20.

1968b.   The 1968 'Ai Excavations. *ASOR Newsletter* 1968-89(5):1-6.

1969a.   The Significance of the Iron Age Village at 'Ai. Vol. 1, pp. 56-61 in *Proceedings of the Fifth World Congress of Jewish Studies,* ed. P. Peli. Jerusalem: R. H. HaCohen.

1969b.   The 1966 'Ai Excavations. *BASOR* 196:2-16.

1969c.   The 1969 'Ai Excavations. *ASOR Newsletter* 1969-70(2):1-5

1970a.   The 1968-1969 'Ai Excavations. *BASOR* 198:7-31.

1970b.   Khirbet Raddanah. *IEJ* 20:230-32.

1970c.   The 1968 'Ai Excavations. *PEQ* 102:42-44.

1973.   The Date of the Raddanah Inscription. Paper presented at the Society for Biblical Literature Annual Meeting.

1974.   Khirbet Raddana. *RB* 81:91-94.

1976.   Excavating 'Ai: 1964-1972. *BA* 39:18-30.

1985a.   A New Perspective on the Hill Country Settlement of Canaan in Iron Age I. Pp. 31-49 in *Palestine in the Bronze and Iron Ages,* ed. J. N. Tubb. University of London Institute of Archaeology Occasional Publications 11. London: University of London Press.

1985b.   Response. Pp. 72-78 in Amitai, 1985.

Callaway, J. A., ed.

n.d.   *Village Life at Ai (et-Tell) and Raddanah in Iron Age I.* = Denyer, 1973 and other essays. Unpublished draft.

Callaway, J. A., and Cooley, R. E.

         A Salvage Excavation at Raddana, in Bireh. *BASOR* 201:9-19.

Camili, E. L., and Ebert, J. F.

1992.   Artifact Reuse and Recycling in Continuous Surface Distributions and

Implications for Interpreting Land Use Patterns. Pp. 113-36 in Rossignol and Wandsnider, 1992.

Caminos, R. A.

1954. *Late Egyptian Miscellanies.* Oxford: Oxford University Press.

Campbell, E. F.

1966. The 1966 Shechem Expedition. *ASOR Newsletter* 1966-67(2):5-10.

1983. Judges 9 and Biblical Archaeology. Pp. 263-71 in *The Word of the Lord Shall Go Forth,* ed. C. L. Meyers and M. O'Connor. Winona Lake: Eisenbrauns.

1991. *Shechem II: Portrait of a Hill Country Valley.* ASOR Archaeological Reports 2. Atlanta: Scholars Press.

1993. Developments in the Excavation and Reexcavation of Shechem/Tell Balatah. Pp. 598-605 in *Biblical Archaeology Today 1990,* ed. A. Biran and J. Aviram. Jerusalem: Israel Exploration Society.

Campbell, E. F., and Wright, G. E.

1965. Sichem. *RB* 72:415-22.

Canaan, T.

1933. The Palestinian Arab House. *JPOS* 13:1-83.

Carr, C.

1991. Left in the Dust: Contextual Information in Model-Focused Archaeology. Pp. 221-56 in Kroll and Price, 1991.

Carter, C. E., and Meyers, C. L., eds.

1996. *Community, Identity, and Ideology.* Sources for Biblical and Theological Study 6. Winona Lake: Eisenbrauns.

Castri, F. di, Goodall, D. W., and Specht, R. L., eds.

1981. *Mediterranean-Type Shrublands.* Ecosystems of the World 11. Amsterdam: Elsevier Scientific Publishing Company.

Castri, F. di, and Mooney, H. A., eds.

1973. *Mediterranean-Type Ecosystems.* Ecological Studies 7. Berlin: Springer.

Cazelles, H.

1993. Clans, état monarchique, et tribus. Pp. 77-92 in *Understanding Poets and Prophets,* ed. A. G. Auld. JSOTSup 152. Sheffield: Sheffield Academic Press.

Chaney, M. L.

1986. Systemic Study of the Israelite Monarchy. *Semeia* 37:53-76.

Chartier, R.

1982. Intellectual History of Sociocultural History? Pp. 13-46 in *Modern Euro-*

pean Intellectual History, ed. D. LaCapra and S. L. Kaplan. Ithaca, NY: Cornell University Press.

Christaller, W.

1966. *Central Places in Southern Germany.* Englewood Cliffs, NJ: Prentice-Hall.

Cliff, A. D., Martin, R. L., and Ord, J. K.

1974. Evaluating the Friction of Distance Parameter in Gravity Models. *Regional Studies* 8:281-86.

Conkey, M. W., and Hastorf, C. A., eds.

1990. *The Uses of Style in Archaeology.* New Directions in Archaeology. Cambridge: Cambridge University Press.

Coogan, M.

1987. Of Cults and Cultures. *PEQ* 119:1-8.

Cooke, F. T.

1925. The Site of Kirjath-Jearim. *AASOR* 5:105-20.

Cooley, R. E.

1975. Four Seasons of Excavations at Khirbet Raddana. *Near East Archaeological Society Bulletin* n.s. 5:5-20.

1997a. Ai. *Oxford Encyclopaedia of the Ancient Near East* 1:32-33.

1997b. Radannah, Khirbet. *Oxford Encyclopaedia of the Ancient Near East* 4:401-2.

Cooley, R. E., and Pratico, G. D.

1994. Gathered to His People. Pp. 70-92 in *Scripture and Other Artifacts,* ed. M. D. Coogan et al. Louisville: Westminster/John Knox.

1995. Tell Dothan: The Western Cemetery. Pp. 147-50 in *Preliminary Excavation Reports,* ed. W. G. Dever. AASOR 52. Baltimore: ASOR Press.

Couturier, G.

1989. Débora: une autorité politico-religieuse aux origines d'Israël. *Studies in Religion/Sciences religieuses* 18:213-28.

Creamer, W., and Haas, J.

1985. Tribe vs. Chiefdom in Lower Central America. *American Antiquity* 50:738-54.

Cross, F. M., ed.

1979. *Symposia.* Zion Research Foundation Occasional Publications 1-2. Cambridge, MA: American Schools of Oriental Research.

Cross, F. M., and Freedman, D. N.

1971. An Inscribed Jar Handle from Raddanah. *BASOR* 201:19-22.

Crumley, C. R.

1979.   Three Locational Models. *Advances in Archaeological Method and Theory* 2:141-73.

Crüsemann, F.

1978.   *Der Widerstand gegen das Konigtum.* Wissenschaftliche Monographien zum Alten und Neuen Testament 49. Neukirchen-Vluyn: Neukirchener.

Curry, L., Griffith, D. A., and Sheppard, E. S.

1975.   Those Gravity Parameters Again. *Regional Studies* 9:289-96.

Dacey, M. F.

1966.   Population of Places in a Central Place Hierarchy. *Journal of Regional Science* 6:27-33.

Dan, J.

1988.   The Soils of the Land of Israel. Pp. 95-128 in *The Zoogeography of Israel,* ed. Y. Yom-Tov and E. Tchernov. Monographiae Biologicae 62. Dordrecht: Dr. W. Junk.

Dar, S.

1986.   *Landscape and Pattern.* 2 vols. BARInt 308. Oxford: British Archaeological Reports.

Darnton, R.

1986.   The Symbolic Element in History. *Journal of Modern History* 58:218-34.

1990.   *The Kiss of Lamourette.* New York: W. W. Norton.

Davies, P. R.

1992.   *In Search of Ancient Israel.* JSOTSup 148. Sheffield: Sheffield Academic Press.

Dearman, J. A.

1992a.   *Religion and Culture in Ancient Israel.* Peabody, MA: Hendrickson.

1992b.   Settlement Patterns and the Beginning of the Iron Age in Moab. Pp. 65-76 in Bienkowski, 1992.

Debo, A.

1934.   *The Rise and Fall of the Chocktaw Republic.* Norman, OK: University of Oklahoma Press.

Denyer, D.

1973.   A Conical Seal from Khirbet Raddanah. Unpublished term paper for Southern Baptist Theological Seminary, Louisville.

Denzin, N. K., and Lincoln, Y. S., eds.

1994.   *Handbook of Qualitative Research.* Thousand Oaks, CA: SAGE Publications.

Bibliography

Derrida, J.

1970.   Structure, Sign, and Play in the Discourse of Human Sciences. Pp. 247-72 in *Structuralist Controversy,* ed. R. Macksey and E. Donato. Baltimore. Johns Hopkins University Press. Repr. 1972.

1981.   *Positions.* Trans. A. Bass. Chicago: University of Chicago Press.

Dever, W. G.

1971.   Archaeological Methods and Results. *Orientalia* 40:459-71. = Review of Albright and Kelso, 1968.

1972.   Middle Bronze Age I Cemeteries at Mirzbaneh and ʿAin-Samiya. *IEJ* 22:93-110.

1973.   Excavations at Shechem at Mt. Gerizim. Pp. 8-9 in Aviram, 1973.

1986.   *Gezer IV.* Annual of the Nelson Glueck School of Biblical Archaeology 4. Jerusalem: Hebrew Union College.

1987.   The Contribution of Archaeology to the Study of Canaanite and Early Is-raelite Religion. Pp. 209-48 in *Ancient Israelite Religion,* ed. P. D. Miller Jr., P. D. Hanson, and S. B. McBride. Philadelphia: Fortress.

1991a.   Archaeology and Israelite Origins. *BASOR* 279:89-96.

1992a.   Archaeological Data on the Israelite Settlement. *BASOR* 284:77-90.

1992b.   The Late Bronze–Early Iron I Horizon in Syria-Palestine. Pp. 99-110 in Ward and Joukowsky, 1992.

1992c.   How to Tell a Canaanite from an Israelite. Pp. 26-61 in *The Rise of Ancient Israel,* ed. H. Shanks. Washington: Biblical Archaeology Society.

1992d.   Unresolved Issues in the Early History of Israel. Pp. 195-209 in *The Bible and the Politics of Exegesis,* ed. P. Day. Cleveland: Pilgrim.

1993a.   Biblical Archaeology: Death and Rebirth. Pp. 706-22 in *Biblical Archaeol-ogy Today 1990,* ed. A. Biran and J. Aviram. Jerusalem: Israel Explora-tion Society.

1993b.   Cultural Continuity, Ethnicity in the Archaeological Record, and the Question of Israelite Origins. *EI* 24:22*-33*.

1994.   Archaeology, Texts, and History-Writing. Pp. 105-18 in *Uncovering An-cient Stones,* ed. L. M. Hopfe. Winona Lake: Eisenbrauns.

1995b.   "Will the Real Israel Please Stand Up?" Archaeology and Israelite Histori-ography. Part 1. *BASOR* 297:61-80.

1996.   Archaeology and the Current Crisis in Israelite Historiography. *EI* 25:18*-27*.

1997a.   Ain es-Samiyeh. *Oxford Encyclopaedia of the Ancient Near East* 1:35-36.

1997b.   Bethel. *Oxford Encyclopaedia of the Ancient Near East* 1:300-301.

1997c.   Archaeology, Urbanism, and the Rise of the Israelite State. Pp. 172-93 in *Urbanism in Antiquity,* ed. W. E. Aufrecht, N. A. Mirau, and S. W. Gauley. JSOTSup 244. Sheffield: Sheffield Academic Press.

1997d.   Philology, Theology, and Archaeology. Pp. 290-310 in Silberman and Small, 1997.

Dewar, R. E., and McBride, K. A.

1992.   Remnant Settlement Patterns. Pp. 227-56 in Rossignol and Wandsnider, 1992.

Dewar, R. E., and Wright, H. T., III

1993.   The Cultural History of Madagascar. *Journal of World Prehistory* 7:417-66.

Donner, H.

1995.   *Geschichte Volkes Israel und seiner Nachbarn in Grundzügen.* Vol. 1. Ergänzungsreihe/Grundrisse zum ATD 4/1. Gottingen: Vandenhoeck & Ruprecht.

Dotan, A.

1981.   A New Light on the Izbet Sartah Ostracon. *TA* 8:160-72.

Dothan, T.

1989.   The Arrival of the Sea Peoples. Pp. 1-14 in *Recent Excavations in Israel,* ed. S. Gitin and W. G. Dever. AASOR 49. Winona Lake, IN: American Schools of Oriental Research.

1990.   Ekron of the Philistines, Part I: Where They Came From, How They Settled Down and the Places They Worshiped In. *BAR* 16(1):26-36.

Dothan, T., and Gitin, S.

1993.   Miqne, Tel (Ekron). *The New Encyclopaedia of Archaeological Excavations in the Holy Land* 3:1051-59.

Dowden, K.

1992.   *The Uses of Greek Mythology.* Approaching the Ancient World 1. London: Routledge.

Drennan, R. D.

1991.   Pre-Hispanic Chiefdom Trajectories in Mesoamerica, Central America, and Northern South America. Pp. 263-87 in Earle, 1991.

Drennan, R. D., and Uribe, C. A., eds.

1987.   *Chiefdoms in the Americas.* Lanham, MD: University Press of America.

Drucker, P.

1951.   *The Northern and Central Nootkan Tribes.* Bureau of American Ethnology Bulletin 144. Washington, DC: Bureau of American Ethnology.

Earle, T. K.

1977.   A Reappraisal of Redistribution. Pp. 213-32 in *Exchange Systems in Prehistory,* ed. T. K. Earle and J. E. Ericson. New York: Academic Press.

1978.   *Economic and Social Organization of a Complex Chiefdom.* University of

Michigan Museum of Anthropology Anthropological Papers 63. Ann Arbor.

1980. A Model of Subsistence Change. Pp. 1-30 in *Modeling Change in Prehistoric Subsistence Economies*, ed. T. K. Earle and A. L. Christenson. Studies in Archaeology 38. New York: Academic Press.

1987a. Specialization and the Production of Wealth. Pp. 64-75 in Brumfiel and Earle, eds., 1987.

1987b. Chiefdoms in Archaeological and Ethnohistorical Perspective. *Annual Review of Anthropology* 16:278-308.

1990. Style and Iconography as Legitimization in Complex Chiefdoms. Pp. 73-81 in Conkey and Hastorf, 1990.

1991a. The Evolution of Chiefdoms. Pp. 1-15 in Earle, ed., 1991.

1991b. Property Rights and the Evolution of Chiefdoms. Pp. 71-99 in Earle, ed., 1991.

Earle, T. K., ed.

1991. *Chiefdoms*, ed. Cambridge: Cambridge University Press.

Edelman, D. V.

1996. Saul ben Kish in History and Tradition. Pp. 142-60 in Fritz and Davies, 1996.

Edelman, D. V., ed.

1991a. *The Fabric of History.* JSOTSup 127. Sheffield: Sheffield Academic Press.

1991b. *Toward a Consensus on the Emergence of Israel in Canaan. = SJOT* 1991(2).

1995. *You Shall Not Abhor an Edomite, for He Is Your Brother.* Archaeological and Biblical Studies 3. Atlanta: Scholars Press.

Elliger, K.

1930. Die Grenze zwischen Ephraim und Manasse. *ZDPV* 53:18-309.

1937. Tappuah. *Palästina Jahrbuch* 33:7-22.

1938. Neues über die Grenze zwischen Ephraim und Manasse. *JPOS* 18:7-16.

1970. Michmethat. Pp. 91-100 in *Archäologie und Altes Testament*, ed. A. Kuschke and E. Kutsch. Tübingen: J. C. B. Mohr.

Eran, A.

1994. Weights from Excavations 1981-1984 at Shiloh. *ZDPV* 110:151-57.

Fecht, G., and Hornung, E.

1983. Die Israelstele des Merneptah. Pp. 224-33 in *Fontes atque Pontes*, ed. M. Görg. Ägypten und Altes Testament 5. Wiesbaden: Otto Harrassowitz.

Feinman, G. M.

1991. Demography, Surplus, and Inequality. Pp. 229-62 in Earle, ed., 1991.

Feinman, G. M., and Neitzel, J.

1984. Too Many Types. *Advances in Archaeological Method and Theory* 7:39-102.

Finkelstein, I.

1978. *Rural Settlement in the Foothills and in the Yarqon Basin in the Israelite-Hellenistic Periods.* M.A. thesis, Tel Aviv.

1981. Israelite and Hellenistic Farms in the Foothills and in the Yarkon Basin. *EI* 15:331-48. In Hebrew.

1983a. *The 'Izbet Sartah Excavations and the Israelite Settlement in the Hill Country.* Diss., Tel Aviv. In Hebrew.

1983b. Tel Shiloh. *ESI* 2:95-100.

1984. The Israelite Population in the Iron Age I. *Cathedra* 32:3-23. In Hebrew.

1985a. *Izbet Sartah.* BARInt 299. Oxford: British Archaeological Reports.

1985b. ed-Dawara, Khirbet. *ESI* 4:20.

1985c. Response. Pp. 80-83 in Amitai, 1985.

1986. *The Archaeology of the Period of the Settlement and Judges.* Tel-Aviv: Ha-Kibbutz Ha-Meuchad Publishing House. In Hebrew.

1987. Khirbet Ed-Dawara. *ESI* 6:48.

1988a. *The Archaeology of the Israelite Settlement.* Jerusalem: Israel Exploration Society.

1988b. Searching for Israelite Origins. *BAR* 14(5):34-45.

1988c. Khirbet ed-Dawwar [*sic*], 1985-86. *IEJ* 38:79-80.

1988-89. The Land of Ephraim Survey 1980-87, Preliminary Report. *TA* 15-16: 117-83.

1990a. Excavations at Kh. Ed-Dawwara. *TA* 17:163-209.

1990b. The Emergence of Early Israel. = Review of Lemche, 1985 and other essays. *JAOS* 110:677-86.

1991. The Emergence of Israel in Canaan. Pp. 47-59 in Edelman, 1991b.

1992a. Ephraim (Archaeology). *ABD* 2:551-55. Garden City: Doubleday.

1992b. Izbet Sartah. *ABD* 3:588-59. Garden City: Doubleday.

1992c. Seilun, Khirbet. *ABD* 5:1069-72. Garden City: Doubleday.

1992d. Pastoralism in the Highlands of Canaan in the Third and Second Millennia B.C.E. Pp. 133-42 in Bar-Yosef and Khazanov, 1992.

1993a. The Sociopolitical Organization of the Central Hill Country in the Second Millennium B.C.E. Pp. 110-31 in *Biblical Archaeology Today 1990 Supplement,* ed. A. Biran and J. Aviram. Jerusalem: Israel Exploration Society.

1993b. Excavations [*sic*] Results in Areas E, G, J, K, L, and M. Pp. 65-80 in Finkelstein, Bunimovitz, and Lederman, 1993.

1993c. The History and Archaeology of Shiloh from the Middle Bronze Age II to the Iron Age II. Pp. 371-93 in Finkelstein, Bunimovitz, and Lederman, 1993.

1994. The Emergence of Israel. Pp. 150-78 in Finkelstein and Naʿaman, 1994.

1995a. The Great Transformation. Pp. 349-65 in Levy, 1995.

1995b. The Date of the Settlement of the Philistines in Canaan. *TA* 22:213-39.

1995c. *Living on the Fringe.* Monographs in Mediterranean Archaeology 6. Sheffield: Sheffield Academic Press.

1996a. The Archaeology of the United Monarchy. *Levant* 28:177-87.

1996b. Ethnicity and Origin of the Iron I Settlers in the Highlands of Canaan. *BA* 59:198-212.

1996c. The Emergence of the Monarchy in Israel. Pp. 377-403 in Carter and Meyers, 1996.

1996d. The Settlement History of the Transjordanian Plateau in the Light of Survey Data. *EI* 25:244-51.

1996e. The Stratigraphy and Chronology of Megiddo and Beth-shean in the 12th-11th Centuries B.C.E. *TA* 23:170-84.

1996f. The Philistine Countryside. *IEJ* 46:225-42.

1997a. Pots and People Revisited. Pp. 216-38 in Silberman and Small, 1997.

1997b. Toward a New Periodization and Nomenclature of the Archaeology of the Southern Levant. Pp. 103-24 in *The Study of the Ancient Near East in the 21st Century,* ed. J. S. Cooper and G. M. Schwartz. Winona Lake: Eisenbrauns.

Finkelstein, I., Bunimovitz, S., and Lederman, Z. eds.

1993. *Shiloh: The Archaeology of a Biblical Site.* Tel Aviv: Institute of Archaeology.

Finkelstein, I., Bunimovitz, S., Lederman, Z., Hellwing, S., and Sadeh, M.

1985. Excavations at Shiloh. *TA* 12:123-80.

Finkelstein, I., Lederman, Z., and Bunimovitz, S.

1997. *Highlands of Many Cultures.* 2 vols. Tel Aviv University Institute of Archaeology Monographs 15. Tel Aviv: Tel Aviv University Press.

Finkelstein, I., and Naʿaman, N., eds.

1994. *From Nomadism to Monarchy.* Washington: Biblical Archaeology Society.

Firth, R.

1950. *Primitive Polynesian Economy.* New York: Humanities Press.

Flanagan, J.

1981a. Chiefs in Israel. *JSOT* 20:47-73.

1981b. Emergence of Empire in the Early Iron Age. *ASOR Newsletter* 1981.2:8-12

1987. Beyond Space-Time Systemics. *JSOT* 39:22-99.

1988. *David's Social Drama.* JSOTSup 129. Sheffield: JSOT Press.

1995. Finding the Arrow of Time. *Currents in Research: Biblical Studies* 3:37-62.

Flannery, K.

1972. The Cultural Evolution of Civilization. *Annual Review of Ecology and Systematics.* 3:399-425.

Flannery, K., and Marcus, J.

1993. Cognitive Archaeology. Pp. 260-67 in Renfrew, 1993.

Foley, J. M.

1994. Folklore and Oral Tradition. Paper presented at the 1994 Annual Meeting of the Society of Biblical Literature, Chicago.

Free, J.

1962. The Seventh Season of Excavation at Dothan. *ADAJ* 6/7:117-20.

Frick, F.

1979. *Religion and Sociopolitical Structure in Early Israel.* SBLSP 17:233-53. Missoula, MT: Scholars Press. = Pp. 448-70 in Carter and Meyers, 1996.

1985. *The Formation of the State in Ancient Israel.* The Social World of Biblical Antiquity 4. Sheffield: Almond/JSOT Press.

1987. Israelite State Formation in Iron I. Pp. 245-58 in *Archaeology and Biblical Interpretation,* ed. L. G. Perdue, L. E. Toombs, and G. L. Johnson. Atlanta: John Knox.

Friedman, J.

1975. Tribes, States, and Transformations. Pp. 161-202 in *Marxist Analyses in Social Anthropology,* ed. M. Bloch. ASA Studies 3. London: Malaby.

Fritz, J. M., and Plog, F. T.

1970. The Nature of Archaeological Explanation. *American Antiquity* 35:105-12.

Fritz, V.

1982. Abimelech und Sichem in Jdc. IX. *VT* 32:129-44. Repr. as pp. 187-204 in Fritz, 1997b.

1987. Conquest or Settlement? *BA* 50:84-100.

1990. Die Landnahme der Israelitischen Stämme in Kanaan. *ZDPV* 106:63-77. Repr. as pp. 143-64 in Fritz, 1997b.

1995. *The City in Ancient Israel.* Biblical Seminar 29. Sheffield: Sheffield Academic Press.

1996. *Die Entstehung Israels im 12. und 11. Jh. v. Chr.* Biblische Enzyklopädie 2. Stuttgart: Kohlhammer.

1997a. Cities of the Bronze and Iron Ages. *Oxford Encyclopaedia of the Ancient Near East* 2:19-25.

1997b. *Studien zur Literatur und Geschichte des alten Israel.* Stuttgarter Biblische Aufsatzbände 22. Stuttgart: Verlag Katholisches Bibelwerk.

Bibliography

Fritz, V., and Davies, P. R., eds.

1996. *The Origins of the Ancient Israelite States.* JSOTSup 228. Sheffield: Sheffield Academic Press.

Frye, N.

1983. *The Great Code.* New York: Harcourt Brace Jovanovich.

Gadamer, H.-G.

1987. The Problem of Historical Consciousness. In *Interpretive Social Science,* ed. Rabinow and Sullivan. Berkeley: University of California Press.

Gal, Z.

1994. Iron I in Lower Galilee and the Margins of the Jezreel Valley. Pp. 35-46 in Finkelstein and Na'aman, 1994.

Galling, K.

1965. Kritische Bemerkungen zur Ausgrabung von el-Jib. *Bibliotheca Orientalis* 22:242-45.

Garbini, G.

1978. Sull'Alfabetario di Izbet Sarta. *OrAn* 17:287-95.

Garstang, J.

1933. Jericho. *Liverpool Annals of Archaeology and Anthropology* 20:3-42.

Gelb, I. J.

1980. Comparative Method in the Study of the Society and Economy of the Ancient Near East. *Rocznik Orientalistyczny* 41:28-36.

Geus, C. H. J. de

1976. *The Tribes of Israel.* Amsterdam: Van Gorcum.

Gibson, D. B., and Geselowitz, M. N.

1988. The Evolution of Complex Society in Late Prehistoric Europe. Pp. 3-37 in *Tribe and Polity in Late Prehistoric Europe,* ed. D. B. Gibson and M. N. Geselowitz. New York: Plenum.

Gibson, S.

1995. *Landscape Archaeology and Ancient Agricultural Field Systems in Palestine.* Diss. University College, London.

1996. Tell el-Ful and the Results of the Northeast Jerusalem Survey. Pp. 9*-23* in *New Studies on Jerusalem,* ed. A. Faust. Ramat Gan: Bar Ilan University Press.

Gilmour, G. H.

1995. *The Archaeology of Cult in the Southern Levant in the Early Iron Age.* Diss., Oxford.

Ginzburg, C.

1989.   *Clues, Myths, and the Historical Method.* Baltimore: Johns Hopkins University Press.

Gitin, S., and Dothan, T.

1987.   The Rise and Fall of Ekron of the Philistines. *BA* 50:197-222.

Giveon, R.

1971.   *Les Bedouins Shosou des documents égyptiens.* Documenta et Monumenta Orientis Antiqui 18. Leiden: E. J. Brill.

Glass, J., Goren, Y., Bunimovitz, S., and Finkelstein, I.

1993.   Petrographic Analysis of Middle Bronze Age III, Late Bronze Age and Iron Age I Ceramic Assemblages. Pp. 271-77 in Finkelstein, Bunimovitz, and Lederman, 1993.

Glock, A. E.

1993.   Taanach. *New Encyclopaedia of Archaeological Excavations of the Holy Land* 4:1428-33.

Goedicke, H.

1977.   The Waning of the Ramessides. *Journal of the Society for the Study of Egyptian Antiquities* 8:73-80.

Goffer, Z.

1996.   *Elsevier's Dictionary of Archaeological Materials and Archaeometry.* Amsterdam: Elsevier.

Goldstein, L. G.

1980.   *Mississippian Mortuary Practices.* Northwestern University Archaeological Scientific Papers 4. Evanston: Northwestern University Press.

Gooding, D. W.

1982.   The Composition of the Book of Judges. *EI* 16:70*-79*.

Gottwald, N. K.

1993.   Recent Studies of the Social World of Premonarchic Israel. *Currents in Research: Biblical Studies* 1:163-89.

Gould, R. A.

1980.   *Living Archaeology.* New Studies in Archaeology 4. Cambridge: Cambridge University Press.

Graham, J. A.

1981.   New Light on the Fortress; and Iron I at Tell el-Ful. Pp. 23-38 in N. Lapp, 1981.

Green, S. W., and Perlman, S. M., eds.

1985.   *The Archaeology of Frontiers and Boundaries.* New York: Academic Press.

Bibliography

Gregg, S. A., Kintigh, K. W., and Whallon, R.
1991.   Linking Ethnoarchaeological Interpretation and Archaeological Data. Pp. 149-96 in Kroll and Price, 1991.

Grosby, S.
1997.   Borders, Territory, and Nationality in the Ancient Near East and Armenia. *JESHO* 40:1-29.

Gunneweg, J., Asaro, F., Michel, H. V., and Perlman, I.
1994.   Interregional Contacts between Tell en-Nasbeh and Littoral Philistine Centers in Canaan during Early Iron Age I. *Archaeometry* 36:227-40.

Guthe, H.
1915.   Beiträge zur Orstkunde Palästinas 13: Naara, Neara. *ZDPV* 38:41-49.

Haas, J.
1982.   *The Evolution of the Prehistoric State.* New York: Columbia University Press.

Hagget, P., Cliff, A. R., and Frey, A.
1977.   *Locational Methods.* Vol. 2 of *Locational Analysis in Human Geography.* London: Edward Arnold.

Hallote, R.
1997.   Gibeon. *Oxford Encyclopaedia of the Ancient Near East* 2:403-4.

Halpern, B.
1983.   *The Emergence of Israel in Canaan.* Chico, CA: Scholars Press.

Harel, M.
1984.   *Journeys and Campaigns in Ancient Times.* Jerusalem: Israel Ministry of Defense. In Hebrew.

Hart, S.
1992.   Iron Age Settlement in the Land of Edom. Pp. 93-98 in Bienkowski, 1992.

Hauer, C., Jr.
1987.   Anthropology in Historiography. *JSOT* 39:15-21.

Hecke, K.-H.
1985.   *Juda und Israel: Untersuchungen zur Geschichte Israels in vor- und frühstaatlicher Zeit.* Forschung zur Bible 52. Wurzburg: Echter Verlag.

Hedeager, L.
1992.   *Iron-Age Societies.* Trans. J. Hines. Social Archaeology Series 3. Oxford: Blackwell.

Hellwing, S., Sadeh, M., and Kishon, V.
1993.   Faunal Remains. Pp. 309-50 in Finkelstein, Bunimovitz, and Lederman, 1993.

Helms, M. W.

1976.   Competition, Power, and Succession to Office in Pre-Columbian Panama. Pp. 25-35 in *Frontier Adaptations in Lower Central America,* ed. M. W. Helms and F. O. Loveland. Philadelphia: ISHI.

1979.   *Ancient Panama.* Austin: University of Texas.

1980.   Succession to High Office in Pre-Columbian, Circum-Caribbean Chiefdoms. *Man* 15:718-31.

1988.   *Ulysses' Sail.* Princeton: Princeton University Press.

1993.   *Craft and the Kingly Ideal.* Austin, TX: University of Texas Press.

Herion, G. A.

1986.   The Impact of Modern and Social Science Assumptions on the Reconstruction of Israelite History. *JSOT* 34:3-33.

Herrmann, S.

1985.   Basic Factors of Israelite Settlement in Canaan. Pp. 47-53 in Amitai, 1985.

Hess, R. S.

1993.   Early Israel in Canaan. *PEQ* 125:125-42.

Hesse, B.

1990.   Pig Lovers and Pig Haters. *Journal of Ethnobiology* 10:195-225.

1995.   Animal Husbandry and Human Diet in the Ancient Near East. *CANE* 1:203-22.

Hesse, B., and Rosen, A. M.

1988.   The Detection of Chronological Mixing in Samples from Stratified Archaeological Sites. Pp. 117-29 in *Recent Developments in Environmental Analysis in Old and New World Archaeology,* ed. R. E. Webb. BARInt 416. Oxford: British Archaeological Reports.

Higgenbotham, C.

1996.   Elite Emulation and Egyptian Governance in Ramesside Canaan. *TA* 23:154-69.

Hodder, I.

1982.   *Symbols in Action.* Cambridge: Cambridge University Press.

1985.   Boundaries as Strategies. Pp. 141-61 in Green and Perlman, 1985.

1987a.   The Contextual Analysis of Symbolic Meanings. Pp. 1-10 in *The Archaeology of Contextual Meanings,* ed. I. Hodder. New Directions in Archaeology. Cambridge: Cambridge University Press.

1989.   This Is Not an Article about Material Culture as Text. *Journal of Anthropological Archaeology* 8:250-69.

1990.   Style as Historical Quality. Pp. 44-51 in Conkey and Hastorf, 1990.

1991.   *Reading the Past.* 2nd ed. Cambridge: Cambridge University Press.

1992. *Theory and Practice in Archaeology.* Material Culture 3. New York: Routledge. Repr. 1995.

1993. Social Cognition. Pp. 253-57 in Renfrew, 1993.

1994. The Interpretation of Documents and Material Culture. Pp. 393-402 in Denzin and Lincoln, 1994.

Hodder, I., ed.

1987. *Archaeology as Long-term History.* New Directions in Archaeology. Cambridge: Cambridge University Press.

Hodder, I., and Orton, C.

1976. *Spatial Analysis.* Cambridge: Cambridge University Press.

Horn, S. H.

1962. Scarabs from Shechem. *JNES* 21:1-14.

1964. Shechem: History and Excavations of a Palestinian City. *Jaarbericht van het Vooraziatisch-Egyptisch Genootschap ex Orient Lux* 18:284-306.

1966. Scarabs and Scarab Impressions from Shechem — II. *JNES* 25:48-56.

1968. Objects from Shechem. *Jaarbericht van het Vooraziatisch-Egyptisch Genootschap ex Orient Lux* 20:17-90.

1973. Scarabs and Scarab Impressions from Shechem — III. *JNES* 32:281-89.

Horn, S. H., ed. and trans.

1960?. *Preliminary Reports of the Excavations of Shechem.* Unpublished manuscript in the Shechem Archive, W. F. Albright Institute of Archaeological Research.

Horowitz, A.

1974. Preliminary Palynological Indications as to the Climate of Israel during the Last 6000 Years. *Paleorient* 2:407-14.

Horwitz, L. K.

1986-87. Faunal Remains from the Early Iron Age Site on Mount Ebal. *TA* 13-14:173-89.

1993. Identification of Bone Raw Material Used in Artifact Manufacture. Pp. 263-64 in Finkelstein, Bunimovitz, and Lederman, 1993.

Huddlestun, J. R.

1991. Merneptah's Revenge. Paper presented at the Annual Meeting of the Society of Biblical Literature, Kansas City, 1991.

Hunt, L.

1989. History, Culture, and Text. Pp. 1-40 in *The New Cultural History.* Berkeley: University of California Press.

Hutton, R. R.

1994.   *Charisma and Authority in Israelite Society.* Minneapolis: Augsburg Fortress.

Iakovides, S.

1979.   The Chronology of LHIIIC. *American Journal of Archaeology* 83:454-62.

Ishida, T.

1973.   The Leaders of the Tribal League "Israel" in the Pre-Monarchic Period. *RB* 80:514-30.

Janesick, V. J.

1994.   The Dance of Qualitative Research Design. Pp. 209-19 in Denzin and Lincoln, 1994.

Jarman, M. R., Vita-Finzi, C., and Higgs, E. S.

1972.   Site Catchment Analysis in Archaeology. Pp. 61-66 in *Man, Settlement, and Urbanism,* ed. P. J. Ucko, R. Tringham, and G. W. Dimbleby. London: Gerald Duckworth.

Jaroš, K.

1976.   *Sichem.* OBO 11. Freiburg: Universitatsverlag.

Jaroš, K., and Deckert, B.

1977.   *Studien zur Sichem-Aera.* OBO 11a. Freiburg: Universitatsverlag.

Jenni, E.

1958.   Historisch-topographische Untersuchungen zur Grenze zwischen Ephraim und Manasse. *ZDPV* 74:35-40.

Johnson, A. W., and Earle, T. K.

1987.   *The Evolution of Human Societies.* Stanford: Stanford University Press.

Johnson, G.

1977.   Aspects of Regional Analysis in Archaeology. *Annual Review of Anthropology* 6:479-508.

Kallai (Kleinmann), Z.

1954.   Beeroth. *EI* 3:111-15. In Hebrew.

1956.   Notes on the Topography of Benjamin. *IEJ* 6:180-87.

1958.   The Town Lists of Judah, Simeon, Benjamin, and Dan. *VT* 8:134-60.

1971.   Baal Shalisha and Ephraim. Pp. 191-206 in *Bible and Jewish History,* ed. B. Uffenheimer. Tel Aviv: Tel Aviv University Press. In Hebrew.

1986a.   The Settlement Traditions of Ephraim. *ZDPV* 102:68-74.

1986b.   *Historical Geography of the Bible.* Leiden: E. J. Brill.

1997.   The Twelve-tribe Systems of Israel. *VT* 47:53-90.

Kappus, S.

1968.   Oberflaechenuntersuchungen im mittleren wadi far'a. *ZDPV* 82:74-82.

Keesing, F. M., and Keesing, M. M.

1956.   *Elite Communication in Samoa.* Stanford Anthropological Series 3. Stanford: Stanford University Press.

Kelso, J. L.

1934.   The Kyle Memorial Excavations at Bethel. *Bibliotheca Sacra* 104:415-20.

1955.   The Second Campaign at Bethel. *BASOR* 137:5-10.

1956.   Excavations at Bethel. *BA* 19:36-43.

1958.   The Third Campaign at Bethel. *BASOR* 151:3-8.

1961a.   The Fourth Campaign at Bethel. *BASOR* 164:5-19.

1961b.   Sensational Finds Made at Bethel. *Pittsburgh Seminary Panorama* 1(4):2.

1962.   Béthel. *Bible et Terre Sainte* 47:8-15.

Kempinski, A.

1979.   Hittites in the Bible. *BAR* 5/5:20-45.

Kennedy, B.

1978.   Review of I. Hodder and C. Orton, 1976. *Journal of Historical Geography* 4:99-100.

Kirkpatrick, P.

1988.   *The Old Testament and Folklore Study.* JSOTSup 62. Sheffield: Sheffield Academic Press.

Kislev, M.

1993.   Food Remains. Pp. 354-61 in Finkelstein, Bunimovitz, and Lederman, 1993.

Knauf(-Belleri), E. A.

1992.   The Cultural Impact of Secondary State Foundation. Pp. 47-54 in Bienkowski, 1992.

1995.   Edom: The Social and Economic History. Pp. 93-118 in Edelman, 1995.

1996.   L'"Historiographie Deuteronomiste" existe-t-elle? Pp. 409-18 in *Israel construit son histoire,* ed. A. de Pury, T. Römer, and J.-D. Macchi. Le Monde de la Bible 34. Geneva: Labor et Fides.

Knierim, R.

1969.   Oberflaechenuntersuchungen im Wadi el-Far'a II. *ZDPV* 85:51-62.

Kochavi, M.

1977.   An Ostracon from the Period of the Judges from 'Izbet Tsartah. *TA* 4:1-13.

1985.   The Israelite Settlement in Canaan in the Light of Archaeological Survey. Pp. 54-60 in Amitai, 1985.

Kochavi, M., and Beit-Arieh, I.

1994.   *Map of Rosh Ha-'Ayin.* Archaeological Survey of Israel 78. Jerusalem: Israel Antiquities Authority.

Kochavi, M., and Demsky, A.

1978.   An Israelite Village from the Days of the Judges. *BAR* 4(3):19-21.

Kramer, C., ed.

1979.   *Ethnoarchaeology.* New York: Columbia University Press.

Kristiansen, K.

1978.   The Consumption of Wealth in Bronze Age Denmark. In *New Directions in Scandinavian Archaeology,* ed. K. Kristiansen and C. Paludan-Miller. Copenhagen.

1982.   Formation of Tribal Systems in European History. In *Theory and Explanation in Archaeology,* ed. C. Renfrew, M. Rowlands, and B. Segraves. London.

1991.   Chiefdoms, States, and Systems of Social Evolution. Pp. 16-43 in Earle, 1991.

Kroll, E. M., and Price, T. D., eds.

1991.   *The Interpretation of Archaeological Spatial Patterning.* Interdisciplinary Contributions to Archaeology 4. New York: Plenum.

Kuhrt, A.

1995.   *The Ancient Near East c. 3000-330 B.C.* Vol. 1. Routledge History of the Ancient World 4. London: Routledge.

Kurinsky, S.

1991.   *The Glassmakers.* New York: Hippocrene Books.

Kuschke, A.

1962.   New Contributions to the Historical Topography of Jordan. *ADAJ* 6/7:90-95.

LaBianca, O., and Younker, R.

1994.   Ammonite Social Structure. Paper presented at the 1994 Annual Meeting of the American Schools of Oriental Research, Chicago.

LaCapra, D.

1978.   Review of White, 1990. *Modern Language Notes* 93:1037-43.

1982.   Rethinking Intellectual History. In *Modern European Intellectual History,* ed. D. LaCapra et al. Ithaca: Cornell University Press.

Lamberg-Karlovsky, C. C.

1993.   The Biography of an Object. Pp. 270-92 in Lubar and Kingery, 1993.

Laperrousaz, E.-M., ed.

1990.   *La Protohistoire d'Israël.* Paris: Les Éditions du Cerf.

Lapp, N. L.

1997.   Ful, Tell el-. *Oxford Encyclopaedia of the Ancient Near East* 2:346-47.

Lapp, N. L., ed.

1981.   *The Third Campaign at Tell el-Ful.* AASOR 45. Cambridge, MA: American Schools of Oriental Research.

Lapp, P. W.

1965.   Tell el-Ful. *BA* 28:2-10.

Larsen, C. S.

1995.   Regional Perspectives on Mortuary Analysis. Pp. 247-64 in Beck, 1995.

Lemaire, A.

1985.   Notes d'Epigraphis Nord-Ouest Semitique. *Semitica* 35:13-17.

1990.   Deu origines d'Israël. Pp. 183-292 in Laperrousaz, 1990.

Lemche, N. P.

1977.   The Greek "Amphictyony" — Could It Be a Prototype for the Israelite State in the Period of the Judges? *JSOT* 4:48-59.

1984a.   Israel in the Period of the Judges. *Studia Theologica* 38:1-28.

1984b.   On the Problem of Studying Israelite History. *Biblische Notizen* 24: 94-124.

1985.   *Early Israel.* VTSup 37. Leiden: E. J. Brill.

1988.   *Ancient Israel.* The Biblical Seminar. Sheffield: JSOT Press.

1991a.   The Development of the Israelite Religion in the Light of Recent Studies on the Early History of Israel. Pp. 97-114 in *Congress Volume Leuven 1989,* ed. J. A. Emerton. VTSup 43. Leiden: E. J. Brill.

1991b.   Sociology, Text, and Religion as Key Factors in Understanding the Emergence of Israel in Canaan. Pp. 7-18 in Edelman, 1991b.

1991c.   *The Canaanites and Their Land.* JSOTSup 110. Sheffield: JSOT Press.

1992.   Israel, History of (Premonarchic Period). *ABD* 3:526-45. Garden City: Doubleday.

1993.   City Dwellers or Administrators. Pp. 76-90 in *History and Traditions of Eretz-Israel,* ed. A. Lemaire. VTSup 50. Leiden: E. J. Brill.

1994.   Is It Still Possible to Write a History of Ancient Israel? *SJOT* 8:105-90.

1996a.   From Patronage Society to Patronage Society. Pp. 106-20 in Fritz and Davies, 1996.

1996b.   On the Use of "System Theory," "Macro Theories," and "Evolutionistic Thinking" in Modern Old Testament Research and Biblical Archaeology. Pp. 273-88 in Carter and Meyers, 1996.

1996c.   *Die Vorgeschichte Israels.* Biblische Enzyklopädie 1. Stuttgart: Kohlhammer.

1996d.   Clio Is Also among the Muses! = Review of Whitelam, 1995. *SJOT* 10:88-114.

Lesko, L. H.

1992.   Egypt in the 12th Century B.C. Pp. 151-56 in Ward and Joukowsky, 1992.

Levy, S.

1962.   Tel ʿAmal. *IEJ* 12:147.

Levy, S., and Edelstein, G.

1972.   Cinq Années de Fouilles a Tel ʿAmal. *RB* 79:325-67.

Levy, T. E., ed.

1995.   *The Archaeology of Society in the Holy Land.* London: Leicester University Press.

Licht, J.

1983.   Biblical Historicism. Pp. 107-20 in Tadmor and Weinfeld, 1983.

Liphschitz, N.

1986-87. Paleobotanical Remains from Mount Ebal. *TA* 13-14:190-91.

1987-89. The Carob in Israel. *Israel — People and Land* 5/6:151-54.

Liphschitz, N., Biger, G., and Mendel, Z.

1987-89. Did Aleppo Pine Cover the Mountains of Eretz-Israel in the Past? *Israel — People and Land* 5/6:141-50.

Livingston, D.

1971-72. Traditional Site of Bethel Questioned. *Westminster Theological Journal* 34:39-50.

1990.   The 1987 and 1990 Excavations at Khirbet Nisya, Israel. *Near East Archaeological Society Bulletin* n.s. 35:2-19.

1994.   Further Considerations on the Location of Bethel and el-Bireh. *PEQ* 126:154-59.

Loffreda, S.

1968.   Typological Sequence of Iron Age Rock-Cut Tombs in Palestine. *Liber Annuus* 18:244-87.

London, G.

1987.   A Comparison of Two Lifestyles in Late Second Millennium B.C. *BASOR* 273:37-55.

Long, B. O.

1976.   Recent Field Studies in Oral Literature and Their Bearing on OT Criticism. *VT* 26:187-98.

Long, V. P.

1994.   *The Art of Biblical History.* Foundations of Contemporary Interpretation 5. Grand Rapids: Zondervan.

Lubar, S., and Kingery, W. D., eds.

1993.   *History from Things.* Washington: Smithsonian Institute.

MacDonald, B.

1994.   *Ammon, Moab, and Edom.* Amman: Al Khutba.

Machinist, P. B.

1994.   Outsiders or Insiders: The Biblical View of Emergent Israel and Its Contexts. Pp. 35-60 in *The Other in Jewish Thought and History,* ed. L. J. Silberman and R. L. Cohn. New York: New York University Press.

MacKay, B.

1983.   The Late Bronze and Iron Age Sites of the Wadi el Hasa Survey 1970. Pp. 18-28 in Sawyer and Clines, 1983.

Maisels, C. K.

1990.   *The Emergence of Civilization.* London: Routledge. Repr. 1993.

Malamat, A.

1973.   Tribal Societies. *Archives Européennes de Sociologie* 14:126-36.

n.a.

1975.   Map of Lod. *HA* 54/55:45-46. In Hebrew.

Marcus, J., ed.

1990.   *Debating Oaxaca Archaeology.* University of Michigan Museum of Anthropology Papers 84. Ann Arbor: University of Michigan Museums.

Marquet-Krause, J.

1935.   La Deuxième Campagne de Fouilles á Ay. *Syria* 16:325-45.

Matthews, V. H.

1978.   *Pastoral Nomadism in the Mari Kingdom.* ASOR Dissertation Series 3. Cambridge, MA: American Schools of Oriental Research.

Mayes, A. D. H.

1974.   *Israel in the Period of the Judges.* SBT n.s. 29. London: SCM.

Mazar, A.

1976.   Khirbet Marjame. *IEJ* 26:138-39.

1977.   An Israelite Fortress-City near 'Ain Samiya. *Qadmoniot* 10:111-13.

1982a.   The Bull Site. *BASOR* 247:27-42.

1982b.   Three Israelite Sites in the Hills of Judah and Ephraim. *BA* 45:167-78.

1982c.   A Cultic Site from the Period of the Judges in the Northern Samarian Hills. *EI* 16:135-35. In Hebrew.

1983.   Bronze Bull Found in Israelite "High Place" from the Time of the Judges. *BAR* 9/5:35-40.

1985.   Evidence of Archaeology. Pp. 61-71 in Amitai, 1985.

1990.   *Archaeology of the Land of the Bible.* Anchor Bible Reference Library. Garden City: Doubleday.

1992.   The Fortifications of the Israelite City at Khirbet Marjama in the Hills of Ephraim. *EI* 23:174-93. In Hebrew.

1994a. The Northern Shephelah during the Iron Age. Pp. 247-67 in *Scripture and Other Artifacts,* ed. M. D. Coogan, J. C. Exum, and L. E. Stager. Louisville: Westminster/John Knox.

1994b. Jerusalem and Its Vicinity in Iron Age I. Trans. N. Panitz-Cohen. Pp. 70-91 in Finkelstein and Naʿaman, 1994.

1994c. The 11th Century in the Land of Israel. Pp. 39-57 in *Cyprus in the 11th Century BC,* ed. V. Karageorghis. Nicosia: University of Cyprus Press.

1997a. Bull Site. *Oxford Encyclopaedia of the Ancient Near East* 1:383-84.

1997b. Palestine: Palestine in the Iron Age. *Oxford Encyclopaedia of the Ancient Near East* 4:217-22.

1997c. Iron Age Chronology. *Levant* 29:157-67.

Mazar, A., and Rosen, S.

1982.   A Cultic Site from the Period of the Judges in the Northern Samaria Hills. *EI* 16:135-45. In Hebrew.

Mazar, B.

1954.   Gath and Gittaim. *IEJ* 4:227-35.

1975.   *Cities and Districts in Eretz-Israel.* Jerusalem: Bialik Institute. In Hebrew.

1982.   *Biblical Israel.* Jerusalem: Magnes.

McClellan, T. L.

1975.   *Quantitative Studies in the Iron Age Pottery of Palestine.* 2 vols. Diss., Pennsylvania.

1985.   Town Planning at Tell en-Nasbeh. *ZDPV* 100:53-69.

McCown, C. C.

1947.   Tell en-Nasbeh. *PEFQSt* 1947:145-50.

McCown, C. C., and Wampler, J. C.

1947.   *Tell en-Nasbeh.* 2 vols. Berkeley: The Palestine Institute of the Pacific School of Religion.

McGuire, R. H., and Paynter, R., eds.

1991.   *The Archaeology of Inequality.* Oxford: Blackwell.

Mellaart, J.

1962.   Preliminary Report of the Archaeological Survey in the Yarmouk and Jordan Valley. *ADAJ* 6-7:126-57.

Mendenhall, G. E.

1973.   Tribe and State in the Ancient World. Pp. 174-97 in *The Tenth Generation.* Baltimore: Johns Hopkins University Press.

1976.   Social Organization in Early Israel. Pp. 132-51 in *Magnalia Dei,* ed. F. M. Cross, W. Lemke, and P. D. Miller Jr. Garden City: Doubleday.

Meron, E.

1985.   *Axes and Adzes in Israel and It's [sic] Surrounding [sic].* M.A. Thesis, Tel Aviv.

Millard, A. R., Hoffmeier, J. K., and Baker, D. W., eds.

1994.   *Faith, Tradition, and History.* Winona Lake: Eisenbrauns.

Miller, J. M.

1987.   In Defense of Writing a History of Israel. *JSOT* 39:53-57.

Miller, R. D., II.

2002a.   Modeling the Farm in Early Iron Age Israel. In *Life and Culture in the Ancient Near East,* ed. R. E. Averbeck, M. W. Chavalas, and D. B. Weisberg. Bethesda, MD: CDL Press.

2002b.   *A Gazetteer of Iron I Sites in the North-central Highlands of Palestine.* AASOR 56. Cambridge, MA: American Schools of Oriental Research.

2004.   Identifying Earliest Israel. *BASOR* 333:55-68.

2005.   Yahweh and His Clio: Critical Theory and the Historical Criticism of the Hebrew Bible. *Currents in Biblical Research* 4.

Moenikes, A.

1995.   *Die grundsätzliche Ablehnung des Königtums in der Hebräischen Bible.* BBB 99. Diss., Rheinische Friedrich-Wilhelms-Universität. Weinheim: Beltz Athenaum.

Monson, J. M.

1983.   *The Land Between.* Rockford, IL: Bible Backgrounds.

Moore, A. M. T.

1997.   Villages. *Oxford Encyclopaedia of the Ancient Near East* 5:301-3.

Moorey, P. R. S.

1971.   A Bronze Statuette of a Bull. *Levant* 3:90-91.

Moors, A.

1989.   Gender Hierarchy in a Palestinian Village. Pp. 195-209 in *The Rural Middle East,* ed. K. Glavanis and P. Glavanis. Birzeit: Birzeit University Press and London: Zed Books.

Mudar, K. M.

1993.   *Prehistoric and Early Historic Settlements on the Central Plain.* Diss., University of Michigan.

Muhly, J. D.

1995.   Mining and Metalwork in Ancient Western Asia. *CANE* 3:1501-22.

Mullen, E. T.

1993.   *Narrative History and Ethnic Boundaries.* Atlanta: Scholars Press.

Müller-Karpe, H.

1977.   Zum Ende der spätkanaanitischen Kultur. Pp. 57-77 in *Jahresberichte des Institut für Vorgeschichte der Universität Frankfurt a. M. 1976,* ed. H. Müller-Karpe. Munich: C. H. Beck.

Naʿaman, N.

1982.   The Inheritance of the Cis-Jordanian Tribes of Israel and the "Land That Yet Remaineth." *EI* 16:152-58.

1985.   Bethel and Beth-Aven. *Zion* 50:15-25. In Hebrew.

1986a.   *Borders and Districts in Biblical Historiography.* Jerusalem Biblical Studies 4. Jerusalem: Simor.

1986b.   Migdal-Shechem and the "House of El-Berith." *Zion* 51:259-80. In Hebrew.

1992.   Canaanite Jerusalem and Its Central Hill Country Neighbours in the Second Millennium BCE. *UF* 24:275-91.

1994.   The Canaanites and Their Land. *UF* 26:397-418.

Naveh, J.

1978.   Some Considerations on the Ostracon from Izbet Sartah. *IEJ* 28:31-35.

Neef, H.-D.

1995.   *Ephraim.* BZAW 238. Berlin: de Gruyter.

Neʿeman, Y.

1990.   *Map of Maʿanit.* Archaeological Survey of Israel 54. Jerusalem: Israel Antiquities Authority.

Negbi, O.

1991.   Were There Sea People in the Central Jordan Valley at the Transition from the Bronze Age to the Iron Age? *TA* 18:205-43.

Neusner, J.

1981.   Beyond Historicism, After Structuralism. *Henoch* 3:171-96.

Newton, R., and Davison, S.

1989.   *Conservation of Glass.* Butterworths Series in Conservation and Museology 5. London: Butterworths.

Nibbi, A.

1989.   *Canaan and Canaanite in Ancient Egypt.* Oxford: Bocardo.

O'Shea, J. M.

1984.   *Mortuary Variability.* New York: Academic Press.

Ofer, A.

1993.   *The Highland of Judah during the Biblical Period.* Diss., Tel Aviv.

n.a.

1978.   The Oldest Known Hebrew Writing. *Bible and Spade* 7:25-30

Oliver, D. L.

1974. *Ancient Tahitian Society.* Honolulu: The University Press of Hawaii.

1981. *Two Tahitian Villages.* Honolulu: Institute for Polynesian Studies.

Orlinsky, H. M.

1962. The Tribal System of Israel and Related Groups in the Period of the Judges. Pp. 375-87 in *Studies and Essays in Honor of A. A. Neuman,* ed. M. Ben-Horin, B. D. Weinryb, and S. Zeitlin. Philadelphia: Dropsie College Press. = *OrAn* 1:11-20.

Otto, E.

1997. *Kontinuum und Proprium.* Orientalia Biblica et Christiana 8. Weisbaden: Otto Harrassowitz.

Ottoson, M.

1994. Ideology, History, and Archaeology in the Old Testament. *SJOT* 8:206-23.

Parsons, J.

1972. Archaeological Settlement Patterns. *Annual Review of Anthropology* 1:127-50.

1990. Critical Reflections on a Decade of Full-Coverage Regional Survey in the Valley of Mexico. Pp. 7-31 in *The Archaeology of Regions,* ed. S. K. Fish and S. Kowalewski. Washington, DC.

Pauketat, T.

1991. *The Dynamics of Pre-State Political Centralization in the North American Midcontinent.* Diss., University of Michigan.

Paynter, R., and McGuire, R. H.

1991. The Archaeology of Inequality. Pp. 1-27 in McGuire and Paynter, 1991.

Peckham, B.

1995. Writing and Editing. Pp. 364-83 in *Fortunate the Eyes That See,* ed. A. Beck, A. H. Bartelt, P. R. Raabe, and C. A. Franke. Grand Rapids: Eerdmans.

Peebles, C. S.

1978. Determinants of Settlement Size and Location in the Moundville Phase. Pp. 369-416 in *Mississippian Settlement Patterns,* ed. B. D. Smith. Studies in Archaeology 27. New York: Academic Press.

1987. Moundville from 1000 to 1500 AD as Seen from 1840 to 1985 AD. Pp. 21-42 in Drennan and Uribe, 1987.

1993. Aspects of Cognitive Archaeology. Pp. 250-53 in Renfrew, 1993.

Peebles, C., and Kus, S.

1977. Some Archaeological Correlates of Ranked Societies. *American Antiquity* 47:421-48.

Peltenburg, E.

1997. Vitreous Materials: Artifacts of the Bronze and Iron Ages. *Oxford Encyclopaedia of the Ancient Near East* 5:309-14.

Peterson, J. L.

1977. *A Topographical Surface Survey of the Levitical Cities of Joshua 21 and 1 Chronicles 6.* Diss., Seabury-Western Theological Seminary.

Plog, S.

1976. Measurement of Prehistoric Interaction between Communities. Pp. 255-71 in *Early Mesoamerican Village,* ed. K. Flannery. New York: Academic Press.

Polanyi, L.

1981. What Stories Can Tell Us about Their Teller's World. *Poetics Today* 2:97-111.

Polzin, R.

1989. *Samuel and the Deuteronomist.* New York: Harper & Row.

Portugali, J.

1982. A Field Method for Regional Archaeology. *TA* 9:170-88.

1984a. *Arim, Banot, Migrashim,* and *Haserim:* Spatial Organization of Eretz-Israel in the 12th-10th Centuries BCE according to the Bible. *EI* 17:282-90. In Hebrew.

1984b. Locational Theory in Geography and Archaeology. *Geography Research Forum* 7:43-60.

1994. Theoretical Speculations on the Transition from Nomadism to Monarchy. Pp. 203-17 in Finkelstein and Na'aman, 1994.

Potts, D. T.

1997. Salt. *Oxford Encyclopaedia of the Ancient Near East* 4:459.

Pritchard, J. B.

1956. The Water System at Gibeon. *BA* 19:66-75.

1957. The Discovery of Biblical Gibeon. *University of Pennsylvania Museum Bulletin* 21.1:3-26.

1958. A Second Season at Gibeon. *University of Pennsylvania Museum Bulletin* 22.2:12-24.

1959. Gabaon. *Bible et Terre Sainte* 18:8-14.

1960a. Gibeon's History in Light of Excavation. Pp. 1-12 in *Congress Volume Oxford.* VTSup 7. Leiden: E. J. Brill.

1960b. Industry and Trade at Biblical Gibeon. *BA* 23:23-29.

1961. *The Water System of Gibeon.* University of Pennsylvania Museum Monographs. Philadelphia: University of Pennsylvania Press.

1962a. *Gibeon.* Princeton: Princeton University Press.

1962b.   Excavations at el-Jib, 1960. *ADAJ* 6/7:121-22.

1963.   Gabaon. *Bible et Terre Sainte* 56:7-15.

1964a.   *Winery, Defense, and Soundings and Gibeon.* Philadelphia: University of Pennsylvania Press.

1964b.   El-Jib Excavations, 1962. *ADAJ* 8/9:86-87.

1976.   Gibeon. In *Archaeological Discoveries in the Holy Land*, ed. J. B. Pritchard. New York: Thomas Y. Crowell.

Provan, I. W.

1995.   Ideologies, Literary and Critical. *JBL* 114:585-606.

Quézel, P.

1981.   The Study of Plant Groupings in the Countries Surrounding the Mediterranean. Pp. 87-93 in di Castri et al., 1981.

Raban, A.

1982.   *Survey of the Nahalal Map.* Archaeological Survey of Israel 28. Jerusalem: Archaeological Survey of Israel.

1991.   The Philistines in the Western Jezreel Valley. *BASOR* 284:17-27.

Rabinovitch-Vin, A.

1983.   Influence of Nutrients on the Composition and Distribution of Plant Communities in Mediterranean-Type Ecosystems of Israel. Pp. 74-85 in *Mediterranean-Type Ecosystems*, ed. F. J. Kruger, D. T. Mitchell, and J. U. M. Jarvis. Ecological Studies 43. Berlin: Springer.

Rabinowitz, I.

1993.   *A Witness Forever.* Occasional Publications of the Department of Near Eastern Studies and the Program of Jewish Studies, Cornell University 1. Bethesda, MD: CDL Press.

Rainey, A. F.

1984.   *A Handbook of Historical Geography.* Jerusalem: American Institute of Holy Land Studies.

Rapp, G., Jr.

1996.   Some Geological Techniques Applied in Eastern Mediterranean Archaeology. Paper presented at "Workshop on the Practical Impact of Science on Field Archaeology," October 1996, Hebrew University, Jerusalem and Tel-Aviv University, Tel-Aviv.

Redford, D. B.

1990.   *Egypt and Canaan in the New Kingdom.* = *Beersheva* 4.

1992.   *Egypt, Canaan, and Israel in Ancient Times.* Princeton: Princeton University Press.

Reisch, G.

1995.   Scientism without Tears. *History and Theory* 34:45-58.

Renfrew, C.

1974.   Beyond Subsistence Economy. Pp. 69-88 in *Reconstructing Complex Societies*, ed. C. B. Moore. BASORSup 20. Cambridge, MA.

1986.   Introduction to *Peer Polity Interaction and Socio-Political Change*, ed. C. Renfrew and J. Cherry. New Directions in Archaeology. Cambridge: Cambridge University Press.

1993.   Cognitive Archaeology. Pp. 248-50 in Renfrew, 1993.

Renfrew, C., ed.

1993.   What Is Cognitive Archaeology? *Cambridge Archaeological Journal* 3:247-70.

Reviv, H.

1966.   The Government of Shechem in the El-Amarna Period and in the Days of Abimelech. *IEJ* 16:252-57.

1989.   *The Elders in Ancient Israel.* Trans. L. Plitmann. Jerusalem: Magnes.

Richter, W.

1963.   *Traditionsgeschichtliche Untersuchungen zum Richterbuch.* BBB 18. Bonn: Peter Hanstein.

Rihll, T. E., and Wilson, A. G.

1987.   Spatial Interaction and Structural Models in Historical Archaeology. *Histoire et Mesure* 2:5-32.

1991.   Spatial Interaction and Structural Models. Pp. 62-95 in *City and Country in the Ancient World*, ed. J. Rich and A. Wallace-Hadrill. Leicester-Nottingham Studies in Ancient Society 2. London: Routledge. Repr. 1994.

Rofé, A.

1982.   The Family-Saga as a Source for the History of the Settlement. *EI* 24:187-91.

Rosen, A. M.

1986.   *Cities of Clay: The Geoarchaeology of Tells.* Prehistoric Archaeology and Ecology 1. Chicago: University of Chicago Press.

Ross, J. F., and Toombs, L.

1961.   Three Campaigns at Biblical Shechem. *Archaeology* 14:171-79.

1962.   Les découvertes effectuées au cors des dernières campaignes de fouilles à Sichem. *Bible et Terre Sainte* 44:6-15.

1976.   Six Campaigns at Biblical Shechem. Pp. 119-28 in *Archaeological Discoveries in the Holy Land*, ed. J. B. Pritchard. New York: Thomas Y. Crowell.

Rossignol, J.

1992.   Concepts, Methods, and Theory Building. Pp. 3-20 in Rossignol and Wandsnider, 1992.

Rossignol, J., and Wandsnider, L., eds.

1992.   *Space, Time, and Archaeological Landscapes.* New York: Plenum.

Rowton, M. B.

1973.   Urban Autonomy in a Nomadic Environment. *JNES* 32:201-15.

1976.   Dimorphic Structure and the Tribal Elite. *Studia Instituti Anthropos* 28:219-58.

1977.   Dimorphic Structure and the Parasocial Element. *JNES* 36:181-98.

Rubin, Z.

1989.   Historical Geography of Eretz-Israel. Pp. 23-36 in *The Land That Became Israel*, ed. R. Kark. New Haven: Yale University Press.

Ruddell, R.

1973.   Chiefs and Commoners. Pp. 254-68 in *Cultural Ecology*, ed. B. Cox. Toronto: McClelland and Stewart.

Sahlins, M.

1963.   Poor Man, Rich Man, Big Man, Chief. *Comparative Studies in Society and History* 3:285-302.

Said, M.

1974.   Letter to E. F. Campbell Jr. Albright Institute of Archaeological Research Archives, Jerusalem.

Saks, R.

1986.   *Human Territoriality.* Cambridge Studies in Historical Geography 7. Cambridge: Cambridge University Press.

Sapin, J.

1968-69. *Le Plateau Central de Benjamin.* Memoire, École Biblique. Jerusalem.

Sawyer, J. F., and Clines, D. J. A., eds.

1983.   *Midian, Moab, and Edom.* JSOTSup 24. Sheffield: Sheffield Academic Press.

Saxe, A. A.

1970.   *Social Dimensions of Mortuary Practices.* Diss., University of Michigan.

Schäfer-Lichtenberger, C.

1996.   Sociological and Biblical Views of the Early State. Pp. 78-105 in Fritz and Davies, 1996.

Schiffer, M. B.

1976.   *Behavioral Archaeology.* New York.

Schloen, J. D.

1993.   Caravans, Kenites, and *casus belli*. *CBQ* 55:18-38.

Schunck, K.-D.

1962.   Bemerkungen zur Orstliste von Benjamin. *ZDPV* 78:143-58.

1963.   *Benjamin*. BZAW 86. Berlin: Alfred Töpelmann.

Schwartz, G. M.

1987.   The Ninevite V Period and the Development of Complex Society in Northern Mesopotamia. *Paleorient* 13:93-100.

1993.   Rural Archaeology in Early Urban Mesopotamia. *National Geographic Research and Exploration* 9:120-22.

1994.   Before Ebla. Pp. 153-74 in *Chiefdoms and Early States in the Near East*, ed. G. Stein and M. S. Rothman. Madison: Prehistory Press.

Schwerin, K. H.

1973.   The Anthropological Antecedents. Pp. 5-17 in *The Caciques*, ed. R. Kern. Albuquerque: University of New Mexico Press.

Seger, J. D.

1997.   Shechem. *Oxford Encyclopaedia of the Ancient Near East* 5:19-23.

Sellin, E.

1922.   *Wie wurde Sichem eine Israelitische Stadt?* Leipzig: A. Deichertsche Verlagsbuchhandlung.

1960?.   Preliminary Report concerning the Results of the Excavations at Balatah-Shechem. In Horn, 1960?. = E.T. of *Anzeiger der Kaiserlichen Akademie der Wissenschaften in Wein* 51 (1914):35-40.

Sellin, E., and Steckeweh, H.

1941.   Kurzer vorlaufiger Bericht über die Ausgrabung von *balata* (Sichem) im Herbst 1934. *ZDPV* 64:1-20.

Service, E. R.

1962.   *Primitive Social Organization*. 2d ed. New York.

1975.   *Origins of the State and Civilization*. New York: Norton.

Shaath, S., ed.

1985-88. *ALESCO: Studies in the History and Archaeology of Palestine*. 3 vols. Aleppo: Aleppo University Press.

Shanks, H.

1997.   Biblical Minimalists Meet Their Challengers Face to Face. = Interview with T. L. Thompson, N. P. Lemche, W. G. Dever, and P. K. McCarter. *BAR* 23(4):26-42, 66.

Shanks, M.

1997.   Archaeological Theory: What's on the Agenda? *American Journal of Archaeology* 101:395-99.

Shanks, M., and Tilley, C.

1987a.   *Social Theory and Archaeology.* Cambridge: Cambridge University Press.

1987b.   *Re-constructing Archaeology.* New Studies in Archaeology 15. Cambridge: Cambridge University Press.

Sharon, I.

1995.   *Models for Stratigraphic Analysis of Tell Sites.* Diss., Hebrew University of Jerusalem.

Shavit, A.

1993.   Tel Malot. *ESI* 12:49-50.

Sherzer, J.

1990.   *Verbal Art in San Blas.* Cambridge Studies in Oral and Literate Culture 21. Cambridge: Cambridge University Press.

Shiloh, Y.

1978.   Elements in the Development of Town Planning in the Israelite City. *IEJ* 28:36-51.

1987.   The Casemate Wall, the Four Room House, and Early Planning in the Israelite City. *BASOR* 268:2-16.

Sigrist, C., and Neu, R., eds.

1989.   Vor- und Frühgeschichte Israels. Vol. 1 of *Ethnologische Texte zum Alten Testament.* Neukirchen-Vluyn: Neukirchener.

Silberman, N. A., and Small, D., eds.

1997.   *The Archaeology of Israel.* JSOTSup 237. Sheffield: Sheffield Academic Press.

Simons, J.

1937.   *Handbook for the Study of Egyptian Topographical Lists Relating to Western Asia.* Leiden: E. J. Brill.

1959.   *The Geographical and Topographical Texts of the Old Testament.* Nederlands Instituut voor het Nabije Oosten Studia Francisci Scholten Memoriae Dicata AB/2. Leiden: E. J. Brill.

Sinclair, L. A.

1960.   *An Archaeological Study of Gibeah (Tell el-Ful).* AASOR 34. New Haven: American Schools of Oriental Research.

Singer, I.

1985.   The Beginning of Philistine Settlement in Canaan and the Northern Boundary of Philistia. *TA* 12:109-22.

1994.   Egyptians, Canaanites, and Philistines in the Period of the Emergence of Israel. Pp. 282-338 in Finkelstein and Na'aman, 1994.

n.a.

1975.   A Site near Tel Menorah. *HA* 56:21. In Hebrew.

Smelik, K. A. D.

1992.   *Converting the Past.* Oudtestamentische Studiën 28. Leiden: E. J. Brill.

Smend, R.

1970.   *Yahweh War and Tribal Confederation.* 2d ed. Trans. M. G. Rogers. Nashville: Abingdon.

Smith, C. A.

1976.   Regional Social Systems. Vol. 2, pp. 3-20 in *Regional Analysis.* Studies in Anthropology 9. New York.

Snodgrass, A. M.

1971.   *The Dark Age of Greece.* Edinburgh: University Press.

Spencer, C.

1987.   Rethinking the Chiefdom. Pp. 369-89 in Drennen and Uribe, 1987.

Spriggs, M.

1988.   The Hawaiian Transformation of Ancestral Polynesian Society. Pp. 57-76 in *State and Society,* ed. J. Gledhill, B. Bender, and M. T. Larson. One World Archaeology 4. London: Unwin Hyman.

Stanhill, G.

1978.   The Fellah's Farm. *Agro-Ecosystems* 4:433-48.

Stager, L. E.

1968.   The Archaeology of Palestine in the 11th Century. Unpublished "Hebrew 200" paper.

1985a.   The Archaeology of the Family in Ancient Israel. *BASOR* 260:1-35.

1985b.   Merneptah, Israel, and Sea Peoples. *EI* 18:56*-64*.

Steponaitis, V.

1978.   Locational Theory and Complex Chiefdoms. Pp. 417-53 in *Mississippian Settlement Patterns,* ed. B. Smith. New York: Academic Press.

1981.   Settlement Hierarchies and Complex Chiefdoms. *American Anthropologist* 83:320-61.

1983.   *Ceramics, Chronology, and Community Pattern.* Studies in Archaeology 60. New York: Academic Press.

Stern, E.

1978.   *Excavations at Tell Mevorakh, Part 1.* Qedem 9. Jerusalem: Hebrew University Press.

Stern, E., and Beit-Arieh, I.
1979. Excavations at Tel Kedesh. *TA* 6:1-25.

Stern, F.
1973. *The Varieties of History.* New York: Vintage.

Steward, D., and Webber, P. J.
1981. The Plant Communities and Their Environments. Pp. 43-68 in *Resource Use by Chaparral and Matarral,* ed. P. C. Miller. Ecological Studies 39. Berlin: Springer.

Steward, J.
1949. Cultural Causality and Law. *American Anthropologist* 51:1-27.

Stolz, F.
1981. *Das erste und zweite Buch Samuels.* Zürcher Bibelkommentare. Zurich: Theologischer Verlag Zürich.

Sumner, W. M.
1990. Full-Coverage Regional Archaeological Survey in the Near East. Pp. 87-115 in *The Archaeology of Regions,* ed. S. K. Fish and S. Kowalewski. Washington, DC.

Swanton, J. R.
1964. An Early Account of the Choctaw Indians. *American Anthropological Association Memoir* 5:53-72.

Tadmor, H.
1979. The Decline of Empires in Western Asia ca. 1200. Pp. 1-14 in Cross, 1979.

Tadmor, H., and Weinfeld, M., eds.
1983. *History, Historiography, and Interpretation.* Jerusalem: Magnes.

Tainter, J.
1973. The Social Correlates of Mortuary Patterning at Kaloko, North Koua, Hawaii. *Archaeology and Physical Anthropology in Oceania* 8:1-11.

1976. Spatial Organization and Social Patterning in the Kaloko Cemetery, North Koua, Hawaii. *Archaeology and Physical Anthropology in Oceania* 11:91-105.

1980. Behavior and Status in a Middle Woodland Mortuary Population from the Illinois Valley. *American Antiquity* 45:308-13.

Tainter, J., and Cordy, R.
1977. An Archaeological Analysis of Social Ranking and Residence Groups in Prehistoric Hawaii. *World Archaeology* 9:94-112.

Talmon, S.
1978. The "Comparative Method" in Biblical Interpretation. Pp. 320ff. in *Congress Volume Göttingen 1977.* VTSup 29. Leiden: E. J. Brill.

Taylor, D.
1975.   *Some Locational Aspects of Middle-Range Hierarchical Societies.* Diss., City University of New York.

Tertel, H. J.
1994.   *Text and Transmission.* BZAW 21. Berlin: Walter de Gruyter.

Thiel, W.
1985.   *Die Soziale Entwicklung Israel in vorstaatlicher Zeit.* 2d ed. Neukirchen-Vluyn: Neukirchener.

Thompson, T. L.
1979.   *The Settlement of Palestine in the Bronze Age.* BTAVO 34. Wiesbaden: Reichert.

1987.   *The Origin Tradition of Ancient Israel.* Vol. 1. JSOTSup 55. Sheffield: JSOT Press.

1991.   Text, Context and Referent in Israelite Historiography. Pp. 65-92 in Edelman, 1991a.

1992.   *The Early History of the Israelite People.* Studies in the History of the Ancient Near East 4. Leiden: E. J. Brill.

1995a.   Gösta Ahlström's History of Palestine. Pp. 420-34 in *The Pitcher Is Broken,* ed. S. W. Holloway and L. K. Handy. JSOTSup 190. Sheffield: Sheffield Academic Press.

1995b.   A Neo-Albrightean School in History and Biblical Scholarship? *JBL* 114:683-705.

1996.   Historiography of Ancient Palestine and Early Jewish Historiography. Pp. 26-43 in Fritz and Davies, 1996.

Thuesen, I.
1996.   Review of Bernbeck, 1994. *JESHO* 39:52-54.

Tomaselli, R.
1981.   Main Physiognomic Types and Geographic Distribution of Shrub Systems Related to Mediterranean Climates. Pp. 95-106 in di Castri et al., 1981.

Toombs, L. E.
1972.   The Stratigraphy of Tell Balatah (Shechem). *ADAJ* 17:99-111.
1992.   Shechem. *ABD* 5:1174-86.

Toombs, L., Campbell, E. F., and Ross, J. F.
1971.   The Eighth Campaign at Balatah (Shechem). *BASOR* 204:2-17.

Toombs, L., and Wright, G. E.
1961.   The Third Campaign at Balatah (Shechem). *BASOR* 161:11-54.
1962.   Sichem. *RB* 69:257-66.
1963.   The Fourth Campaign at Balatah (Shechem). *BASOR* 169:1-60.

Bibliography

Townsend, T. P.

1972.   *Historiography and the Time of the Judges.* Diss., University of Michigan.

Trinkaus, K. M.

1995.   Mortuary Behavior, Labor Organization, and Social Rank. Pp. 53-75 in Beck, 1995.

Tuchman, G.

1994.   Historical Social Science. Pp. 306-23 in Denzin and Lincoln, 1994.

Turkowski, L.

1969.   Peasant Agriculture in the Judaean Hills. *PEQ* 101:21-33, 101-13.

Van Beek, G. W.

1951.   Cypriote Chronology and the Dating of Iron I Sites in Palestine. *BASOR* 124:26-29.

Van Seters, J.

1983.   *In Search of History.* New Haven: Yale University Press.

1995.   The Historiography of the Ancient Near East. *CANE* 4:2433-44. New York: Charles Scribner's Sons.

Vansina, J.

1985.   *Oral Tradition as History.* Madison: University of Wisconsin Press.

Vanstiphout, H.

1995.   Memory and Literacy in Western Asia. *CANE* 4:2181-96. New York: Charles Scribner's Sons.

Van Zeist, W.

1985.   Past and Present Environments of the Jordan Valley. *Studies in the History and Archaeology of Jordan* 2:199-204.

Vaux, R. de

1971.   La Thèse de l'Amphictyoni Israëlite. *HTR* 64:415-36.

1973.   *La Period des Juges.* Vol. 2 of *Histoire ancienne d'Israël.* Études Bibliques 13. Paris: Libraire Lecoffre.

Vermeule, E.

1972.   *Greece in the Bronze Age.* Chicago: University of Chicago Press.

Veyne, P.

1988.   *Did the Greeks Believe in Their Myths?.* Chicago: University of Chicago Press.

Wagstaff, M., ed.

1987.   *Landscape and Culture.* London: Basil Blackwell.

Waldbaum, J. C.

1978.   *From Bronze to Iron.* Studies in Mediterranean Archaeology 54. Göteborg: Paul Åströms.

Walton, J. H.

1989.   *Ancient Israelite Literature in Its Cultural Context.* Grand Rapids: Zondervan. Repr. 1990.

Wandsnider, L.

1992.   The Spatial Dimension of Time. Pp. 257-84 in Rossignol and Wandsnider, 1992.

Wapnish, P., and Hesse, B.

1988.   The Contribution and Organization of Pastoral Systems. Pp. 29-39 in *Early Israelite Agriculture,* ed. O. S. LaBianca and D. C. Hopkins. Occasional Papers of the Institute of Archaeology 1. Berrien Springs, MI: Andrews University Press.

Ward, W. A., and Joukowsky, M. S., eds.

1992.   *The Crisis Years: The Twelfth Century* B.C. Dubuque, IA: Kendall/Hunt.

Wason, P. K.

1994.   *The Archaeology of Rank.* New Studies in Archaeology. Cambridge: Cambridge University Press.

Watkins, L.

1997.   Izbet Sartah. *Oxford Encyclopaedia of the Ancient Near East* 3:198-99.

Webley, D.

1972.   Soils and Site Location in Prehistoric Palestine. Pp. 169-80 in *Papers in Economic Prehistory,* ed. E. S. Higgs. British Academy Major Research Project: The Early History of Agriculture. Cambridge: University Press.

Weinstein, J.

1992.   The Collapse of the Egyptian Empire in the Twelfth Century B.C. Pp. 142-50 in Ward and Joukowsky, 1992.

Weippert, H.

1988.   *Palästina in Vorhellenistischer Zeit.* Handbuch der Archäologie Vorderasien 2.1. Munich: C. H. Beck'sche Verlagsbuchhandlung.

Weippert, H. and M.

1976.   Jericho in der Eisenzeit. *ZDPV* 92:105-48.

Welch, P. D.

1986.   *Models of Chiefdom Economy.* Diss., University of Michigan.

1991.   *Moundville's Economy.* Tuscaloosa: University of Alabama Press.

Wenning, R., and Zenger, E.

1986.   Ein bauerliches Baal-Heiligtum im samarischen Gebirge aus der Zeit der Anfange Israels. *ZDPV* 102:75-86.

White, H.

1990.   *Tropics of Discourse.* Rev. ed. Baltimore: Johns Hopkins University Press.

Whitelam, K.

1989.   Israel's Traditions of Origin. *JSOT* 44:19-42.

Wilson, R. R.

1984.   *Sociological Approaches to the Old Testament.* Philadelphia: Fortress.

Wobst, H. M.

1977.   Stylistic Behavior and Information Exchange. Pp. 317-43 in *For the Director. . . .* Anthropological Paper 6. Ann Arbor: University of Michigan Museum of Anthropology.

Wolf, E. R.

1966.   *Peasants.* Foundations of Modern Anthropology 10. Englewood Cliffs, NJ: Prentice-Hall.

Wolff, S.

1994.   Senior Fellow Report. *ASOR Newsletter* 44:3.

1995.   Ein Haggit. *HA* 104:53-54. In Hebrew.

Wright, G. E.

1941.   Archaeological Observations on the Period of the Judges and the Early Monarchy. *JBL* 60:27-42.

1957.   The Second Campaign at Tell Balatah. *BASOR* 148:11-28.

Wright, G. R. H.

1967.   Some Cypriote and Aegean Pottery Recovered from the Shechem Excavations 1964. *Opuscula Atheniensia* 7:47-80.

1968.   Temples at Shechem. *ZAW* 80:1-35.

1970.   The "Granary" at Shechem and the Underlying Storage Pits. *ZAW* 82:275-78.

1971.   Shechem and League Shrines. *VT* 21:572-603.

1985.   *Ancient Building in South Syria and Palestine.* 2 vols. Handbuch der Orientalistik 7. Leiden: E. J. Brill.

1987.   Temple and Gate in Palestine. Vol. 2, pp. 173-83. Shaath, 1985-88.

1992a.   The Place Name Balatah and the Excavation at Shechem. Pp. 1-9 in *Obiter Dicta.* London: Aquiline; Leiden: Netherlands Institute for Near East; and Nicosia: Spectrum. = *ZDPV* 83 (1967):199-202.

1992b.   The Mythology of Pre-Israelite Shechem. Pp. 10-21 in *Obiter Dicta.* London: Aquiline; Leiden: Netherlands Institute for Near East; and Nicosia: Spectrum. = *VT* 20 (1970):75-82.

1993-94. Section Drawing at Shechem. *Archiv für Orientforschung* 40/41:320-37.
1994. Mensuration and Monuments at Shechem. Pp. 321-28 in *Beiträge zur Altorientalischen Archaeologie und Altertumskunde,* ed. P. Calmeyer, K. Hecker, L. Jakob-Rost, and C. B. F. Walker. Wiesbaden: Harrassowitz.
1997. Building Materials and Techniques: Bronze and Iron Ages. *Oxford Encyclopaedia of the Ancient Near East* 1:363-67.

Wright, H. T.
1984. Prestate Political Formations. In *On the Evolution of Complex Societies,* ed. T. K. Earle. Malibu: Undena.
1985. The Evolution of Civilizations. Pp. 323-65 in *American Archaeology Past and Future,* ed. D. J. Meltzer, D. D. Fowler, and J. A. Sabloff. Washington: Smithsonian Institute.
1987. Regional Socio-Economic Organization in Southern Mesopotamia. Pp. 317-29 in *Prehistoire de la Mesopotamie,* ed. J.-L. Huot. Paris: Editions du Centre National de Recherche Scientifique.

Wright, H. T., ed.
1986. The Evolution of Complex Societies in Southwestern Iran. *Paleorient* 11(2):2-127.

Wright, H. T., and Johnson, G.
1975. Population, Exchange, and Early State Formation in Southwest Iran. *American Anthropologist* 77:267-89.

Würthwein, E.
1994. Abimelech und der Untergang Sichems. Pp. 12-28 in his *Studien zum Deuteronomistischen Geschichteswerk.* BZAW 227. Berlin: de Gruyter.

Yamauchi, E.
1994. The Current State of Old Testament Historiography. Pp. 1-36 in Millard, Hoffmeier, and Baker, 1994.

Yannai, E.
1995. A Group of Early Iron Age Lamps from the Northern Sharon Valley. *TA* 22:279-81.

Yeivin, S.
1971. *The Israelite Conquest of Canaan.* Publications de l'Institut historique et archaeologique nëerlandais de Stamboul 27. Istanbul: Nederlands Historisch-Archaeologisch Instituut in het Nabije Oosten.

Yoffee, N.
1979. The Decline and Rise of Mesopotamian Civilization. *American Antiquity* 44:5-35.
1981. *Explaining Trade in Ancient West Asia.* MANE 2/2. Malibu: Undena.

1992.   Too Many Chiefs? Pp. 60-78 in *Archaeological Method and Theory: Who Sets the Agenda?*, ed. N. Yoffee and A. Sherratt. Cambridge: Cambridge University Press.

Yoyotte, J.

1990.   La campaigne palastinienne du Pharaon Merneptah. Pp. 109-20 in Laperrousaz, 1990.

Yurco, F. J.

1986.   Merneptah's Canaan Campaign. *JARCE* 23:189-215.

Zertal, A.

1983a.   Har Menashe, Survey — 1982. *ESI* 2:43-44.

1983b.   Mount Ebal. *ESI* 2:72.

1984.   *Arruboth, Hefer, and the Third Solomonic District.* Tel Aviv: Kibbutz Meuchad.

1985.   Has Joshua's Altar Been Found on Mt. Ebal? *BAR* 11(1):26-43.

1986.   How Can Kempinski Be So Wrong! *BAR* 12(1):43, 49-53.

1986-87.   An Early Iron Age Cultic Site on Mount Ebal. *TA* 13-14:105-66.

1987.   The Cultivation and Economics of Olives during the Iron Age in the Hill Country of Manasseh. Pp. 196-203 in *Olive Oil in Antiquity*, ed. M. Helter and D. Eitam. Haifa: Haifa University Press.

1988a.   *The Israelite Settlement in the Hill Country of Manasseh.* Haifa: Haifa University. In Hebrew.

1988b.   The Water Factor during the Israelite Settlement Process in Canaan. Pp. 341-52 in *Society and Economy in the Eastern Mediterranean 1500-1000 b.c.*, ed. M. Heltzer and E. Lipiński. Analecta Lovaniensia Orientalia 23. Leuven.

1991.   Israel Enters Canaan. *BAR* 17(5):28-49.

1992.   *The Manasseh Hill Country Survey.* Haifa: Israel Exploration Society and Israel Defense Department. In Hebrew.

1994.   "To the Land of the Perizzites and the Giants": On the Israelite Settlement in the Hill Country of Manasseh. Pp. 47-69 in Finkelstein and Na'aman, 1994.

1996.   *The Manasseh Hill Country Survey.* Vol. 2 (The Eastern Valleys and the Fringes of the Desert). Haifa: Haifa University Press. In Hebrew.

1997.   Northern Samaria, Survey of. *Oxford Encyclopaedia of the Ancient Near East* 4:164-66.

Zohary, M.

1966-86.   *Flora Palaestina.* 4 vols. Jerusalem: Israel Academy of Sciences and Humanities.

Zori, N. (= Tsori, N.)

1962.   An Archaeological Survey of the Beth Shean Valley. Pp. 135-98 in *The Beth Shean Valley, The 17th Archaeological Convention*. Jerusalem: Israel Exploration Society. In Hebrew.

1971.   *Tel-Josef Area in Antiquity*. Tel-Aviv: Neographica. In Hebrew.

1975.   Middle Bronze I and Early Iron I Tombs near Tel Rehov in the Beth Shean Valley. *EI* 12:9-17. In Hebrew.

1977.   *The Land of Issachar Archaeological Survey*. Archaeological Survey of Israel. Jerusalem: Israel Exploration Society. In Hebrew.

Zorn, J.

1993.   *Tell en-Nasbeh*. 4 vols. Diss., Berkeley.

Zvelevil, M., Green, S. W., and Macklin, M. G.

1992.   Archaeological Landscapes, Lithic Scatters, and Human Behavior. Pp. 193-226 in Rossignol and Wandsnider, 1992.

Index